The Business of Hacking

Creating, Developing, and Maintaining an Effective Penetration Testing Team

Michael Butler
Jacob G. Oakley

Apress®

The Business of Hacking: Creating, Developing, and Maintaining an Effective Penetration Testing Team

Michael Butler
Falls Church, VA, USA

Jacob G. Oakley
Owens Cross Roads, AL, USA

ISBN-13 (pbk): 979-8-8688-0173-0
https://doi.org/10.1007/979-8-8688-0174-7

ISBN-13 (electronic): 979-8-8688-0174-7

Managing Director, Apress Media LLC: Welmoed Spahr
Acquisitions Editor: Susan McDermott
Development Editor: Laura Berendson
Project Manager: Jessica Vakili

Distributed to the book trade worldwide by Springer Science+Business Media New York, 1 New York Plaza, New York, NY 10004. Phone 1-800-SPRINGER, fax (201) 348-4505, e-mail orders-ny@springer-sbm.com, or visit www.springeronline.com. Apress Media, LLC is a California LLC and the sole member (owner) is Springer Science + Business Media Finance Inc (SSBM Finance Inc). SSBM Finance Inc is a **Delaware** corporation.

For information on translations, please e-mail booktranslations@springernature.com; for reprint, paperback, or audio rights, please e-mail bookpermissions@springernature.com.

Apress titles may be purchased in bulk for academic, corporate, or promotional use. eBook versions and licenses are also available for most titles. For more information, reference our Print and eBook Bulk Sales web page at http://www.apress.com/bulk-sales.

Any source code or other supplementary material referenced by the author in this book is available to readers on the Github repository: https://github.com/Apress/The-Business-of-Hacking. For more detailed information, please visit https://www.apress.com/gp/services/source-code.

If disposing of this product, please recycle the paper

Table of Contents

About the Authors

Michael Butler is a 14-year veteran of the offensive cybersecurity industry. He got his start by conducting cyber warfare operations with the US Army and NSA. He then went on to build two commercial penetration testing teams, teach multiple offensive cybersecurity classes at Black Hat and other conferences, and become an expert in hacking cloud environments. In 2023, he founded Final Frontier Security to elevate quality assessments and client experience through all aspects of offensive cybersecurity. He has previously collaborated with Dr. Oakley as the technical reviewer for the book *Professional Red Teaming* and is the co-author of *Theoretical Cybersecurity: Principles and Advanced Concepts* (Apress, 2022).

Dr. Jacob G. Oakley is a cybersecurity journeyman, author, speaker and educator with 17 years of experience. A foremost expert on offensive cybersecurity, cyber warfare, and space system cybersecurity, he has advised Department of Defense (DoD) and Fortune 500 executives on strategic mitigation of risks and threats to globally distributed, multi-domain network architectures. He is an adjunct professor at Embry-Riddle Aeronautical University and Steering Committee member for the IEEE Space System Cybersecurity Standards Working Group. His books, *Professional Red Teaming*, *Waging Cyber War*, *Cybersecurity for Space*, *Theoretical Cybersecurity*, and *The Business of Hacking* are published by Springer/Apress.

CHAPTER 1

Introduction

Hacking Is Different

There aren't many books on the subject of leading hackers. Trust me, I've looked. But if you look for a book on how to hack, you'll find them by the truckload. In fact, if you took the number of books on offensive cybersecurity and compared it to the number of books written about other areas of cybersecurity or even information technology (IT) in general, you could easily assume that the field of hacking is one of the largest within IT. Of course, anyone familiar with the field will tell you that penetration testing is a relatively small subset within the cybersecurity industry. The majority of cybersecurity professionals are working to identify, defend, detect, and respond to threats. So why then is the literature on the technical subject of offensive cybersecurity so prolific?

The answer might be fairly obvious – hacking is exciting! It's interesting and flashy. The idea of getting paid to break into IT systems can be very attractive, especially when compared to jobs that may seem more mundane on the surface such as security analysis and engineering. The profession is also very different from its sister professions. To the initiate in cybersecurity, this difference is first made clear by the diverging paths of education. At some point early in the development of their cybersecurity skills, a professional will have to choose whether to focus on the offensive

© Michael Butler and Jacob G. Oakley 2024
M. Butler and J. G. Oakley, *The Business of Hacking*,
https://doi.org/10.1007/979-8-8688-0174-7_1

or defensive side of the house. While there is some overlap, the tools, techniques, and even mindsets of professionals on these paths are radically different.

Hacking is different. The skill repertoire a professional hacker cultivates includes identifying a vulnerable server hidden within thousands of data points, deceiving people into giving up sensitive data, and hiding in the noise on a network wire to stay under the threshold of detection. It is understandable that this would require a different approach and mindset than other areas of cybersecurity. While this difference seems to be generally accepted, my years in building and leading offensive cybersecurity teams have led me to another conclusion – leading hackers is different.

Recruiting, motivating, developing, and retaining offensive cybersecurity professionals come with unique challenges, but the differences don't end there. They extend into team scaling, marketing, and sales. The needs of the clients of an offensive cybersecurity team are different and require different strategies to meet. The operational flow is different. The parameters for success are different. The way in which an engagement is approached mentally is different.

These differences arise from the place that hacking has within an organization's cybersecurity programs. It is used to set the direction for the next iteration in security engineering and as the last step in validating the progress that each iteration has made. This is starkly different from other cybersecurity disciplines that are concerned with either the operation and monitoring of defenses (security analysts) or the construction of new defenses to meet threats identified through hacking or other means.

The management-level differences hide pitfalls that catch those new to building and managing an offensive cybersecurity capability by surprise. The differences aren't obvious, making them difficult to anticipate and adequately address. It can take years of stumbling, experimentation, and stressful nights to find the way to navigate the pitfalls. I'm speaking from experience. Even the years I spent as an offensive cybersecurity

professional did not prepare me for leading a team and then later building
a capability from the ground up. I can look back now on my experiences
and see myself groping in the dark for an adequate solution that wouldn't
appear for years. I have no doubt that I am not the first person to
encounter many of these challenges. In fact, I have spoken to and heard
of other teams struggling with the same things I have struggled with. And
I often see the same sense of lost frustration in leaders that I had and, to
some degree, still have. I am also certain that I am not the first person to
find solutions to many of these challenges, but as mentioned at the start
of this chapter, I haven't found many that wrote their solutions down
afterward.

Bad Team, Good Team

My experience in offensive cybersecurity capability (OCC) management
comes from building and leading two different teams over the course of
roughly 10 years each. Both teams represented the offensive offering of
small cybersecurity consulting firms.

I joined the first team as a penetration tester executing long-term staff
augmentation contracts. For the uninitiated, staff augmentation is when a
member of a consultant company's staff joins the client's team in a semi-
permanent position that is renewed typically on a 6-month to 1-year basis.
Before long, I was the contract director, team lead, and senior penetration
tester for a contract with a very large commercial organization and a
second contract with a very large government agency. I was very busy.

My time building that team helped me to develop an appreciation of
the variety of clients that needed offensive cybersecurity services, how
their requirements differed, and the techniques that seemed to work
best for each. While I very much enjoyed my time on that first team, the
team's construction was flawed from the start. The team was created as
a reaction to client requests for offensive cybersecurity services. There

was no structure, vision, or collaboration. The pentesters on the team were handed engagements by the management and then executed them in a silo.

Much like the team's construction, its management was also reactive in nature. Problems were addressed when they became significant enough to warrant attention. New pentesters were only hired when new work needed to be executed. Tools and techniques were not actively developed unless a team member wanted to put in their own time outside of the contract requirements.

In that team, there were few efforts to foster a connected, supportive, and growing team environment. The team members met once weekly via video call. The call was rather awkward, and the testers retreated to their contract silos the moment it ended.

I am not criticizing any one person other than myself with the lackluster leadership of that team. As one of the earliest testers on the team and the director of the largest contract that included an offensive cybersecurity component, I became one of the de facto leaders of the team. I had a lot to learn about leading an offensive cybersecurity capability (OCC), and my lack of experience and vision did the team no favors. What I did obtain from that experience was an understanding of the problems and challenges inherent to leading that kind of team, a few good ideas, and a lot of knowing what not to do.

I was given a second chance when I was asked to build an offensive cybersecurity capability from the ground up at a new cybersecurity startup. I had a vision and I had learned enough from the first team to know what I didn't want. Over the next several years, the team grew and went through several phases of maturity. From our infancy with just two testers doing whatever it took to make our clients happy to the startup phase of a small team building internal tooling and improving processes to the professional phase with a large team and fine-tuned practices and automation. These phases of growth each presented a unique set of challenges and required me and the leaders within the capability to mature to address them. Our vision developed to include a deeper understanding of the following areas of management:

- Agile experimentation
- Client management
- Capability structure
- Development of team members
- Inspiring collaboration and camaraderie
- Standards of deliverables
- General penetration testing standards

Through this book, we will discuss each of those management domains and their place within the framework of building a successful team that is also capable of growing to meet new challenges.

The difference between these teams is stark but it comes down to two things: a defined vision and a willingness to engage with challenges proactively. I believe these two principles are the bedrock of successful management both in and out of the offensive security world.

In the chapters to come, I will refer back to these two teams, their successes and failures, to demonstrate the right and wrong ways to approach challenges.

Why This Book Matters

My hope and goal for this book is to clearly frame the challenges that anyone involved in the creation, development, and management of an offensive cybersecurity capability will encounter. I will present my own experiences, mistakes, and solutions as I have developed them thus far in my career. This book is not intended to be the definitive source of solutions; rather, it is intended to help begin a larger conversation about leadership in the offensive cybersecurity world.

To that end, I have enlisted the help of my good friend and colleague, Dr. Jacob Oakley. Together we bring 30 years of experience in the offensive cybersecurity industry. That experience spans military leadership, the US intelligence community, defense and non-defense contracting, cybersecurity for space vehicles, and commercial companies that run the gamut from local startups to those listed on the Fortune 100 not to mention extensive time within academia.

Together, we will cover how to build an offensive cybersecurity capability from the ground up, develop it, scale it, and understand your stakeholders. We'll discuss effective assessment practices and how to develop reports and touch a bit on marketing. Finally, we will look to the future of our industry with topics such as cyber arms, cybersecurity in space, and artificial intelligence (AI).

CHAPTER 2

The Service

Definitions

Our exploration of building and managing an offensive cybersecurity service begins with a few definitions to establish a common language between the various types of services.

Offensive Cybersecurity Service (OCS)

An offensive cybersecurity service is the mechanism by which an organization is able to acquire, manage, and execute offensive cybersecurity tasking as well as all elements involved in the management, development, and growth of the service and its personnel. This is not the same as a red team or a penetration testing team although it encompasses such teams. An OCS represents all elements of the service to perform offensive cybersecurity within an organization including elements that are not usually directly associated with a red team or penetration testing team such as sales, marketing, client management, team management, capability development, and more.

This book will explore all areas of an offensive cybersecurity service and not only the topics that are important to the penetration testing team itself. Therefore, you will often see this term used.

© Michael Butler and Jacob G. Oakley 2024
M. Butler and J. G. Oakley, *The Business of Hacking*,
https://doi.org/10.1007/979-8-8688-0174-7_2

The definition of this term is broad by design because within the offensive cybersecurity field, there are few subtypes of teams and professionals. In my experience, the various subtypes are far more similar than they are different, and for most of the points in this book, they can be grouped together under the offensive cybersecurity banner. There are of course a few notable exceptions. For example, internal red teams may not find the content on marketing particularly useful. But generally speaking, all types of professionals and teams can benefit from an exploration of the topics in this book.

Team Types

There are two primary labels given to teams of offensive cybersecurity professionals: red teams and penetration testing teams. These terms are often used interchangeably and sometimes one team will fill both roles, but there is an important difference in the objectives for each type of team. We will explore each one to gain an understanding of the differences and where they overlap.

Penetration Testing Team

A penetration testing team consists of IT professionals trained in offensive cybersecurity techniques. The objective of a penetration test is to identify vulnerabilities within the engagement scope. Once vulnerabilities are identified, the team will work to demonstrate the impact of the vulnerabilities through exploitation if the client allows.

The outcomes of a penetration test for the client are

- Identification of previously unknown vulnerabilities

- A deeper understanding of the risks the environment faces

- Identification of weaknesses in the systems and processes that develop and deploy the environment

Let's look at an analogy to express these outcomes. A penetration testing team is assigned to assess a web application. The team identifies a low complexity SQL injection vulnerability and uses it to access sensitive client information. In the engagement report, the team provides the details of the vulnerability and makes recommendations on how to remediate it. In addition, the team suggests more robust dynamic and static scanning be added to the lifecycle of the application to help prevent similar vulnerabilities in the future.

In this analogy, the client would work to remediate the identified vulnerability and improve the application development pipeline to include better security practices, and they would have a greater understanding of the potential impact of a real-world attack.

A penetration test is an important part of the security of any application, system, or environment. They give a real-world perspective and leverage the attacker's mindset. This isn't something that those involved with the development or securing of the system can do. They will not usually have the skills or mindset to carry out an offensive cybersecurity assessment of their environment, and they will most likely make assumptions about the system due to their understanding of it.

Red Team

A red team also consists of IT professionals trained in offensive cybersecurity techniques, but their objective is quite different. The objective of a red team is to test and assess the detection and response capabilities of an environment.

The outcomes of a red team assessment for the client are

- Identification of blind spots in the environment's ability to detect a compromise

- Identification of weaknesses in an environment's ability to respond to a compromise scenario

- An understanding of the level of sophistication required to bypass detection and response measures

As an example, a red team is given access to a host that is joined to the internal network of an organization. The members of the red team emulate the actions of a sophisticated adversary by slowly and stealthily enumerating the aspects of the network that the compromised host gives them access to. This is what is known as an "assumed breach" scenario.

By moving slowly and blending in with normal network traffic, the red team is able to stay under the threshold of detection and thereby cirvumvent network defenses. They work to identify hosts within the network that could provide the team with additional access, escalated privileges, and/or access to services or processes that are critically important to the business of the organization (commonly referred to as "critical terrain"). Once identified, the red team will attempt to find vulnerabilities within these hosts and exploit them to demonstrate the impact of flawed detection and response mechanisms.

As the engagement proceeds, the red team will use less and less stealth and sophistication until they are caught. This provides the client with a real-world understanding of the level of attacker their current defenses are capable of detecting and the level of sophistication necessary to bypass them.

After the engagement is complete, the client can use the results to drive improvements in their internal network's detection and response systems and processes with the goal of detecting attackers that operate at a higher level of sophistication.

Purple Team

One final team type that we need to discuss is the purple team. The purple team is a more collaborative approach to the assessment of the blue team's capabilities. It combines the blue and red teams; therefore, purple! In a purple team engagement, the offensive side executes attacks and other actions within the protected network and the defensive side makes sure that (1) the action is detected and (2) the response is adequate. The great benefit of this approach is the real-time improvement of defenses.

Purple team engagements can go a step further by leveraging frameworks of documented behavior by various groups of attackers. For example, the MITRE ATT&CK framework is a knowledge base for adversary tactics and techniques based on real-world observations. A purple team can use the MITRE ATT&CK framework to emulate the behavior of an adversary that is likely to target the organization. This allows the organization to prioritize efforts to defend itself against specific threats that it most likely faces rather than attempting to be secure against all threats simultaneously.

It is not common for organizations to staff a dedicated purple team, and since the skillset of the red team significantly overlaps with that of the purple team, the red team will often be given both responsibilities. In my experience, when a red team performs purple team engagements, it has an unexpected benefit. It can cool tensions between the red and blue teams who are usually seen as adversarial in their work and can easily become adversarial in their relationship.

Some competition is good. It helps to keep both team sharp when they have some skin in the game. However, I have witnessed organizations that allowed this natural competitiveness to grow to an unhealthy level, which negatively affected the usefulness of the engagements. The collaborative aspect of purple team engagements helps re-establish healthy relationships between the security teams and reminds them that they are all on the same side.

Team Differences

The primary differences between these two types of offensive cybersecurity teams lie within their objectives and client outcomes, but there are secondary differences as well. Red team engagements are most effective when the blue team (the defenders of the environment) are not alerted that the assessment is happening. This creates a more real-world scenario where the blue team must identify and respond to any alerts from the red team as if they are an actual compromise.

On the other hand, pentesting engagements do not require any level of secrecy. In fact, it is often beneficial to have all parties involved in the development and maintenance of the target environment included in the test so that they can provide feedback and suggestions to the testers.

When a pentester identifies a vulnerability, they will report it and may attempt to exploit it to determine the severity of the vulnerability. Red teams test a system until they find a vulnerability that grants a higher level of access, and then they move on to testing the next system. While this methodology does not thoroughly test each system the red team member encounters, it does simulate how a real-world threat actor would move through the environment.

The end product of each engagement, the engagement report, also contains some differences. While both teams will produce a report that highlights vulnerabilities and impact, the red team report will primarily evaluate the alerts and actions that occurred in response to their testing.

We have discussed these two teams as if they are two separate entities, but in practice, both engagements are almost always the responsibility of the same team due to the significant overlap of skills required. Not only does one team handle both types of engagements, but both types of engagements may be found in the same assessment. For example, a team may perform an assessment of a web application and find a significant vulnerability that gives them access to the server that hosts the application. With the client's approval, the team may pivot into the client's internal network and evaluate the blue team's response or lack thereof. A pentester can simultaneously evaluate an environment and evade detection.

Internal vs. Consultative

The second major difference between the teams within offensive cybersecurity is their client base. Some teams serve the needs of a single client. These teams are either contractors or employees brought on board to consistently provide offensive cybersecurity services to the organization. These kinds of teams only exist in rather large organizations who have a need for a dedicated internal team. My first exposure to commercial penetration testing was with such a team. I worked for a small cybersecurity firm that had a contract to supply fulltime offensive cybersecurity professionals to a very large commercial company.

Other teams serve a variety of clients. These clients only need the services occasionally, perhaps annually or quarterly. These kinds of teams exist at services-based cybersecurity companies who market their capabilities and services to bring in clients and scale the team to meet the market demand. The engagements these teams perform typically last anywhere from 2 weeks to a few months before the pentesters involved move on to another client. The second team I joined was primarily consultative. The team executed engagements for multiple clients every week.

It's important to recognize that although there are some differences, these two types of teams are more alike than they are different. The challenges present in one type are generally present in other type with a few notable exceptions. The differences between internal and consultative teams are significantly reduced once you consider that even when serving a single organization, an internal team is responsible for testing multiple departments, networks, and applications. Interacting with those various departments is no different than a services-based team interacting with multiple clients. For ease, I will refer to anyone who requires offensive cybersecurity services and to whom the final report is delivered as a client, whether that party is an internal department or an external customer.

Establishing the Service Vision

If you've worked within the offensive cybersecurity field for a few years, you'll most likely have encountered teams that were started without any real consideration as to their structure. This lack of vision results in a structure that is developed in reaction to the needs of the work. The outcome is a haphazard patchwork of short-term band-aid solutions put in place to solve immediate problems without consideration for the long-term health of the service.

The first commercial penetration testing team that I joined took this approach, or lack of an approach, and the result was the following team dynamic that has become all too familiar in our industry:

A single senior technical leader begrudgingly takes the responsibility of organizing the team and their engagements while, often publicly, wishing they were able to spend more time on the technical side of the job and less time doing project management. The team itself is made up of mostly mid- to senior-level pentesters who work remotely and rarely communicate unless they are collaborating on a given project. The team meets once a week or less to discuss projects and possible operational issues in a video call where very few team members turn on their camera. The call contains many awkward pauses that go on for just a little too long, and the team members are happy to end it as quickly as possible.

This service structure is less than ideal. It results in team members having little reason to remain on the team other than their paycheck. It does not attract motivated and hungry testers to join the team. It does not produce engaged testers who are passionate about their work and who develop tools to assist the team as a whole. The quality of the engagement output drops over time, and team member turnover becomes a serious challenge.

Of course, no one sets out to build this kind of team structure. It is the result of there being no planned structure, no vision. It can begin from an upper management-level decision to create an offensive cybersecurity service due to an internal or market requirement. The management then hires someone who knows a lot about the technical aspects of offensive cybersecurity to lead the new team, and then they consider the job done as the requirement has been met. If the construction of the service lacks vision from the onset, it is unlikely to suddenly attain a purpose once it is established. As a friend of mine once said, "You can't accidentally do well for the long term."

So we have to start with a vision. The vision needs to be clear and simple enough to be easily communicated and implicitly understood. This might seem a bit daunting at first, but it's not as intense as you might initially assume. In fact, it is preferrable that the initial service vision is very simple.

The vision should consist at minimum of the basic priorities of the service and an idea of what the service and its team will look like in one year. Even this very simple vision will give the team a much higher chance of success than a team without a vision.

The service vision will change and be adapted over time as the service members and their leader mature and develop a greater understanding of their mission, what works, and what doesn't work. A basic vision will lend itself to this growth and adaptability from the start.

Structure

Management of an offensive cybersecurity service consists of five domains:

- Lead

- Project

- Client

- Team
- Capability

When an OCS is first established, its structure will be rather simple. This is not because some of these five domains do not exist in new OCCs. Rather, it is because multiple domains are managed by the same person or people. This is casually referred to as wearing multiple hats. So even though a new OCS will not require dedicated personnel or as much dedicated effort to each domain as a more mature OCS, it is still important to note the domains and track the service's maturity across them.

Lead

The lead domain is concerned with all operations that occur between the initial notification that a lead exists and the lead becoming a schedulable project. This domain exists even for internal OCCs even though they do not require a traditional sales/lead pipeline. A lead for an internal team is defined as a request or requirement to execute an assessment of a specific environment. For example, a product may have a new update that requires a pentest before it can be pushed to production. A lead for a team of consultants is defined as a potential project from a client who is interested in the services of the OCC.

For consultative teams, this domain may seem misplaced. You may be thinking, "aren't leads the responsibility of the sales team?" While that idea is mostly correct for teams that work with a sales team, the sales team will need technical support from the OCS to communicate the technical details of the project's requirements and the types of assessments the service provides to the client. Sales people rarely possess the technical education to convince clients of the service's quality and to adequately scope the client's project. They will often lean on the members of the OCS to provide that support.

Within the lead domain, the OCS develops processes to educate clients (even internal clients) on OCS services, help the client develop project requirements, establish project scope, discuss testing requirements (access, credentials, lists of target IP addresses, etc.), ensure the paperwork contains language necessary for project execution, establish a schedule for the project, and select a calendar date for the project to begin.

Project

A lead becomes a project once any necessary paperwork is signed and a date on the calendar is selected. The project domain is responsible for ensuring that the team is ready and able to execute the given engagement. That means that there is space on the team's calendar, team members with the skills that the engagement requires are assigned to it, any special considerations or objectives are communicated with the assigned team members, and all technical requirements such as scope and access have been negotiated and provided to the team.

Once the engagement begins, project management is responsible for monitoring the engagement to ensure that all aspects of it are executed and that any unique client requirement is met. At the end of the engagement, the project management handles the deliverables and communication of findings to the client and discusses any further activities that might be necessary before the engagement is closed. An example of further activities would be re-testing identified vulnerabilities once the developers of a given system have implemented patches.

Client

Clients are the single most important factor for any offensive cybersecurity service, and client satisfaction is the primary metric for team success and output quality. This might be difficult to swallow for many offensive cybersecurity professionals. Our job is technical. We find vulnerabilities, exploit them, and report. Someone else can manage the clients! This

17

attitude is common and understandable. After all, we spend our careers developing our technical skillset. The classes we attend don't mention client satisfaction and the list of requirements in job postings we apply to make no mention of babysitting customers.

But the fact remains that a team's strong technical skills will not make up for a lack of attention to client needs, communication, and general management. Clients of consultative teams will prefer working with a team that makes an effort to understand them, be transparent with them, and help them through the testing process over a team that provides more vulnerability findings. Internal clients will provide better feedback for a team that they feel they can collaborate with. They may become suspicious or even confrontational with a team that excludes them from an assessment of their environment.

Without solid client management and communication processes, an assessment becomes a black box. It is performed with an unknown level of quality and produces results without context from the client's perspective. What's worse is that the client's requirements may shift or become better defined as the assessment progresses. If a lack of communication prevents the team from adapting to changes in the requirements, the output of the assessment may not be relevant to the client's needs regardless of how technically successful the engagement was.

Client management is present through all other areas of management and represents the standards and practices of how the client is communicated with and how their needs are addressed.

Team

The team domain contains all activities and processes related to acquiring, developing, and motivating members of the offensive cybersecurity service. Much like our approach to the OCS in general, any vision is better than no vision because it shifts the management of this domain from reactive to proactive. Staffing the OCS will not be easy since staffing any IT role is difficult in the current market and we work within a small sector of the cybersecurity industry. OCS leadership will need to develop a multi-prong approach to finding and selecting its members.

A strong internal development strategy can alleviate a lot of difficulties related to staffing by lowering the bar of skill required for entry into the team. The trade-off is of course time. Regardless of the efficacy of its development program, the OCS will need time to get junior team members to the point that they can reliably contribute to the team's output at the level required.

Additionally, internal development is absolutely essential to push and keep the team at the cutting edge of their craft. This is a split responsibility since the professionals that make up the OCS should be proactive in their own education and maintenance of their skillset. However, OCS leadership cannot choose the direction of development that its members pursue in their own time. So if you want your team to develop skills within a certain domain, you will have to create processes that allow them to do so within the OCC.

Motivation is a topic that is rarely addressed on teams with more reactive leadership. The attitude seems to boil down to, "I have work. I hired professionals to do the work. My job is done." While this simplistic approach does solve the immediate problem, it will cause long-term team disruptions, a higher turnover rate, and a generally less happy workforce. The team must feel that it has a mission that is collaboratively achieved. Each member knows what they must do to reach the next level within the team and what is expected from them in the maintenance of their skills. By allowing team members to have a say in how things are done and providing transparency in the fruit of their labors, you will create a drive within the team to accomplish great things.

Capability

The sophistication and quality of the capabilities of an OCS are what differentiate it from its competitors and allow it to deliver high-quality results. An OCC's capabilities are categorized by the domains in which the OCS performs assessments, for example, external network, internal network, cloud, web application, etc. Some teams will have clients that require testing against all domains including some of the less common such as physical pentesting and hardware hacking. Other teams, typically internal teams, will be focused on just a few. Outside of the assessment domains, an OCS also has internal capabilities such as reporting, infrastructure management, and data control. In this book, we will group these non-assessment categories into the "team tooling" domain.

The offensive cybersecurity industry is constantly improving and adding new tools and techniques to all assessment domains. Likewise, the capabilities of an OCS will require constant improvement or risk becoming atrophied and less relevant with time. The eroding of the quality and relevance of a capability can be subtle. I have personally experienced a capability that became so eroded that it caused significant client-facing issues before I realized that development was needed.

Team Structure

Leadership

The management and execution structure of an OCS are fairly straightforward if all the management domains established in the previous section are considered. Each domain is vital to the success of the overall service and will require time, strategy, and effort from the leadership of the service. However, the real-world implementation of service leadership is going to look very different. At the initial establishment of the service, it isn't necessary or helpful to have a dedicated leader for each domain. Most likely, you will have one or at most two leaders overseeing all aspects of the service when the team is small.

The simplest and most natural way to group the management of these domains is to put those related to typical project management tasks under a leader with project management experience and to group the domains that are more technical under a senior offensive cybersecurity professional with team leadership experience. So the lead, client, and project management domains would fall under the project manager, and team and service management would fall under the technical leader. These leaders will have to work very closely together and will often overlap each other while building processes that affect every domain within the service.

As the team grows, additional members will join the leadership team as needed. What is interesting about these new members is that a much lower bar of experience in management and leadership skill is required for them. This is because by the time the team is ready to bring new members into its leadership team, most of the processes of the team will have already been established and the team will have built a clear understanding and some momentum toward its vision. Therefore, less creativity and innovation are required of these new leaders at least not in the broad strokes of the service's management. Instead, they focus on maintaining and enforcing the established processes in order to take tasking off the plate of the senior project and technical management.

Member Composition

The OCS team will be responsible for executing projects and developing service capabilities. Its composition and how it is managed as it scales will have a significant impact on every aspect of OCS management and service success. With that in mind, the OCS leadership might assume that the best possible way to staff the team is to select senior professionals in the field. While budgeting limitations might cut these dreams short, in my experience this is far from the best approach. A team made up of a variety of skill and experience levels is easier to motivate, more effective, and overall delivers better results than a team staffed exclusively with senior-level talent. The goal is to build the best team which is not necessarily a team of the best testers.

There is a quality that junior professionals possess that seems to dim as years of experience are added – hunger. Someone straight out of college who has dreams of becoming a professional hacker is hungry. They'll do what it takes, learn whatever they have to, and adapt to the team environment in order to realize those dreams. They do not have preconceived ideas about how pentesting should be done or how projects should be executed. They are ready to learn, and as long as the OCS provides a robust avenue to do so, they will quickly flourish into the direction the OCS requires

This is not to say that senior professionals are useless and unwieldy or that they are no longer hungry to learn new things. Rather, the place of a senior professional is to set the standard of what good hacking looks like, to mentor the hungry junior talent, and to determine the next evolution of the service's capabilities. While junior talent is focused on the requirements of project execution that are directly in front of them, senior talent participates in guiding the future of the OCS and its capabilities with the leadership as well as growing the juniors.

CHAPTER 3

Finding and Retaining Talent

After developing your vision and a basic idea of where you want your OCS to be in a year, the first challenge that you will need to overcome is staffing the service. Acquiring talent is a two-phase project. The first phase is proactively finding or more passively attracting candidates who are interested in joining your service, and the second phase is evaluating them to make sure they are a good fit.

As any job market survey will tell you, it's difficult staffing IT positions today. There is a significant gap between the jobs that are available and the professionals ready to fill them. There are a few factors that will determine the level of difficulty you face. The first factor is the level of skill required for the position you are trying to fill. Predictably, there are far more junior-level professionals seeking a job than there are senior level. The second factor is the type of work and the industry sector your team works in. If the work is considered exciting, new, or challenging, then you have a greater likelihood of attracting talent. Finally, the benefits and compensation package you offer candidates are going to either give you an advantage or disadvantage when making a competitive offer to a candidate.

In my experience, an OCS that works as a third-party contractor performing short-term consultative engagements will usually be able to offer higher salaries to candidates. This is because the OCS is a driving force of revenue within the organization. An OCS in an internal corporate

© Michael Butler and Jacob G. Oakley 2024
M. Butler and J. G. Oakley, *The Business of Hacking*,
https://doi.org/10.1007/979-8-8688-0174-7_3

environment will usually struggle a bit with raw salary numbers but can become competitive with a total compensation package that includes benefits such as a yearly bonus and stock options. Corporate teams are also able to offer a better work–life balance since the service isn't being squeezed to provide every possible drop of revenue via billable hours.

When you are ready to start finding the professionals that will staff your team, start by taking stock of your OCC's total compensation package. Identify where your package has advantages over competitors and what elements of the work would be considered exciting for a prospective team member. This last element may seem a bit unrealistic. Do cybersecurity professionals really choose a position with a lower salary because the work is more interesting? The answer is a definite yes. In fact, the kind of professional that is passionate enough to forego a higher salary for more interesting work is exactly the kind of team member you want. I have personally hired and retained team members who were very aware that they could get significantly higher salaries with other companies but chose to stay on my team because they loved the work. You won't always be able to win a numbers competition against larger, better-funded companies but the exciting work that your team performs can be just as attractive.

While the current state of the IT talent market can be daunting, we on the offensive cybersecurity side of the house do have one significant advantage – everyone wants to be a hacker. I can't tell you how many interviews I have conducted with IT professionals who wanted to switch from some other IT field into offensive cybersecurity, even when they knew that switching career fields would result in them losing a bit of salary. This means that even though we work within a fairly small subset of cybersecurity, our job opportunities get attention across IT.

There is a direct relationship between the level of talent you require and the level of effort required to obtain that talent. If you are looking for a junior member to join your team because your OCS has a strong internal development program that will get them to the skill level you need quickly, you will find dozens of recent college graduates applying for the position. On the other hand, it can take months to find senior-level talent especially if there is a specific skillset or type of experience that you are looking for. As an example, I once had a requirement to staff a position with a penetration tester who was also familiar with cloud environments and had experience either attacking or securing cloud environments. At the time, this was a rather rare skillset in the offensive cybersecurity world. After attempting to fill this requirement for 4 months, I finally decided to hire a junior pentester who was very intelligent and eager to learn. Within the next few months, they had learned everything I needed them to know about performing assessments on cloud environments.

If time allows, I almost always prefer to develop internal team members or to hire junior testers and develop them into the skill level that I need. Not only does this give back to the community and help foster new professionals in their development, it allows you to create the exact skillset you need instead of looking for someone that already has it. The downside of developing a pentester's skillset to fill a role is that you miss out on the new perspectives that an outside hire can bring to the team. You will have to balance these two benefits since both are quite important. A team that relies on developing junior testers to fill roles will become stale over time. In the worst scenario, team members become overly confident in their skills since there is no new blood to challenge them. Additionally, it may not be feasible in many situations to develop internal talent. You may not have the time or the ability to train someone up to the level that you need.

Sourcing Talent

To develop a talent acquisition strategy, you'll need to be familiar with the various avenues of engaging with professionals and getting word of your requirement out there.

Community Engagement

When you are first standing up your OCC, the first team members will most likely come from friends, previous coworkers, and acquittances that the leadership of the OCS has made through the community. The offensive cybersecurity field has always enjoyed a very active and engaged community. Hacking is fun, and collaborating in skills and knowledge at conferences and other community events is very attractive to people from all over. By becoming personally engaged in the community, the leadership of the OCS will be able to tap directly into the relationships that exist there. While you may not directly know someone who fits the bill for your current requirement, someone does, and if you put the word out into the community, you have a good chance of getting a response.

There are several ways to engage with the community. The most obvious is cybersecurity conferences. Conferences can be very large like Defcon or be quite small such as local BSides conferences. You and your team can participate in conferences by giving talks, providing training, or sponsoring the conference and setting up a booth to talk with potential applicants.

Conferences can also serve as a sort of condensed interview. You're able to meet with a candidate in person and discuss technical subjects. This informal way of getting to know a potential candidate helps reduce a lot of the pressure of a formal interview process.

Referrals

Referrals are one of the best sources of finding mid- to senior-level talent especially when those referrals come from current team members. Experienced penetration testers will often move from job to job based on the recommendations of friends instead of hunting through job postings. Friends may be aware that a good pentester is interested in work long before that pentester would ever apply to a job you have posted.

There is of course a significant bias in referrals because it's usually a team member referring a friend of theirs. This is why it is important that referral applicants are not able to bypass a thorough interview process just because they have a friend on the team.

I have had more success identifying high-quality testers from referrals than any other means. Referrals should be encouraged, and those providing the referral should receive some form of reward if the referred individual is brought on board the team.

While referrals are a great way to find talent especially in the first few years of the OCC, they are not scalable nor reliable. You cannot build a talent acquisition strategy around referrals because there will be times that no adequate referrals are provided.

Job Requisition Postings

Posting a job requisition to your corporate website is one of the least expensive ways of finding talent, but unless your corporation is rather large and well known, it's unlikely that the post will get much traffic. If this is the case, a job posting on your site can still be useful if it is marketed through various communities and networks via social media, especially LinkedIn. The more people within your organization that advertise your posting to their network, the more traffic the post will experience.

If you're not seeing the traffic you would like or you don't have the time to wait and find out if community connections will bear fruit, you can spread a wider net by posting the given job requisition to what are essentially job promotion websites. There are many options for job promotion websites with varying degrees of efficacy, but they do require an investment which can sometimes get pricey.

The talent acquisition strategy changes a bit with this option because it becomes more of a numbers game that is very similar to standard marketing. The goal is to determine how much money needs to be spent to reach the applicants you need. The answer will change depending on the requirements of the position you are currently trying to fill, and it will take some experimentation to find.

Referrals are going to give you applicants that are at least fairly close to meeting the requirements of the position. Job postings, especially those that are advertised on well-known job promotion sites, are going to result in dozens, perhaps hundreds, of applications, but most will not meet the minimum requirements. In my experience, I found that at least 75% of the applicants of my job postings were totally unqualified for the work described in the posting, another 20% were only a mediocre match with the final 5% or less being applicants that I could actually pursue. It will take more time and effort to go through the applicants of advertised job postings than previously discussed techniques so your leadership team will need to be prepared for that workload.

The upside to job postings is that they are a reliable and scalable method of reaching applicants. Additionally, job postings allow you to reach professionals outside of your network.

Third-Party Recruiters

Third-party recruiters are a mixed bag. There are good agencies that will work with you to develop an accurate idea of your ideal candidate and then use their own familiarity with cybersecurity to identify resumes from their resources that are in line with the team's expectations. There are also not so great agencies who seem more intent on providing you any resume that might fit and have little understanding of why they don't. I believe the biggest difference between helpful and unhelpful headhunter agencies is the understanding they have of the field and the effort they put into understanding what you are looking for. Overall, I have not had much success with headhunter agencies, but I believe they are most useful when your team is looking for senior-level talent and your organization does not have its own dedicated recruiters.

Internal Recruiting Team

Staffing dedicated recruiters to assist with all aspects of talent acquisition, processing, and assessment can be an incredible help, but not all offensive cybersecurity services will be part of an organization large enough to justify the expense.

While I'm sure that some service leaders have struggled with internal recruitment teams, I have personally had very positive experiences. Even when members of the recruitment team are not well versed in cybersecurity or even computing in general for that matter, they can take a lot of the repetitive work off the shoulders of the service leaders and filter out candidates that don't meet the requirements of the position. They can streamline the interview process, which allows the service leaders to focus on the technical and personal aspects of the interview. If they have the support, the recruitment team can act as dedicated headhunters who proactively seek out individuals that fit the position's requirements. This can be invaluable especially when hunting for senior-level talent or a nonstandard skillset.

Summary

The previous five options for finding candidates follow an increasing scale of cost, effort, and / or time required that is directly related to the number of potential team members you will reach and applications you will receive. Your team may never grow to the size of needing the services of a headhunter agency or an internal recruiting team, but it is important to know what options are available as you scale to prevent the team from clinging to options it has outgrown.

While working at my first pentest team, I became stuck on the idea that applicants coming from referrals or community connections were often the highest quality and were the most likely to join the team. While I wasn't necessarily incorrect, my fixation on one solution meant that my team was slow to scale and provide staffing to new contracts. Investing in job marketing sites and more robust corporate job application management software would have given me access to many more applicants and most likely would have led to a service that was better prepared to scale to demand.

Assessing Candidates

After you have gathered a number of applicants, it's time to assess and select the individual that best fits the role requirements. Interviews are difficult for both the interviewer and the interviewee. In a short time, you are trying to assess the interviewee's technical skills and team compatibility in an environment that naturally encourages the interviewee to feel pressured and to behave in a nontypical, borderline deceptive way. It's important to prepare for the interview process with these challenges in mind.

Conducting the Interview

Interviews should never be conducted alone. One interviewer most likely does not have all the technical skills necessary to fully evaluate the candidate and having more than one perspective is invaluable. At the same time, bringing too many interviewers to the interview can be intimidating. I believe the magic number is two. Any more than that feels like an interrogation panel to the interviewee, and it becomes more difficult for the interviewers to coordinate.

A member of the OCS management leading the interview with a senior technical team member conducting most of the technical questions has been the best combination for me. This pair does a good job of representing life on the team and the technical requirements of the work. The interviewee gets a window into team life, which is hopefully inspiring and interesting to them if the team has a strong internal dynamic.

Interview questions can either be small scope such as the question, "what port does MySQL servers typically use?" or open-ended such as "how would you conduct an assessment of a database server listening on port 3306?" Small questions produce small answers. They give a pinpoint understanding of the applicant's knowledge and don't encourage further conversation. Depending on the requirements of the position, there may be specific pinpoints of knowledge that are necessary, but in most cases, open-ended questions are preferrable.

Open-ended questions encourage a more conversational interview, and the more that the applicant discusses their testing process, the more you are able to determine their technical and personal aptitude. During my interviews, I would ask very broad questions, and then, as the applicant explained their process, my interview partner and I would ask clarifying and technical questions to make sure we got the data we needed. For example:

"You have been assigned to an external assessment. All paper-work is completed, and you are approved to begin. The client has only provided the domains and IP ranges that they own. From a high level, how do you conduct the assessment, what tools do you use, and what data are you attempting to obtain?"

This is big question with a lot of scope. At first, it may feel overwhelming to the applicant, and as such, it is critical that the interviewers voice encouragement to the applicant as they talk through their process. Even small affirmations such as "yeah, that's how we do it too" can help the applicant feel that they are making progress in their answer.

If open-ended and large-scope questions are your friend, anxiety is your enemy. I think most of us have been the nervous interviewee at some point in our career. It's not fun when your interview questions cause that kind of anxiety in someone else. More practically, anxious applicants do not convey a good picture of their technical nor interpersonal skills.

Some professionals are naturally prone to anxiety during interviews and there's not much you can do to prevent it. However, the interview process should be constructed to do what you can to prevent unnecessary pressure, and you should have strategies available to calm the interviewee if you sense they are becoming anxious.

The two-interviewer system works well for this. If the interview questions are beginning to make the interviewee nervous, then the interviewer that is not asking the questions can step in and offer some clarification, suggest a break, or even help the interviewee through a question they are struggling with. Helping an interviewee through a question is not a bad thing. While this might seem counterintuitive since the point of the interview is to gauge applicant responses to questions, it is more important that the applicant is relaxed and able to converse normally.

All interviewers should provide authentic positive feedback when possible during the interview. I have been on both sides of interviews where the interviewer felt it was important to not give any reaction whatsoever. The result is a pressurized environment where the applicant has no idea if they're doing well or not.

Technical Assessment

Technical skill requirements are the easier side of the interview. As the interviewer, you are attempting to answer the following questions:

- To what degree does this individual meet the requirements of the work they will be expected to execute?

- To what degree will this individual be able to make meaningful technical contributions to the service?

The first question relates to the immediate need that the position is intended to satisfy, and the second question relates to the long-term value added to the team as a whole that the candidate is expected to provide. Prior to the interview, the requirements for satisfying both of these questions should be established through collaboration between the technical and project leadership of the team. As an example of these requirements, if an OCS is attempting to fill a junior team role with a focus on web application pentesting, their short-term requirements would look something like:

- Familiar with BurpSuite

- Understands basic web application vulnerabilities and how to identify and exploit

- Understands the general flow of a penetration test flow

From these requirements, OCS leadership would derive questions such as

- Can you tell me about a vulnerability you identified using BurpSuite? Please highlight the BurpSuite tools you used to identify and exploit the vulnerability and walk me through the process you used to do both.

- Can you define Cross-Site Scripting vulnerabilities, their various types, and how testing for them is generally done?

- If you were to conduct a penetration test, what are the phases of testing that you would go through and what is the goal of each phase?

Long-term requirements for senior positions will be more focused on team capability development and the technical direction of the team. We'll discuss this more in-depth later in this book. For junior team members, long-term requirements are focused on their self-development.

Since the position in our example is a junior position, the long-term requirements might look something like

- Will most likely be capable of becoming OSCP (Offensive Security Certified Professional) certified within 1 year

- Will provide assistance in coding new testing techniques developed by team seniors

From which, the following questions are derived:

- How well did you perform on your last certification/ degree/class?

- What do you do to develop your skills in offensive cybersecurity?

- What coding languages are you familiar with?

- Do you have any publicly viewable code projects?

Hands-on practical examinations are a great way to get a real look at what the applicant can do with their technical skills instead of just discussing it. The second team that I built developed a Capture the Flag (CTF) scenario. This CTF consisted of six machines hosted in the cloud. Three of the machines were available to the applicant via the Internet, and the remaining three machines made up an internal network. Each machine contained a unique flag that the applicant needed to retrieve to get credit for the host.

The CTF was very useful especially when evaluating junior candidates. It can be difficult to get a thorough understanding of the abilities of junior- or entry-level candidates since their resumes are fairly empty. Some of my most successful team members joined the team with no degree, no certifications, and no experience, but they were able to demonstrate their skills and ability through large-scope interview questions and completion of the CTF.

Team Compatibility Assessment

With a little time and funding, technical skills can be taught, whereas motivation, passion, a willingness to work with others, ability to challenge the status quo when appropriate, and the intellect to learn quickly and adapt cannot be. Therefore, an applicant's personality and their compatibility with the team should receive a slightly higher priority when selecting a new team member.

Team compatibility does not mean that the new team member will play nice and never cause a disruption. Disruptions are a good thing. All teams will grow stale and overly reliant on old processes. The best new team member is not necessarily the one that will readily accept the status quo. New team members bring a fresh take on your team's established processes and have an ability to identify flaws that have been missed for years. The difference between a team member who adds value with their challenges and a disruptive team member is timing and acceptance. Processes should be challenged when the team is ready to address the challenge. There are meetings specifically for this purpose that we'll talk in the chapter on team management. Once a decision has been made by OCS leadership, the team members accept and execute that decision.

Team compatibility evaluation is more difficult than technical evaluation. There are no CTFs for things like emotional intelligence, conflict resolution, professionalism, and ego management. Adding to the difficulty, applicants are incentivized to present their best behavior during the interview process. The way they behave during the interview is not fully indicative of how they will interact with your team.

Like the technical evaluation, team compatibility evaluation begins by establishing the questions we are trying to answer:

- Is the applicant able to learn and adapt to new scenarios and gain new skills quickly?

- Will they collaborate well on projects and effectively assist other team members when needed?

- Will this individual connect well with the rest of the team and be inspired by the team's vision?

The first requirement can be assessed by giving the candidate nonstandard scenario-based questions or by asking them about a time in their testing experience where they identified an interesting or unique vulnerability. I have found a lot of success with the latter option. Interviewees will often become energetic and lose some anxiety while explaining the work they did to identify and exploit a vulnerability. The question helps to smooth out any interview anxiety and gives the interviewers a great view into the interviewee's testing process and ability to react to difficult situations.

The second requirement can also be answered through scenario-based questions or previous testing experience. If the applicant has worked in technical team environments before, the interviewers can ask about how he interacted and collaborated with his peers.

The last requirement requires the table to turn a bit because the interviewers are the ones providing information to the interviewee. Most of the time, the interviewee will ask about the team environment and the work that is to be done unprompted, but regardless of who starts the conversation, the interviewers should give the interviewee a detailed description of the work that would be immediately expected and the long-term opportunities. I have conducted a few interviews where the applicant was particularly good at one domain of testing (e.g., web application testing) but considered that domain to be boring. When I let the applicant know that while work in web applications would be expected, the team had lots of other types of testing available. The applicants were excited at the possibility of learning testing outside of the domain they were already familiar with.

Retaining Talent

Once you have hired a new team member, work begins on developing and maintaining an environment that encourages and inspires that team member to remain with your OCC. You might assume that compensation is the primary driver when it comes to team retention, but in my experience, there are several factors that are more impactful than raw compensation numbers.

The Mission Mindset

I have personally never been more passionate for the mission of a team than when I was a soldier assigned to work at the National Security Agency (NSA). The team was made up of military members and civilian employees, and they were all just as passionate as I was. The mission was personal to each of us. Not only was the work very challenging, but the team members challenged each other and themselves. We expected each of us to bring our best. When I wasn't actively working the mission, I was developing my skills so that I could rise to the challenge and do my best to push the mission forward.

You might be thinking that this doesn't apply to you or your team. Your team is probably not directly involved in the defense of the nation. Even if it is, that may not feel like enough to spark passion.

The truth is that there were several other teams at the NSA with an identical mission to the team I was assigned to. The other teams did very good work, but most did not have the level of passion and dedication that my team had. They didn't challenge each other, and some were even apathetic toward their mission.

When your team's mission has an obvious importance tied to it (defense of the nation, landing a man on the moon, stopping a wildfire, etc.), you have a significant advantage in cultivating a mission mindset. The importance of the mission is obvious. Its definition of success is clear cut. The leader of the team doesn't have to do as much to create a mission mindset because the mission has done a lot of the work for them. But even such important and obvious missions aren't enough. Without a clear vision, a standard to rise to, and observable progress, no mission will be important enough on its own. It is these elements, not the mission itself, that create the mission mindset.

Constructing a Mission

What is the mission of any professional sports team? The obvious answer would be, "to win the trophy." But if that were the mission, then a team would win the trophy and then not return the following year. Why come back the next year to do it all over again when the mission was accomplished? A mission can't inspire team members to the same degree the second time around, can it?

Winning the trophy is not the mission of a sports team. Becoming the kind of team that wins trophies is. It's personal. It's not based on getting one trophy. It's not based on a finite amount of time (the sports season). Rather, it is an infinite mission of challenging oneself and each other to rise to the standard that the game sets. The games won and the trophies earned are just the observable progress toward that goal.

The mission that you develop for your team is likewise infinite. It is about becoming the kind of team that gets the results that are important to it. It is not about the results themselves.

My second team had the following goals:

1. Deliver the most value to our clients

2. Perfect team management processes

3. Push team capabilities to the next level

4. Develop team member skills to the next level

These goals should work for most consultative teams. They are the team's vision, and they give each team member an understanding of the direction that the team is moving in.

On its own, the vision is rather meaningless. I've worked for many companies with illustrious vision statements that had no impact on my work or the culture of the company. Vision becomes a mission when a standard is applied. As the team leader, you are responsible for determining and enforcing the standard.

Setting the Standard

A standard is made up of the expectations placed on the work of each team member. It is the level of quality that is considered acceptable within the team. Developing a standard is deceptively simple. Team leaders across all industries have tried to set a standard by demanding motivation and raising the bar of what is considered acceptable over and over. We hear about these kinds of toxic leaders all the time. Their teams put in the lowest amount of effort required, and their turnover rate is unacceptably high. This is not only unethical, it is unnecessary, and in the close knit community of offensive cybersecurity, it can be deadly to your team's future.

If you set your standard too high, team members will become overwhelmed and frustrated. If you set it too low, they will become overly comfortable and not challenge themselves.

Developing a standard is an iterative process. You start with the broad strokes, and as you and your team learn, experiment, and mature, you add the finer details. The broad strokes should be simple and self-evidently good for the team and its business. They should be expressed in a single sentence, and there should be one broad standard for each area of management. These broad standards should not require much change, only growth as the team matures.

As an exercise in the inception of a team standard, let's break down and apply a broad standard to the five management domains we discussed in Chapter 2:

- Lead

- Project

- Client

- Team

- Capability

Lead

Lead management may be outside of your responsibilities depending on the type of team you manage. For my second team, we worked closely with our sales team. This served us well because we developed our understanding of client expectations, their environment, and the scope directly from the client.

We set the standard that a tester would attend all sales calls. It didn't matter if it was an initial sales call or a quick final meeting before the sale, a tester was present. This is a standard I often had to enforce against the intuition of my upper management. They felt that a tester's time would be best spent testing. However, my team believed that we did more than provide technical assistance in getting a sale. We were putting our best foot forward and impressing the client from the start. Our clients were almost always fairly technical. Allowing a client to speak directly with a tester who would be involved in their assessment put them at ease especially since their experience with other teams consisted of only nontechnical salespeople and surveys they were required to fill out. As the revenue my team generated grew by leaps and bounds year after year, my upper management eventually relented.

Project

The standards you set in the project management domain will determine what is most important in the setup and execution of a project. While it's always better to have at least a broad standard from the beginning, I did not set one for project/engagement management. I don't believe I was educated enough on what good engagement management looked like at the start of my second team to determine a standard. Rather, the engagement standard was developed over time as my team, and I learned to boil down the essentials of good engagement management processes.

The broad standard we eventually adopted was "give the tester the best chance for success." From this standard came ideas such as ensuring testers had access to all engagement data formatted intelligently and located in one place, not assigning a tester to more than one project at a time, and more.

Client

The client standard I set for my team was "we are successful when a significant number of clients are referring us to their colleagues." To me, that was the ultimate sign of success. A client was so impressed and satisfied with the quality of our work that they were excited to tell their friends about it. Anytime my sales team received a lead from a referral, I shared that success with the OCS team. It was our most significant form of observable progress. Our second broad standard was "always keep the client and tester informed through strong communication channels," which is a principle this book will discuss in great detail.

Team

You might assume that the team management domain is where you apply a standard to the team but that is not the case. You will apply a standard to how you will manage the team. It is something you will openly discuss with your team and something they will call you out on if you fail to live up to it. For example, all members of my second team knew that I would never require them to work beyond their 40 hours a week. Requesting or requiring team members to work beyond the hours set for the team is a band aid to cover up poor management processes and a lack of foresight. Last-minute changes and the chaos of the business are not an excuse. As leaders in the offensive cybersecurity industry, we are expected to understand the chaos and account for it. Therefore, I consider it a personal failure as the leader of a team if I have to ask them to work over 40 hours. That is not to say that I did not have occasional failures in my management and foresight. There were times that I requested extra support to cover overbooked assessments. But in those times, I acknowledged my failure to meet the standard of team management that I had set. I held meetings with my team and explained to them how the failure occurred and what I was going to do to ensure it didn't happen again.

42

The team management standards are some of the most important ones you will set. They communicate to the team what they can expect from their leadership. The standards set the groundwork for your relationship with the team. You are not a manager pushing down requirements and expecting results. Instead, you are in the trenches with them, a leader that expects as much from himself as he does from them.

Capability

Capability is the management domain dedicated to the processes of developing and maintaining the team's tools and techniques across testing domains. A broad standard for this management domain encompasses the expectations the team will have for the state of each of its capabilities and the outcomes of development effort. For example, your team might set the following expectation:

All capability techniques must be learnable without help and usable without direction.

This standard is not set to avoid team mentorship and internal training. It is set to ensure that the documentation standards and the final state of any capability are at the stage where the team can actually use it and self-educate.

Technical Challenges

Like most consultative companies, the projects that my second team executed were very diverse. Every client's environment was different as was their expectations for our work. It kept my team on their toes. Any time they felt comfortable in their skillset, some new challenge would emerge that they weren't prepared for.

In the moment, these dynamic challenges and expectations could be stressful, but overall, they led to my team members placing greater value on their work and greater faith in their abilities. More than one team member who chose to accept a job in the corporate or government world would later tell me that they missed the work that they did on my team.

IT is a creative industry. IT professionals solve unique problems in new ways every day. Problem solving through creativity is the core of what makes IT professionals passionate about their work, and offensive cybersecurity is no different.

More often than not, offensive cybersecurity professionals will choose to accept a position with a lower salary if they know the work is interesting and challenging. This works for retention too. I once had three members of my team choose to stay on the team even knowing that other companies would happily give them a much higher salary than what my budget could allow. I eventually asked each of them to apply to other positions because it was better for their careers.

Diverse and interesting technical challenges come easy in the world of consulting, but it might not come as easily in your field. Healthcare, infrastructure, and other more regulated industries require paperwork and stiff procedures that stifle creativity in favor of predictability and reliability. The work can become boring, repetitive, and paperwork-heavy. So how do you provide your team with opportunities for creativity and passion?

The first way is that you take advantage of an opportunity within your team's work to provide exposure to new challenges. For example, if your team works in a healthcare field that is rolling out new medical devices, perhaps your team could validate the security of the devices before they are implemented. Look for new and creative ways to leverage your team's skillset beyond the strict requirements of the job.

Second, you can schedule regular team collaboration exercises with platforms like HackTheBox or OffSec's Cyber Range. These platforms provide opportunities for training and team building while also giving your team an escape from the possible monotony of their requirements.

Compensation

The likelihood that a team member stays with your service for the long term is not directly proportional to their compensation. I have both hired and retained members of my team at salaries that were lower than what they could get elsewhere, and they knew it. Interesting work, an investment in education, dedication to individual development, and a strong team environment are the best tools you have in retaining talent. I am not advocating paying team members less than they are worth, but budget and industry restrictions will most likely prevent you from being the highest-paying team in the field. You will have to offer more than just compensation in order to attract and retain talent.

That being said, compensation is still an obvious and important factor. Regardless of how great your team gets along members aren't going to stay around if they are paid significantly less than the current typical salary for their skill level. As the leader of the OCC, you have two responsibilities in this regard. You need to stay relatively up to date on the current market value for the skillsets of your team members, and you will have to present a strong argument for compensation increases to the upper management when the time comes.

Staying current on compensation trends is part of community engagement. Establishing connections between your OCS leadership team and other leaders or members of management in the field will help you stay current. There are also several websites that proport to track salary trends in several fields. These sites can offer some general idea of where salaries are, but they seem to be overly generalized and do not take into account other forms of compensation.

When working with upper management to adjust compensation, it's helpful to understand their point of view. Upper management will view the OCS through the lens of its metrics. For consultative teams, the metrics will be related to revenue generation. How many engagements were successfully executed? How many clients have returned for repeat business? Is the team maintaining an acceptable level of billable time? For internal teams, the metrics will be more related to the security improvements that have been enabled and driven by the efforts of the OCC.

With the metrics that are important to upper management in hand, the next step is to associate the given team member with those metrics and to demonstrate how their efforts have pushed the metrics forward. Has the team member received any new certifications that allow the OCS to enter new markets? Have they developed new techniques that have resulted in an increase to the number and quality of vulnerabilities identified? Have they developed strong relationships with clients and are the reason that the team is able to better interface with those clients?

In addition to the metrics, upper management will need an understanding of average industry compensation and where the OCS falls on that scale. You cannot expect upper management to be familiar enough with the offensive cybersecurity marketplace to be able to accurately determine an appropriate salary. They will need data and experience that reinforce your recommendations.

When there simply isn't room in the budget for increased compensation, attempt to work with upper management to provide other forms of compensation. Additional training time, training material, and paid conference attendance can go a long way.

Burnout

Developing an OCS is a long-term endeavor, and considering the level of effort that is put into developing your team's skillsets, it is best that new team members stay with the team for at least a few years. If your management style is focused on short-term gains, you will face long-term damage and team member burnout.

The most common way that burnout occurs is when team members are overworked. This can be due to management over-allocating work to team members who are then forced to put in the extra hours to accomplish it or due to individual team members not knowing when to stop. You can prevent both sources of overwork by developing a healthy work culture in your team.

When managing my second team, I created a policy where I would not ask anyone to work more than their 40 hours. This directly eliminated the possibility of management causing burnout through too much work, but it didn't do much to stop team members from burning themselves out. What I discovered is that my team began to naturally police themselves. By setting a strong anti-burnout stance, I informed my team of what was acceptable. From that point, if any team member noticed another team member consistently putting a significantly high number of hours into a project, they would raise it at the next team meeting and voice their concern.

The second anti-burnout policy I created was mandatory paid time off (PTO). My second team had an unlimited PTO policy, meaning that as long as time off was approved, an employee was allowed to take it. Although the unlimited PTO policy was intended to encourage employees to take more time off, my team did just the opposite. After the policy was put into place, I noticed how little time off the team members were taking. The risk of burnout was increasing. To combat this, I threatened my team that if they did not schedule their own PTO, I would schedule it for them. I expected every team member to take at least three weeks off per year.

These two policies were the basis of my anti-burnout approach, but they did a lot more than that. They let my team know that I wanted to create a healthy working environment, something that is not easy to find at many employers. It was a major contributing factor in my ability to retain my team members for years even when they were given better compensation offers from my competitors.

CHAPTER 4

Team Management

In this chapter, we'll take a look at how to manage an offensive cybersecurity service. We will review a few of the standard agile principles but this is not a chapter on the theories of project management. My goal is to discuss the real-world challenges that pentesting teams will encounter, present the ways in which I have overcome them, and discuss the lessons that I drew from those encounters.

Time Management

Time management doesn't get the respect it deserves. Whether or not the most qualified resource is assigned to work a given project is the first and most significant indicator of whether the project will be successful, and the client satisfied. When leading my second team, I learned that if I failed to adequately deploy my resources to meet the demands of each project, the client's response was far more likely to be mediocre at best. I couldn't expect that client to talk about how crazy good my hackers were. I couldn't expect future clients to reach out, interested after they heard about my team's work.

Time management can be deceptively simple. On the surface, it seems that the team leader is simply aligning a tester with the correct skillset to the requirements of the project. What could be difficult about putting a square peg into a square hole? There are two challenges that can add a significant amount of complexity. The first is that you may not have

© Michael Butler and Jacob G. Oakley 2024
M. Butler and J. G. Oakley, *The Business of Hacking*,
https://doi.org/10.1007/979-8-8688-0174-7_4

the appropriate skillset available. For example, if there is a particularly large and difficult web application that needs an assessment, you may want to schedule your most senior web application tester to the task. Unfortunately, you find that the tester is already scheduled for another project and won't be available. Now you must either delay the web application assessment, assign a less-qualified tester and risk a less than desirable outcome, hire a new tester, or attempt to find some way to have the senior tester participate in both assessments.

Depending on your organization, some of these options will be more possible than others. For corporate internal teams, delaying a project due to insufficient resourcing might be more possible than it is in the world of consulting where delays mean a loss of revenue. But the solution cannot always be to delay project. Hiring additional resources will fix a lot of these problems if you are fortunate enough to be in an organization that provides enough budget to do so. For the rest of us, we have to get creative.

The second challenge is that while a simple pairing of skills to requirements is functional, it is often not the best fit. Skillset is the most important factor, but it is only one factor in determining which tester is the best fit for a project. Other factors include

- Client communication skills

- Prior experience and rapport with the client

- Prior experience with the technologies involved in this project

- Tester interest in the project

A team leader can either ignore these other factors and wonder why the team output quality is inconsistent or they can spend a great deal of time creating and adjusting team schedules that consider each one. This last option gets worse with time because the team lead has to be familiar with all the testers on a growing team. Neither option is wonderful. Believe me, I've tried both.

What is needed is a low-overhead system that maximizes the efficiency of the team's work hours while accounting for the unique needs of our clients and applies the specific tangible and intangible skills of testers to those needs. We need this system to not rely solely on the team leader but to be capable of scaling as the team grows. Finally, the system must be very flexible and adaptable to changes in project schedules and scope.

This system sounds like a fantasy that couldn't exist in the real world.

The System

We have a hefty list of requirements for a system that's going to manage our team resources. Before we begin to tackle them, we need a few rules for the system. These rules are based on my experience with what creates an environment of team camaraderie (discussed more in depth later in this chapter).

Rules

- If a tester is assigned to a project, they must not be moved from that project until it is complete or there is a work stoppage.

- Testers must not be asked to work more than a 40-hour work week.

The first rule came from realizing that whenever a tester was jumped from project to project, their concentration was broken. They were frustrated because they weren't able to complete something they had started and now they had to start over with a whole different assessment. Testers need time to understand the environment they are working in. It is not helpful for them or good for assessment quality to move them around before the project is complete. The assessment's report suffers when multiple testers are moved in and out of the project. Finally, the client feels uneasy when the tester they are working with shifts to someone new that they have not built rapport with yet.

The second rule may seem obvious to some and ignorant to others. Tech fields in general seem to have a love of working more than the time allotted, and some team leaders rely on this fact. As a team lead, I appreciated my testers' motivation and dedication to their craft. If they wanted to work extra hours to educate themselves, solve a difficult problem in an assessment, or build something new for the team, they were certainly allowed to do so. However, I never asked nor required them to work extra hours. The only exception to this rule occurred at times when an unforeseen circumstance resulted in the team no longer having the resources that were expected and left our hours short. In these circumstances, I worked with my upper management to pay testers for any extra hours they choose to put in, but once again, it was not required. I also viewed these occurrences as a failure on my part to adequately prepare and staff my team for the work that was assigned, and I informed the team of the changes I was implementing to make sure it would not happen again in the future.

Having an expectation for testers to work beyond their normal number of work hours per week is planning to eventually burnout the tester while simultaneously reducing the quality of the work due to increased stress and reduced rest.

Staffing

The exact mix of skills needed on a team is going to be highly situational. However, the general principle should be that the junior-level testers outnumber the senior-level testers by at least three to one. This does two things. It allows the team leader to have more team members on their team while still meeting budget limitations, giving the leader more flexibility in scheduling. Secondly, it keeps senior testers focused on tasks that require their level of skill.

Teams that are more top-heavy skill-wise require their seniors to spend more time on tasks that junior-level testers can accomplish. Additionally, they require that the seniors spend more time performing assessments instead of performing research into capability evolutions (more on that in the next chapter). The result is senior testers that are somewhat bogged down with junior-level tasks and possibly even bored with the lack of challenge in much more of their work.

But won't less senior testers naturally result in lower-quality team output? This was my question when I began shifting the skill ratio of my team more toward the junior side. The answer is no as long as the team leader takes the steps to ensure that senior testers perform senior tasks and junior testers perform junior tasks. As an example, let's say a particularly complicated web application requires an assessment. The assessment infrastructure must be created, initial scans need to be run, and a catalog of web application endpoints and pages needs to be assembled. These tasks do not require a senior tester's time. A junior tester can perform them and then provide the results to the senior tester for review and manual testing.

This is the simple principle behind maximizing the efficient utilization of team resources – senior testers perform senior tasks; junior testers perform junior tasks. With this approach, we maximize the effectiveness of the senior tester and free them up for ensuring the success of multiple projects simultaneously. This last point is important. Instead of assigning a senior tester to a single project, they can be assigned to a small subteam of junior-level testers.

This is a unique paradigm that I haven't seen used in many teams, but it is the most effective use of tester time. The junior-level testers are focused on individual projects. A single application, network, or whatever other target type gets their full attention. The senior-level tester is responsible for ensuring success of two or three projects instead of putting their effort entirely into a single project. The senior tester applies their experience and knowledge to make sure that the clients of all projects are satisfied instead of focusing on one project and one client.

This approach has the added benefit of making the quality of several testers consistent. The senior tester is familiar with the standards set by the team lead and will make sure that all the assessment under their watch adhere to them.

This is not necessarily a one-size-fits-all approach. There are some projects that require senior attention from beginning to end. For example, if the team receives a contract to assess the security of a piece of hardware and the team's junior testers are not familiar with the process, then a senior tester will have to conduct a larger portion of the test. However, even in these scenarios junior testers should be involved. They are learning opportunities and should result in more educated junior testers and new team documentation on how to conduct hardware-based assessments.

Cheap and Scalable

The last two requirements we have to satisfy for our system is to make the system easily scalable to any team size and to keep the time and financial costs low. Scalability is achieved through simple repeatable architectures. If a system is sufficiently simplified, then it will not require the constant attention of the team leader. Instead, low-cost resources will be able to perform the majority of scheduling tasks.

A senior tester who is assigned to ensure the success of a subteam of several junior- or mid-level testers will become intimately familiar with the skillsets, experience, and client communication capabilities of each of the testers. As the team adds new members, new subteams are constructed and assigned resources. Instead of the team leader scheduling the time of each individual resource, the leader assigns projects to a subteam that has the skillset to execute the project. The senior tester in charge of that subteam then determines how the team will approach the assignment and ensures that the team standards of quality are met in all assigned projects.

Once the team consists of more than one subteam, the team leader should hand off the responsibility of assigning projects to a low-cost resource. I have had success using college students or recent graduates to run project scheduling for the entire team. By providing the scheduler with a basic idea of what each project requires and the general skills of each team, the scheduler can perform the broad strokes of project assignments. Then the senior leader of the team to which a project is assigned can determine who in their subteam is best suited to tackle the project.

Handling Disruptions

Our system is theoretically sound so far. As the team receives projects, they are assigned out to subteams and then assigned to the appropriate individual(s). This might work for a lot of teams especially if they are serving one predictable customer and don't need to account for a lot of changes. In the contracting world, my team expected at least three significant changes to scheduling and resources on a weekly basis. These changes can come from any piece in the contract pipeline. Here are a few of the more common root causes for changes that I have experienced:

- The client is not ready for the test at the agreed upon kickoff date.

- The contract paperwork was delayed due to negotiations, legal concerns, etc.

- A team member is not able to perform the work due to an unexpected personal situation.

- A project that has already started cannot continue because some element is not ready for the next phase of testing.

- The amount of time initially scoped for a project is insufficient and the project must be extended.

If you are in charge of a team that is going to experience a good amount of instability in scheduling expectations, you have two choices. You can either build a rigid or a flexible system. A rigid system handles unexpected changes by simply rescheduling the project into a new slot to give whatever is causing the delay time to be remedied. This is the best approach from a process point of view. It is simple, it solves the problem, and it's scalable. Unfortunately, it may also be totally unacceptable when considering client deadlines for security assessments and the potential for lost revenue due to pushing back projects.

In a flexible system, the team leader must find ways to adapt to changes in scheduling. A flexible system requires flexibility in the resources that execute it. In an offensive cybersecurity service, the primary resource is tester time. If testers are expected to be executing work during 90–100% of their available work hours, there is not enough resource flexibility for the schedulers to adapt quickly to changes in schedules and client requirements.

The team leader should establish early on how scheduling will respond to the level of expected changes. If the team is going to use a flexible system, then the leader must set a billable hour threshold. Once crossed, this threshold triggers the process for bringing an additional resource on to the team. I typically set my threshold at 80%. If 80% of my team's available work hours were assigned to projects for more than three weeks in a row, I informed my upper management that we needed to begin interviews. The 80% worked for me, but it's not a hard rule. It's going to fluctuate based on how predictable your team's workload is and how often changes that require flexibility are going to occur.

Team Coordination

Coordinating your team is the process of aligning, preparing, and supporting team members for and through their assessments. The team leader is responsible for creating, enforcing, and managing the framework in which these processes take place, but the team leader does not conduct all the processes themselves, especially when it comes to providing support.

One of the core ideas of agile teams is that they are self-organizing. They can also be self-supporting if given the correct tools. The ability of a team to self-support is directly linked to the connection and camaraderie felt between the team members. It is the team leader's job to foster camaraderie and then leverage it to provide support to the members of the team.

At one point in my career, I worked on a team where tests were conducted in a vacuum. The assessments were assigned out, and other than a short awkward weekly meeting, there was no assistance readily available for me from my peers or more senior testers. Any technical challenges that I encountered were mine to overcome alone. As you would imagine, this siloed approach to team coordination negatively affected my ability to conduct assessments, and consequently, the quality of my work was less than it could have been.

I wasn't the only one in the dark. I was siloed from my team and my client was siloed from me. My focus was on the technical challenges of my daily work on the project. I did not have the vision nor the time to think about things from the client's point of view and determine if they were going to be happy with the end product. This meant that my team lead only found out about project issues at the end of the assessment when it was too late to do anything about it.

A lack of camaraderie will result in a lack internal self-supporting coordination. As we construct our team's internal processes, our focus should be to create an environment where team members are encouraged to work together and work with clients.

If we've done our job correctly, then all the testers on the team will know which projects they are assigned to in advance. Of course, last-minute changes happen, pentesting is a field with a fair bit of chaos mixed in, but once a tester is assigned to a project, they cannot be reassigned unless work on that project is halted. This allows them to really dig in and understand the target environment, the unique requirements of the client, and the tech they will be attempting to circumvent.

Along the path of the assessment, the team leader has a number of tools and touchpoints to address issues early on, provide support to each tester, and gain an understanding of the quality of each ongoing assessment. If the team leader isn't happy with the level of quality from a certain assessment, they are given enough time to do something about it.

Preparing for Client Communication

Communicating directly with clients is not something that is taught in offensive security courses, and it doesn't always come naturally. In fact, tech professionals are often discouraged from speaking directly with clients. But the benefits of a client being directly involved and providing influence into the progress of the assessment are too great to have walls between them and their tester.

If testers are going to communicate with clients, then they need guidance on how to do so. First and foremost, there can't be too much expected from the tester. As a team leader, we cannot put the burden of managing the client through the whole pre- and post-engagement process on a tester. The scope of their client communication requirements needs to be narrowly defined and simply formatted so that the tester can spend as much time testing as possible and the client gets the information they need.

For the handoff and kickoff meetings, communication is pretty straightforward for the assigned tester. The tester doesn't need to do more than introduce themselves and maybe give a short bio. A low-cost operations assistant or a senior member of the team should be responsible for ensuring all important topics are covered and both parties understand what is needed for the test to begin.

Daily updates are where testers start contributing more to client communication. This might make some testers nervous and other testers annoyed. Providing a simple format should address both reactions by showing the tester what needs to be sent to the client and then allowing them to get back to the work they enjoy. An example format would be

- Three bullet points of what testing occurred the previous day and what the results were

- Three bullet points of what testing is planned for the current day

- Any blockers that are preventing the tester from performing aspects of the assessment

Daily Standup

The daily standup is a tool straight from the agile toolbox. It is a short meeting, usually no more than 15 minutes, where team members discuss their projects and list any blockers preventing them from being more successful. For teams that work together in an office, conduct the daily standup by physically meeting and going through the projects. For remote teams, the daily standup is usually conducted over a video call.

The daily standup is a great tool for agile project management, but team leads need to recognize that it has another very important quality – it is the first time that the team meets every day. This meeting sets the tone for internal team communication and collaboration. If at the end of the standup, the testers go back to their various corners of the office or turn off their webcams and return to their assessments, it breeds an environment of tester isolation. This is especially concerning for remote teams who already have a difficult time establishing team camaraderie without face-to-face contact.

As I mentioned in the introduction to this book, I have experience in both highly isolated and highly collaborative teams. All team members on both teams worked remotely. Without a doubt, highly collaborative teams are far more successful in their assessments and far more happy with their work. Testers on highly collaborative teams are easier to retain because they enjoy their team environment. That's worth something to them, so much so that they will even forego a higher salary at another company to stay with a highly collaborative team.

The primary difference between the two teams that I managed was how they leveraged team meetings. The isolated team had one weekly meeting for one hour where team members would talk about their projects and how things were going. They received little feedback or interest because they rarely talked to each other.

My second, more collaborative, team started every day with a daily standup call and then crucially did not end that call. We will discuss this technique in greater detail in a few pages.

Vulnerability Sharing

While leading a highly collaborative team, I came up with an activity that supported both team camaraderie and development. Typically, when a tester identifies a vulnerability, they notify the client and document the finding. They might mention the vulnerability at the next morning's team standup, but other than that, they move on with their testing. I realized that any time a vulnerability is identified, it is an opportunity for learning and development for the rest of the team.

With vulnerability sharing, when a tester identifies a vulnerability, they let the team know and then show them the area of the environment in which the vulnerability was identified. Any team members with a few hours to spare would attempt to find the vulnerability themselves. This creates a moment where a team member's assessment process is examined by his peers. If the team member is unable to find the vulnerability, then the original tester walks them through how the vulnerability was found and makes sure that any missing techniques are added to the team member's process.

Alternatively, when a tester finds a vulnerability they can go through a show-and-tell session where they walk the team through how it was identified and answer any questions. Of course, all of this must be done with prior client approval to make sure there isn't an issue with other testers working on the environment.

Retrospective

Another tool from the agile toolbox is the retrospective or "retro." This is a monthly meeting where the team reviews the successes and difficulties of projects that were completed during the previous month. The team identifies areas for improvement and process that are functioning well. Retros are guided by the team leader, but as a team leader, you should not expect to emerge unscathed. I often have found myself answering questions regarding why certain project management decisions were made. Retros are not limited in their critique of a project's handling. Team members are not required to stick to the technical side of the test, and the team leader should be prepared to answer management questions and take suggestions for improvements.

Retrospectives are the most important tool you have to identify weaknesses in team processes.

The retro results in a list of ideas for process improvements. This is where process experimentation begins. Ideas are just theories for improvement and they may fail in practice. You and your team should prioritize the ideas by the expected improvement a given idea will hopefully generate. No process should have more than one experiment running at a time so that the results of the experiment can be are not contaminated by the effects of another experiment.

As an example of how this works, let's say your team brings up an issue with how engagement data is being communicated to testers before an engagement. Client requests aren't making their way to the tester, and more than one client has complained that minor requests that they made early in the pipeline were not completed. The team determines that an improvement to the client data communication process would be to have testers assigned to a project present at all meetings prior to the project's start date. You agree and start an experiment. For the following month, all projects will have their assigned tester present at all client meetings prior to the project's execution.

As the experiment is executed, you note the process change appears to be a success. Testers are generally more aware of specific client requests than they previously were. However, you also find that this new process improvement comes with some drawbacks. It isn't always possible for the assigned tester to attend all client meetings. It is somewhat distracting to the tester to attend these meetings when they are in the middle of executing a totally separate contract. Finally, assigning a tester to a contact is not a guarantee that the tester will actually be the one who executes it. Things change and schedules shift.

During the following month's retrospective meeting, you note the success of the process change but also bring up the drawbacks. Your team is now better educated concerning what works and what doesn't work with the given process. A new improvement is developed that addresses both the original concern and the new concerns that were previously unknown.

Through this process of iteration, the retrospective and experimentation will gradually you and your team and improve all aspects of project execution. It is also the most effective tool in making your team members feel they have a voice and an impact in the direction of the team.

Team Climate

Building a team with a strong sense of camaraderie is hard. The difficulty is exacerbated by modern teams primarily working remotely. A team leader can't rely on physical proximity to do most of the work for them anymore. Inaction will lead to a team without connection. Team members will likely retreat to their own corners and perform their assigned tasks in isolation when left to their own devices.

Connected teams work together. They leverage the skillset of each member to ensure the success of all projects. And they're more fun. Building these kinds of teams is something that many industries are struggling with, not just those in tech. How do we get our teams to connect and work together especially when they are not physically co-located?

Getting Started

There is a running theme in a lot of the management principles this book discusses. The idea is that you as the team leader are responsible for sparking a process, generating moment for the process, and then getting the team behind it. Once the team buys into it, they will continue the momentum. Attempting to enforce a process that the team is not buying into is a losing battle. Your answers to team issues must fit with the team so that they become integrated and a natural flow of the daily life of each team member.

Team climate is one of these processes. In order to successfully build a connected team, you will need to build team processes that encourage connection and implement the processes in the team's daily life until momentum builds and the process becomes natural. If the team resists or the process seems to fizzle, then it may not be a good fit for your team. Being heavy-handed with your enforcement of a process that is not being accepted will not work out. You can't order the team into building camaraderie.

All-Day Call

The all-day call is the most successful technique that I have used to build team connection. The idea is simple. The team begins the day with their morning standup meeting. They discuss their projects, any successes, and any blockers they have encountered. Once standup is finished, the call does not end. Instead, the call continues for the rest of the day. Team members are free to hop on and off the call. They are not required to have their cameras turned on. This is to make the work environment for each team member as comfortable as possible for them while still maintaining a connection with the rest of the team.

Of course, the team also has text communication that they can use. But it feels a little odd to type something out to a team member that you are in a call with. So instead, team members talk. For a remote team, getting team members to talk to each other at least a little everyday after standup ends is a huge win. Once they start discussing their work and giving each other guidance and advice, they have started to become collaborative, and they are building camaraderie.

Implementing this idea can be difficult especially in a team that is not used to having an open door to collaborating. The ice needs to be broken so that it becomes second nature for a tester to bring up an issue in the all-day call and know that they will receive support.

For the first week that this technique is implemented, all team members should be required to be on the call all day. Again, they don't need to turn on their cameras. It doesn't need to be an uncomfortable nuisance that they will happily abandon once the required week is over. During that first week, the team leader and the senior testers should proactively offer help to the other team members, ask them how the project is going, and generally take an interest in the work of the junior- and mid-level testers.

The all-day call should become the first place that testers go when they want to bounce an idea off their team or need help figuring out the last step to a vulnerability. New members to the team should also have the one-week requirement to be on the call all day so that they too can see how the team collaborates.

If you are successful at implementing the all-day call in your team, you find that they begin to discuss other things than just their current project. They'll discuss their personal lives, interests, hobbies, etc. The all-day call becomes the office water cooler. This is not a bad thing. While you might feel that time is being wasted, this is no different than what occurs in a typical office environment. In fact, it is a necessary part of building team camaraderie and is the most significant evidence that you have been successful in doing so.

Team Building Activities

Like many of you, I groan when I hear the words "team building activity." In the military, it was called "forced fun," which doesn't sound very fun. I've been through a good number of these activities with the different teams I've worked with and led. My general takeaway has been that team building activities work well for the teams that don't need them. Teams that already have a strong sense of connection will have a lot of fun. Teams where each member is siloed from the rest and barely even knows the names of the other members will want it to be over as quickly as possible.

The point is you cannot rely on team building activities to take a team from 0 to 60. Team connection begins with daily interactions becoming second nature and can then be developed by additional activities.

Negative Team Members

There is nothing more destructive to a strong team climate than a consistently negative team member. I am not referring to members who have occasional complaints about a team process or management decision. This kind of feedback is valuable to identifying ways that your processes may be improved. I am talking about team members who consistently bring a negative and pessimistic attitude to team meetings and new ideas.

You may not notice the amount of damage one consistently negative team member can cause. It wasn't obvious to me at first, but the moment a negative team member would accept a job elsewhere, the whole team seemed to breathe easier. New ideas were presented more freely, and team meetings became more optimistic and effective.

The most common issues that create negative team members are

- They aren't aware of the effect their negativity has.

- They are disgruntled by some issue.

- They don't enjoy their work.

The first two can be addressed more easily than the third. Both require discussions with the team member to help them become aware of how they are affecting the team and to determine if there is any core issue that you can help solve. In my own experience, this works most of the time. Most people don't want to bring the team down and aren't aware of doing so. Once they are made aware, they are apologetic and attempt to have a more positive impact.

The variety of the work that your team executes will limit how much you can do for someone who doesn't enjoy their assignments. We all have to do the work we don't enjoy from time to time. For example, I have yet to meet a pentester who enjoys writing reports, but the reports still need to be written. However, you may have some flexibility within those limitations to assign work to the tester that is more in line with what they enjoy doing.

For example, I have had several testers who enjoyed internal network assessments far more than web application assessments. In those cases, I did what I could to assign them internal network assessments more often and was transparent with them when it wasn't possible. These efforts were appreciated and they improved the testers' attitudes.

It's important that you put the effort and try to improve a negative team member's attitude even if you believe that it's not possible. Your team needs to see that their leader attempts to work with a difficult team member instead of jumping directly to administrative action.

Player Over Pawn: Transparent and Inclusive Management Practices

The fastest way to stifle collaborative momentum is to cause your team members to feel that their input and efforts are not valued. This can be a difficult line for a team leader to walk. On the one hand, you should encourage your team to question everything so that improvements can be identified. On the other hand, your team needs to follow your direction and respect when a decision is made. Your team needs to simultaneously feel encouraged to voice their ideas and criticisms and expected to execute the tasks that are assigned to them.

Allowing your team too much freedom results in having to debate every decision. You will find yourself justifying your project plans to the satisfaction of each team member. If you restrict their ability to understand and criticize team processes, you will lose one of your most valuable resources for improvement.

The solution is to provide designated times where decisions are discussed and feedback is provided. An example of this is the retrospective meeting that we talked earlier in this chapter. When my team and I would have a retrospective meeting, the team members would bring up and discuss the issues and successes of previous projects. As the team leader, I explained the business processes involved in the projects. If a team member felt that a business process could be improved, the team would discuss it and I would provide the perspective of management as to why the process was constructed the way it was. Criticisms of business processes ended it two ways. Either my team's feedback was not accepted due to a stronger business case that required the process to remain as it was or the feedback was accepted and the process was improved. Either way, the team would at least understand how the process functioned, why it functioned that way, and why their feedback was accepted or not.

Providing a time and place for transparency and consideration of improvements allows team members to get involved and to feel that they are not pawns in their workplace destiny. Even if it is not always immediately implemented, their feedback is valued, considered, and responded to. There are no hidden processes or powers-that-be that cannot be explained.

The retrospective meeting is an open forum for discussion of previous projects and the processes that support them. It's a great place for the team to brainstorm solutions and improvements. When a team has a strong sense of collaboration, the retrospective meeting will often go beyond the time it is scheduled for as team members get excited building out new ideas. But the retro is not the only place where constructive criticism and management transparency can be communicated. One-on-one meetings between team leaders and individual team members offer a place where more specific feedback can be provided and discussed.

The scope for retros is team and project wide. The scope for a one-on-one is small and focused on a team member. Both scopes are important for understanding the health and areas needing improvement and transparency within the team.

The idea of opening the door to criticism of business, management, and team processes might make some team leaders nervous. It's important to remember that our job is to align the team and move it toward a vision. If a process that we have constructed or have inherited from upper management is flawed, then it is holding the team back from moving forward as effectively as it could. Criticism and feedback should be allowed up until the point that it begins to affect team alignment, and it is up to the team leader to set that boundary. Processes are not personal.

You have to walk a fine line. On one side, being open to criticism and suggestions about management processes will help you understand and address the difficulties the team is having. I wouldn't have been as successful with my second team if I was the only one coming up with ideas on how to manage all our operations. But on the other side, an openness to criticism can result in a breakdown of authority as the team becomes more and more comfortable with questioning your decisions and the decisions of leaders above you.

You can address this issue by tightly defining when and how criticism and suggestions are to be presented and by moving on from them after they are addressed. For example, I had one very good senior tester on my second team complain that our clients would often change the scope of the assessment shortly before or even during the assessment's execution. I shared his frustration. The clients would often shift the scope but not significantly enough to affect the assessment's time window. However, it reduced the predictability of the assessment and made it more difficult to ensure that a tester with the right skillset was assigned to the project.

The senior tester suggested that clients should be required to sign a scoping document that would be unchangeable without a delay in testing. Other teams used this method to reduce the chaos of their scheduling. After considering the issue for some time, I decided to do nothing. I valued the satisfaction of our clients more than the predictability of our engagements. At that time, the revenue my team generated was increasing by close to 100% every year. I felt that the flexibility we gave to our clients was one of the major reasons that we had been so successful. However, I did suggest that we be more rigid when clients changed the scope in such a way that it would require additional testing time by requiring additional time to be added to the project.

I fully explained my decision and reasoning to the team. The senior tester and several other members of the team were not fans of my approach, but after my explanation was given, we moved on to the next issue. The testers accepted the decision and executed their work accordingly because the time to criticize management processes had ended.

By tightly defining when and how criticism and suggestions will be accepted, you can benefit from the suggestions of your team and help your team members feel that they are players in the success of the team, while still maintaining a leadership position.

Experimentation

About half-way through my time leading my second team, my good friend and boss came up with something he wanted to try. He wanted to nearly double the price per hour for our pentesting services. I disagreed strongly with him. The team had only existed for about 3 years. I did not feel we had built the industry recognition and reputation to ask for higher prices. My boss argued that he had performed market research and determined that our competitors were charging within the range he suggested.

We came to an agreement. We would run an experiment for a short time and see if our clients would accept the new prices. At the time, I attended nearly all sales calls with both new and established clients. I learned that our cliental was highly technical and appreciated having a technical individual on the call. This gave me a front-row seat to view the results of the experiment.

After a few very promising sales calls, we sent out the quotes with the new higher prices. I cringed inside, waiting for the rejection emails to begin filling my inbox. To my very great surprise, I found that I was receiving signed offers instead.

This experience caused me to confront the limitations of my experience and knowledge in my field. I felt I was very familiar with our clients. If I missed the fact that we were grossly undercharging, what else could I be missing? What other experiments could I run not just in the area of sales but in service delivery, management, team structure, and more to identify flawed assumptions?

I was very fortunate to have a team technical director who was very familiar with and supportive of this kind of iterative, experimental, agile-ish approach. From that point forward, when a member of my team had an idea for how something could be improved, the seniors of the team would first debate it to determine if it had enough merit for experimentation. If so, then we would create the parameters for a small experiment to find the truth.

Experimentation is how a team learns. It is the tip of the pioneering spear. Through experiments, a team is able to explore and develop ideas and test assumptions. Once a team realizes how powerful this tool can be, the sky is the limit. You can run experiments on all aspects of client satisfaction, operational management, team management, team structure and composition, time management, communication style and mediums, and much more. After a few of your assumptions are proven wrong or at least misguided, you and your team will learn to test assumptions in-depth before building processes on top of them.

Experimentation gives your team confidence to move in a new direction because they demonstrated a likelihood of success. It generates support from upper management because, if tracked correctly, an experiment will generate hard evidence supporting team decisions.

There are only two limitations that should be placed on experimentation. First, do not overlap experiments or run so many simultaneously that you cannot trust the results from each. As an example, when my boss and I were running that experiment on increasing the hourly price of our assessments, my team requested that we run an experiment on requiring additional documentation from clients before an engagement could begin. I postponed this second experiment because I did not want the possibly negative client reaction to the new requirement to be perceived as a negative reaction to the higher prices. I completed the first experiment and then proceed to the second.

If the base within which you are performing the experiment is large enough, you can run two or more experiments simultaneously. This is commonly called A/B testing in the world of software development. You just have to be sure not to cross the lines.

Second, do not perform frivolous experiments. Each experiment should have a tightly defined hypothesis that it is attempting to prove or disprove. Each experiment should be capable of affecting a decision or a process in how the team operates. The results of each experiment should be verifiable and actionable.

Much of the lessons that I learned and that led me to write this book came about from my team experimenting with ideas I would not have considered and probably wouldn't have given time. Years later, I read the book *The Lean Startup* by Eric Ries. The book is a great source for anyone wanting to learn how to approach a tech startup. It talks a great deal about experimentation and verified learning. I found that the book echoed a lot of my experiences with the benefits of experimentation and how to encourage the practice within a team. I strongly recommend it to any team leader and at every level of management.

CHAPTER 5

Operational Management

The execution of offensive cybersecurity projects requires a coordinated team, communication with the client, and a properly prepared project. Each of these requirements contributes to the overall success of the project and ignoring any of them comes with consequences.

Client Management

Client communication is the most important factor in understanding, preparing for, and directing an assessment. This might seem somewhat obvious, after all who other than the client is going to tell us what they want? But teams, especially larger teams, tend to move toward a consistent standard of assessment rather than adapting each assessment to the specific needs of the client. A one-size-fits-all approach is easy to manage, easy to explain to new testers, easy to justify with upper management, and easy to track. It's a very satisfying way of conducting business because it removes the chaos that is inherent to performing an assessment of an unknown environment.

© Michael Butler and Jacob G. Oakley 2024
M. Butler and J. G. Oakley, *The Business of Hacking*,
https://doi.org/10.1007/979-8-8688-0174-7_5

·   There's nothing wrong with this standardized approach to assessments as long as you acknowledge that a deeper level of quality is being sacrificed for predictability and speed. There are many pentesting companies that offer quick and inexpensive assessments. A friend of mine referred to this style of pentest team a "pentest puppy mill."

If you and your clients expect your team to perform a high-quality assessment that considers the unique factors present in their environment, you will have to take a different approach. This idea is difficult to swallow for tech people, especially those with a background in software development. As tech people, we want to standardize. We want to automate. We want to take humans out of the process where possible and replace it with efficient machines. As team leaders, we want to create a predictable process. We want to remove all chaos from the project. But the more standardized our testing methodology, the less we are able to adapt to different and changing requirements.

This is a difficulty in the management of an offensive cybersecurity service, but it is also an opportunity for differentiation. Most competitors will find it too difficult to or too expensive to develop a team capable of addressing the unique requirements of its clients. Their clients will receive a standardized pentest and a standardized report in a timely manner. But the clients will not know what went into developing the report, and since they were not asked to communicate more fully with the testers, they must assume that their concerns were not addressed. Their confidence in their security is shaky at best.

We'll talk about these ideas more in the chapter on understanding clients. For now, we're going to focus on implementing a client communication strategy that captures unique client requirements prior to the engagement and uses continuous communication to give a client a full understanding of what was tested. This will result in the client being confident in the resulting report and in their understanding of the threats that face their environment.

Initial Handoff

The first step in our strategy is to engage the client early. The team leader or a senior member of the team has a meeting with the client as soon as possible after the engagement has been scheduled. For a consultative team, this would be immediately after the sales and contracts team have finished the paperwork with the client and are able to hand the assessment off to the team for delivery.

The tester who is scheduled to perform the work should attend this meeting. Meeting minutes and notes are great, but there is no replacement for getting the information directly from the client to the tester. Additionally, allowing the tester to build a relationship with the client early makes future communication more smooth.

The handoff meeting is intended to introduce the client to the team and the tester who they will be working with. It also provides a chance for the team to reiterate scope of the assessment as they currently understand it and give the client a chance to point out any errors that might have slipped in during previous steps in the pipeline. At all points in the pipeline, the client should be aware of who they can reach out to regarding the assessment.

Kickoff

The kickoff meeting is conducted between the client, a senior member of the team, and any testers who will be performing the work. It can be combined with the handoff meeting if there isn't much time before the engagement starts. The timing of the kickoff meeting will vary depending on the client and the size of the engagement; however, clients will need time to prepare their environments for testing. I have found that clients generally need about 2 weeks to conduct this preparation but your mileage may vary.

The kickoff meeting has several goals:

- Reiterate scope expectations and assessment phases

- Discuss and highlight any special requirements, requests, or limitations

- Establish communication medium(s) and cadence

- Discuss and develop access requirements for each phase of the engagement

- Ensure the client is aware of when the environment must be ready so that the assessment may begin on time

The most important outcome from this meeting is that communication mediums and frequency are established. Once you have that, you can work out the details of the other items instead of relying upon what was said at the meeting. In my experience, the most effective client communication medium during an assessment is a chat channel (Slack, Teams, etc.). Chat channels are ad hoc and fluid. You don't have to obtain calendar information from everyone in the channel before sending a message like you do when setting up a video call. They allow the team to ask questions about the environment or the assessment requirements without interrupting work. Chat channels provide a more informal, work-focused communication method.

Engagement Time

The goal of client management during pre-engagement work and meetings is to gather detailed requirements, sync on expectations, and setup communication. During the engagement, the goal of client management becomes to ensure that the client is aware of what they are getting for their money. Of course, for internal corporate teams "money" isn't really involved since no one is paying for the engagement. This doesn't make a difference in the way client management should be conducted. Internal teams have just as much to gain from providing their clients visibility into the testing as teams of consultants do.

Communication is the key to ensuring the client is satisfied with the result. When I worked as a contractor on the internal red team at a very large corporation, the lead of the team demanded one thing in every assessment – external remote code execution (RCE). RCE vulnerabilities aren't necessarily rare, but large tech corporations are usually pretty good at updating their software in response to serious known vulnerabilities. That meant that I was expected to find external, 0-day, RCE vulnerabilities in each and every assessment. What made matters worse was that the corporation implemented iron-clad authentication mechanisms before any of the content of their applications were viewable. I was expected to find access without credentials. I saw my available attack surface shrinking.

The reason that such a high standard was required was because it was the only way the assessment would be considered impactful. If I was given access to a server, then management wouldn't view the assessment as meaningful because it started with an assumed compromise. Any work I did identifying other types of vulnerabilities (cross-site scripting [XSS], SQLi, IDOR, etc.) was largely ignored because they did not demonstrate a critical compromise event. As a contractor member of the team, I did not have a way to show value to my client outside of the report.

This is an issue that teams who do not communicate with their clients regularly will encounter. The only window into the quality of the test the client is given is the end report. This is not enough, and it encourages the client to judge the worth of the team entirely off of the number and severity of vulnerabilities listed.

The worth of a pentest is not judged by the number and severity of vulnerabilities in the report but by the skill applied, the range of techniques leveraged, and the completeness of the assessment. If your team does not communicate these metrics to the client, then you leave the client to assume that assessment quality is directly proportional to the number of vulnerabilities in the report.

After my experience at that corporation, I gave myself the goal of creating a system where my team could provide a client with a report that contained 0 findings and the client would still feel that the test was worth their money and my team was one of the best they had ever worked with. This may seem ridiculous. First, why would an assessment not be able to identify any vulnerabilities, and second, why would the client be happy about it?

To answer the first question, it is possible, though rare, that an environment is hardened to the point that assessments cannot find significant vulnerabilities in the weeks of testing. This is especially true for assessments with limited scope that have been thoroughly tested for years with very few updates to the environment.

To answer the second question, clients who are aware of the level of skill that went into attacking the environment will be satisfied even if those attacks did not result in identified vulnerabilities. They are getting what they paid for – an accurate understanding of the security of their environment against a highly skilled adversary within a limited time frame.

The key to providing clients with this level of insight into the value that they are receiving by choosing your team is daily updates. Every morning, each tester that is assigned to a given project uses the established communication medium (hopefully a chat channel) to inform the client of three things:

1. What testing was conducted the previous day?

2. What testing is planned for today?

3. Any blockers that could impact the tester's ability to conduct the planned testing.

These daily updates are not formal. They are a chance for the tester to share his thoughts directly with the client and obtain feedback. By providing a daily update, the client is able to weigh in and perhaps give the tester advice for further testing. The client is made fully aware of the work that is being done to support their goals and is able to influence it toward even greater success.

This is a best-case scenario, but the opposite end of the spectrum isn't bad either. If the client decides to say nothing in response to the daily updates and not participate at all, they are still at least made aware of the progress of the test.

Another benefit of communicating with the client is that the client is already aware of what is in the report before it is in their hands. The client has seen from the daily updates and other discussions with the testing team what vulnerabilities have been identified. Therefore, there are no surprises waiting for them when it comes to the outbrief.

Outbrief

When the engagement is complete and your team is ready to present their findings to the client, you schedule the outbrief meeting. I have found that outbrief is best scheduled for some time during the week following the end of the engagement. The details of the engagement will still be fresh in the minds of the testers who participated in it and the client will appreciate receiving the findings without a significant delay.

Any member of the team who contributed to the report or performed some aspect of the assessment should attend the meeting. Results of an assessment are best presented when they come from the tester who performed the actual testing that produced the results. There are a few exceptions to this rule. If a tester is so anxious about speaking to a client in a formal setting, their section of the report should be presented by the team lead or a senior team member who has been briefed by the tester prior to the outbrief. The anxious tester should still attend the meeting to address any questions. Similarly, if you have determined that a tester does not present well in formal settings, then you should have a senior member of the team handle that tester's outbrief section and separately work with the tester to improve their client communication skills.

As we've previously discussed, client communication is not a skill domain that is taught to hackers going through standard educational paths. However, it is a vital skill for the success of both the team and the individual team members. This means that you can't expect all testers to be immediately successful in communicating with clients. But if you set high-quality client communications as an important team value and demonstrate and work with your team to understand what high-quality communication looks like, your team members will improve.

Outbriefs should be conducted in person if possible and over a video call if not. Even if the client does not turn on their cameras during a video call, every member of your team should. There is no replacement for the value of the client seeing the professionals who performed the work discuss their findings. It allows the client to view you as people that they trust, instead of a faceless testing entity.

The flow of the outbrief should be simple and consistent. This will help you and your team become more comfortable and confident in handling outbriefs over time because you know what to expect. The following format is what a typical outbrief flow looked like for my team:

- Testing team and client introductions – roughly 5 minutes.

- The leader of the outbrief ensures that everyone has a current version of the report and opens the formal outbrief with basic information about the engagement (scope, time, etc.).

- The leader passes the "mic" to each member of the team who wrote a section of the report as their section comes up.

- The leader summarizes the findings and remediation recommendations.

- The meeting is opened to a conversation about the test and its results.

- The leader closes the meeting.

I strongly recommend having a technical team member who is confident in their ability to communicate with the client lead the call. While sales representatives, members of management, and others from your side may attend the call, it is best to put a strong technical foot forward. The outbrief is one of the most significant opportunities to impress the client from a technical point of view and directly build their trust in your team.

While your first instinct might be to have rigid, formal outbriefs, it builds more trust with your client when your team is able to relax while remaining professional. Clients should feel free to interrupt and ask questions at any point throughout the outbrief. They may provide clarification or bring context that your team was not aware of to the findings.

Most outbriefs are civil and relaxed, but occasionally, pentesting results can ruffle feathers and even make some members of the client team or organization adversarial. After all, the outbrief is essentially a detailed list of flaws in the target environment. Those that are responsible for the environment may view this as a criticism of their skill and ability and respond.

The best strategy for adversarial clients is professionalism, respect, neutrality, and attempts to diffuse the situation. Your team members will need to understand that their work will be questioned and even ridiculed at times by members of the client's team. They must remain neutral and professional, address the client's concerns with the findings, and ignore any negative personal or professional remarks. While this may seem counterintuitive, it is not the job of the team members to defend the findings in the report. Instead, the team's focus should be on ensuring the report and the findings it contains are accurate. If the team is fixated on defending their findings against an adversarial client, the situation will escalate and your team will lose a lot of the professional impression you have made on your client.

At times, an upset client may be bringing an important issue that your team was not aware to light. For example, let's say a tester finds a serious vulnerability in a web application in a testing environment. The person responsible for application security becomes enraged when hearing about this vulnerability at the outbrief and explains that it only exists in the testing environment and production is not configured the same way. This is an important piece of information that will certainly affect the severity rating of the vulnerability and perhaps invalidates the vulnerability altogether. If your team members are focused on report accuracy over defending findings, they will recognize this and diffuse the situation by informing the client that they were not aware of the configuration difference and they will get the report updated.

It is the job of the team leader or the most senior team member in the meeting to not allow a client to become outright disrespectful to the team. While some emotion is understandable and manageable, there is a line that shouldn't be crossed, and if it is, the meeting ends and is rescheduled after further discussions with the client.

Project Execution

It is the job of a team lead to keep the testers testing as much as is reasonably possible. We listed a few additional tasks that we are putting on the tester's plate such as team meetings and client communication. These are necessary tasks and they are worth the time that they take from actual testing. Management of the project, including the pre- and post-engagement phases, is something the testers should not have to worry about with the exception of the outbrief meeting. A tester should be able to show up for work, glance at the schedule to see what project they are assigned to, and find that everything they need to get started has already been worked out the client.

Single Point of Information

Engagements produce a lot of data, and it can get messy. A team has to keep track of the scope, Rules of Engagement, access requirements, application credentials, network maps, application source code, client point-of-contact, scheduled start and end date, unique requirements and client requests, special reporting requirements (Letter of Attestation, Executive Summary, etc.), assigned tester(s), communication channel(s), and more. This information is either critical to client satisfaction and a high-quality final report or required for the assessment to be conducted at all. Some of this data comes from teams outside of the offensive service such as sales, contracts, and upper management. If a tester is spending time during the engagement chasing down the data they need from an internal team or from the client, they are not testing. Worse, they are interrupted, and it will take time for the tester's full concentration to return to assessment.

Engagements go through a pipeline whether that pipeline is sales to contracts to service delivery like it is in the world of consultative teams or it is an internal corporate pipeline. At each stage of the pipeline, data is generated that is necessary to the successful execution of the engagement. It might be as small as note from upper management stating that this engagement is in support of verification of PCI security standards or as much as an entire Rules of Engagement document signed by the client. The data helps to paint a clear picture of what the tester needs to do to satisfy the client.

The team needs a system that collects all necessary pieces of data and makes them available to the tester in a simple consistent format, a one-stop shop that is the source of truth for project information.

I first began developing a solution to this data issue when my testers complained they weren't aware of critical client requests until well into the engagement. I realized that the lack of easy access to project data was going to start creating client-facing issues. A client could tell a sales representative an important detail about how the test needs to be conducted. The sales rep might make a note on it, but there was no process making sure that the note would get to the tester.

We were already using a ticketing application to track and schedule team projects with a kanban approach. I informed the company sales and contracting teams that we would begin creating project tickets the moment a sales call was scheduled. Then, for the life of the project, all teams involved in the project would attach information necessary to the execution of the engagement to the ticket. This solves one of our problems. All the data is now in one place but it isn't organized. The next step was to assign my operations assistant, a low-cost resource, to the task of formatting and cleaning up the data on the ticket so that it was simple and accessible for testers. This made sure that I wasn't wasting valuable (and expensive) tester time or my own time working through data. Of course, a better long-term solution was to train all teams who interacted with my team on how to properly format the data they provided to ensure the tester would have what they needed. But process improvement is an iterative process, and I knew my team would use our retrospectives to identify additional improvements.

We quickly found that the sales and contracts team were not the most consistent about providing the data we needed. This was understandable. When a sales representative has achieved a sale, it's time to move onto the next one. That's their job. So, I implemented two policies to respond to this issue. First, I strongly enforced an interface between other teams in the pipeline and our team. If the basic required data for executing an engagement was not provided by the time the engagement ticket got to my team, then it was rejected with an explanation. Second, I assigned my operations assistant to proactively work with the other teams to make sure that we got the data we needed without testers being involved. My hope was that this inter-team interaction would be a gentle start to educating the other teams on how best to interface with my team.

I think ticketing applications work very well for project data management. One ticket that represents the project and exists from the initial sales call all the way until the engagement is complete and the ticket is archived. You may find a different implementation, but the point is to provide testers with one clear place to find the data they need to do their job.

Pre-engagement

Pre-engagement processes are the domain of the team leader in coordination with other teams within the organization such as sales, legal, and customer service. The goal when developing these processes is to make something simple and repeatable that can be documented and executed by a low-cost resource. Most of us who have spent a good amount of time in any tech field have heard the lamenting of senior technical people who were promoted into management and now feel they waste their time everyday in endless meetings and pointless processes. I've been that guy but it isn't necessary.

When an engagement is picked up on Monday morning by a tester, we want our processes to have assured that everything is good to go. Nothing is worse and more disruptive than telling a tester to get an assessment started only to find that vital information is missing. If we as the team lead are taking all the processes on our shoulders, then we are bound to fail as our team's workload increases or as we receive tasking from elsewhere. Something is wrong when we are spending all of our time on processes that do not require our level of skill and experience. Our processes are fragile if they require the constant involvement of senior team members. Therefore, the question we should ask as we complete each process is, "could an intern handle this?" If we cannot answer "yes" to this question, we need to further break the process down.

After going through the process of acquiring everything needed for a test a few times, a team leader can write a checklist of what is needed from the client and then provide that to future clients. A low-cost resource, such as an intern, should be responsible for following up with the client, establishing communication mediums (such as chat channels), and making sure that the testers get everything they need before the scheduled start date.

Scope Creep

If there's one principle I hope you take away from this chapter it is that you and your team should be communicating with your clients. But there is a downside to increasing the volume of communication. It opens the door for the client to easily make suggestions about areas of the environment that should be added to the engagement and thereby cause scope creep. By the time your team is executing a project, it's not easy to change or extend the project timeline. Paperwork has been signed or agreement has been made. The team has a schedule to keep and a client who is modifying the scope that was agreed upon can become a disruption.

Scope creep can occur without the client realizing it. Client representatives with some sort of a technical background are especially prone to getting invested in the engagement and making suggestions for testing that would require additional time. Scope creep is addressed by providing the client with transparency and communication. When a client makes a suggestion for a change in the scope of the engagement, they should be informed how that change will affect the test. If the test is consultative, then there should be a requirement for additional funding in order for the team to take on the new requirement. If the test is internal, the new requirement might need more time than was previously scheduled. If the funding or time cannot be modified (due to budget or schedule restrictions), something else from the assessment must be sacrificed to accomplish this new requirement.

As long as the request is formalized, documented, and the engagement scope updated to reflect it, there is nothing wrong with the client wanting to pivot the goals of the assessment. This is especially true for consultative teams where the client has purchased the time. The client will appreciate the team's ability to switch gears and tackle new objectives as the engagement develops as long as the team communicates the cost/benefit of the pivot.

While the client may appreciate a team's flexibility, the testers may not. However, the priority is to produce a report that is valuable to the client. If the original scope is no longer considered valuable, then a report produced based on that scope is worthless to the client.

Daily Reporting

Disruptions can occur at any time during engagement execution. The client may call a stop to the testing. The tester may have a personal emergency and need to be taken off the project. An outage may occur that prevents completion of a phase of the engagement. Whatever the reason, the team will need to be able to handle project disruptions. The assessment process must be resilient enough to handle an extended pause in execution or a new tester taking over in the middle of a project.

If you have ever taken over an engagement in progress from another tester or had to resume a project after a week-long delay, then you will have experienced how difficult it can be. The environment is unfamiliar, and you can't recall the details of what testing occurred. You're not sure how much work has been completed, and your only source of information is your own memory or the notes from the previous tester.

If your team has implemented a single point of information and provides daily updates to the client, then project data and a general idea of what testing has occurred will be available. But this still leaves out a lot of the details. Missing details means that the tester who is new to the project will waste some time getting back up to speed. Even worse, when it comes time to write the report, the tester will have to report on a period of the test that they are not familiar with.

After encountering this problem several times myself, I realized that my processes were too fragile. They were dependent on a dedicated tester being able to perform the test through an unchanging time period. To build resilience, I needed to change processes so that tests could be halted and restarted or shifted to a new tester with very little down time. I developed the idea of daily reporting. Testers were expected to spend the last 30 minutes of every day updating the report. They would write both a narrative of the testing they performed and summary of the findings they identified. This accomplished two goals. First, it meant that the report was always up to date with what had occurred during the test and could be used to get a replacement tester up to spend quickly. Second, it meant that at the end of the testing time frame, the report would already be completed. My team wouldn't need additional time to prepare the report, and the report would be highly accurate since it wasn't based on the memories of the testers.

Reporting and pentesting should occur in small batches not unlike unit testing in software development. When software developers complete a section of code, they write a unit test to both document and verify the functionality of that code. This concept applies to pentesting and makes the engagement process more resilient to interruptions.

Post-engagement

After an engagement has concluded and the report is ready for the out brief, all that's left for operational management is a few cleanup tasks. The most obvious is that an outbrief needs to be scheduled. Once again, this is an area where we can leverage a low-cost operations assistant to interface with the client and align the calendars of all the stakeholders who need to be at the meeting.

One question that quickly becomes apparent is what to do with all the project data that has been accumulated in our single point of information? At the end of the engagement, this ticket, or however else the point has been implemented, contains a wealth of information about the engagement, the technical details of what was requested and what occurred, and most importantly, information about the client's desires. The priority with this data must be to protect client confidentiality and adhere to any agreed upon processes of identifying and managing sensitive information. But after we've done so, we can use the data to inform future engagements with the client.

The data collected during an engagement can be used to perform a better assessment the next time the client reaches out to your team. Your team will begin the assessment already aware of the details of the environment, the desires of the client, and the unique challenges of the project. This helps cut down on time spent on familiarization, client introduction, and data gathering. It lets the testers focus on what matters and helps the team begin executing quickly.

From a client management perspective, data gathered during an engagement builds a portrait of the client, their unique goals, and their communication preferences. With this data, future interactions with the client are likely to be more successful.

Lastly, the engagement should be marked for inclusion in the next team retrospective meeting.

Operational Checklists

As you and your team become more mature and familiar with what works best for your engagements, the idea of operational checklists may come up organically. The concept is that in order to standardize the quality of the team's work and output, a checklist should be developed that encompasses all activities from the beginning to the end of a phase of the engagement. In theory, this makes sense, and it scratches that itch that tech professionals have to optimize and simplify, to remove the human, and thereby make the engagement predictable and controllable.

Operational checklists can be very helpful by providing a guide of the minimum expectations to testers, especially those that are new to the team and less familiar with how an assessment flows. However, as the checklists become more detailed and specific, they begin to work against the goal of high-quality output.

Penetration testing is a balance between creativity and logic. We follow a logical path, but we have to use creativity to overcome the obstacles that we encounter. Every client environment is unique. If this wasn't the case, then there would be no need for pentesters since the process of pentesting could be handled purely through automation. While automaton can provide a great baseline, a pentester is able to evaluate and correlate the unique details of an environment and select the most likely path to exploitation. Operational checklists that are overly detailed stifle the creativity that is necessary for quality testing.

That being said, broad operational checklists should be a part of your team's operations. They should be used to define areas of testing that are required for a complete test. For example, when I was new to the commercial offensive cybersecurity field, I regularly encountered servers that allowed SSH traffic. After several engagements, I realized that for at least my targets, SSH services were always patched or at least they were never old enough for me to find a version with a serious vulnerability. As a result I started stop performing in-depth checks on SSH services and spent my time on other services that I felt had a higher chance of presenting a vulnerability.

In some ways, this kind of service prioritization based on what is most likely to be vulnerable is one of the pentester's most valuable tools. But it must be balanced against the necessity to execute a complete assessment. An operational checklist can be used to create that balance. It provides the tester with what must be done for the assessment to be considered complete and then allows the tester to use their creativity and experience to target what they feel is most likely to be vulnerable.

Good Penetration Testing vs. Effective Penetration Testing

I once was put in charge of executing a penetration test contract for a very large company. The company was in the process of acquiring a slightly less large company, and my client wanted an assessment of their new acquisition. The results of the test would give the client a broad idea of the effort required to bring the new acquisition into their environment and up to their cybersecurity standard. The test would be used to inform and drive the security team's prioritization of tasks as they onboarded the new environment.

One of the members of my team was an exceptionally good hacker. He was miles ahead of me in technical knowledge and testing experience. I assigned him to this contract with a few other team members and got to work on it myself. I was confident that my team would find a way to compromise the external network of the acquisition and gain access to their internal network. After all, the acquisition was huge, and its attack surface was significant. There had to be something vulnerable hidden in it somewhere.

After a few weeks on the project, I was worried. My team had not yet gained access, and so I met with each of them and discussed how the test was going. I found that the exceptional hacker had spent the majority of his time working on one vulnerability. He couldn't quite get his exploit to work, but he felt certain that the vulnerability existed and he was close to exploiting it.

We talked through the other targets that he had been tasked to assess. He admitted that he found a few targets that were hosting old custom web applications that might be vulnerable, but he hadn't put much time into them since his focus was on this one vulnerability. He intended to take a closer look at them after he successfully developed and executed his exploit.

I let him return to his work and reviewed a few of the other targets. One of them piqued my interest. It was an application that the acquisition company had bought several years prior from a small business. An acquisition of an acquisition seemed like a good place to find vulnerabilities since it would be further removed from the established security program of the larger companies. After putting a day or two into testing this application, I found a vulnerability that disclosed cloud credentials without authentication. It was a huge finding, and the vulnerability was rather simple. If I were a better tester, I probably could have exploited it within a few hours. I showed it to my team and they turned it into a massive compromise of the acquisition's cloud environment.

This is the difference between good penetration testing and effective penetration testing. Good penetration testers are incredibly skilled and experienced. They can identify and exploit vulnerabilities in their sleep. If you're fortunate, you might have a few on your team.

The difficulty with good penetration testers is that they come with tunnel vision. The more skilled they are, the worse the tunnel vision seems to get. They either find it difficult to consider the bigger picture or simply have no interest in doing so due to their focus on the technical challenges. Hacking is a series of challenges that may or may not have a solution. When a good penetration tester encounters a challenge, they want to solve it. They aren't done with a vulnerability until they have built a working exploit. They do not consider the larger goal of delivering value to the client because they are so focused on the challenge immediately before them.

Effective penetration testing means prioritizing targets based off the likelihood that they have significant vulnerabilities and the impact that the target will have to your client's goals. In the acquisition assessment, I was not concerned with whether the vulnerability my tester was spending their time on could be exploited. I was only thinking about how we could best move the assessment forward and deliver something of value to my client. The vulnerability had already taken too much time.

This is something that new team leaders struggle with. They can't understand why their senior tester spend the two weeks of a web application assessment struggling with a single vulnerability and came away with a barely acceptable report. The senior tester would look at the same assessment with satisfaction because they finally got the exploit to work. They learned something and were proud to document the complicated exploit that they developed.

From the point of view of your team members, the big picture is your problem. They have their hands full with their work, which is often very difficult. You can involve them to some degree in the big picture by communicating client goals and prioritizing client satisfaction when considering the direction of the team's development. But at the end of the day, they are correct. The big picture is the responsibility of leaders of the team.

The perfect scenario is when good penetration testers are guided by those that have the big picture in mind. This leverages their skills and experience and points them in the direction of what is most beneficial to the assessment. This will require the direct involvement of team leadership, but it will result in effective penetration testing.

Later in this book, we will discuss each of the most common testing domains and highlight how to prioritize targets and develop likelihoods for an effective assessment.

CHAPTER 6

Developing Hackers

Disclaimer

Before we dive into creating a team development strategy, building out
capability evolutions, and discussing how to ensure a team maintains both
its skill and its competitive edge via education, I wanted to note that I am
not personally endorsing any specific training course. Courses change over
time and may become more or less relevant and helpful to a given team.
Each team is different, and it is up to the team leader with the support of
the senior team members to identify what will work best for your unique
situation.

If You're Not Getting Better, You're Getting Worse and Fast

In December 2022, the offensive cybersecurity team that I led was
winding down for the year. Most of the team was out of the office for the
holidays. As with most pentesting teams, our work slowed down during
the holidays for two reasons – retail companies didn't want to take the risk
that their applications would go down during their biggest payday of the
year due to any technical reason and any company needing a pentest for
compliance reasons had already received it. I didn't take the time off since

© Michael Butler and Jacob G. Oakley 2024
M. Butler and J. G. Oakley, *The Business of Hacking*,
https://doi.org/10.1007/979-8-8688-0174-7_6

work was so slow it was basically a vacation either way. Unfortunately for me, a large client of ours reached out and requested a mobile application penetration test to be conducted over the holidays and into the new year. I accepted the contract even though I knew I would have to perform the mobile app pentest and I wasn't quite as familiar with that particular type of engagement as I would have liked. I felt confident in the fact that my team had conducted many similar assessments and they were excellent at documenting their processes. I thought that the worst-case scenario would be a desperate call to one of my testers to get some pointers and guidance on the assessment process.

The engagement began and I received the mobile application that I was expected to assess. I'll skip the technical details, but it was a very difficult application in a number of ways. Mobile testing in general at that time was becoming increasingly difficult, especially in the world of iOS applications which of course my target application was. Mobile testing had relied on being able to root a device and then thoroughly test the application from the rooted device. But the increased security and the bounties offered by major mobile operating system developers meant that public exploits for gaining root-level access were decreasing. I found that I was stuck in a situation where I did not have a platform that was adequate for the testing required. I turned to my team's documentation. I found that the situation I was in was something that had been a team issue for some time, but they had so far found ways to work around it. There was no answer for how I was to test this particular application.

I had a good relationship with the client and so I immediately informed them of the situation and let them know I was working on a solution. I called various members of my team to get options, but there were very few. Despite my best efforts and putting in some serious holiday overtime to try to provide a quality assessment, I found that by the first few weeks of the new year, I had disappointed the client and failed to deliver a quality assessment within the time I was given.

There were two outcomes from this experience. First, the client sent my team significantly less contracts during the following year. Second, I learned a hard lesson – when you aren't getting better, you're getting worse and fast. Before this assessment, I was under the impression that my team's mobile app testing capability was strong. Perhaps not as strong as it could be, but good enough to not need direct attention to improving it for the time being. I was wrong. I had failed to identify when a core team capability was not keeping pace with the developing requirements of the market and the evolution of cybersecurity. Additionally, I had failed to improve team and tester capabilities regardless of the current perception of program strength. These two failures directly led to a client-facing event and an impact on the team's bottom line.

I think most IT professionals have either had a similar experience or witnessed one. A point where an individual's skill did not live up to their perception of it or when a team lead believed things were in good hands because he had staffed his team with highly skilled individuals only to find that skills and capabilities that are not maintained are prone to atrophy and get left behind by an evolving industry.

As leaders within offensive security, we must be aware of this concept and actively work to improve our teams and prepare them for the new challenges in each domain of our craft. Fortunately, there is almost always a wide variety of tools and educational content that addresses at least most of a team's needs. It is the leader's responsibility to develop strategies to both ensure that the skills of individual testers are being improved and that the team is staying on the cutting edge of vulnerabilities as they develop across all domains that the team practices in.

Self-development Is Not Enough

Some leaders may understandably take a less engaged approach to the development of their testers' skills. While I think it can be generally agreed upon that it is the leader's responsibility to ensure the continued development of the capabilities of the team, it may seem less apparent that individual development is also our responsibility. Aren't professionals responsible for maintaining their own skills? Can't we as leaders expect that much from them?

While I understand the theory, in practice, being unengaged in the development of team members results in skill atrophy at worst and development in a direction that is not necessarily helpful to team goals at best. If you do not direct the professional growth of your team, you cannot expect them to grow in alignment with your vision.

As an example, before I understood the importance of directing the growth of my team members, I would impress upon my junior testers the need for them to develop their skills. The testers were motivated and intelligent self-starters, and I was confident that they would be able to quickly develop skills in offensive cybersecurity that would directly benefit the team. To my surprise, one of my junior testers decided to put his effort into learning radiofrequency identification (RFID) technology, got a chip implanted in his arm to allow him to interface with any RFID station, and became quite the expert on the technology. Of course, this skillset was entirely useless to me and the team. We did not have any physical penetration testing engagements, and even if we did, the target organization may not be using RFID. I realized that although professionals should and do seek to improve their skills in their own time, a team cannot base its team member development strategy on the motivations of its members.

Once leaders understand the importance of directing the development of their team members, they may attempt to make a compromise that allows them to keep the team member fully engaged in work during work hours and then direct them as to how they should develop themselves in their own time. Aside from the obvious ethical issues with tasking team members outside of work hours, this attempt at a compromise really results in less motivated development, less focused testing, and the potential for burnout.

It can be difficult for a leader to find the hours necessary to develop the members of his team. I have personally battled with my leadership over complaints that my team did not put in enough billable hours and skepticism at the team's need for additional resources when the current resources were not tasked at 100% of their capacity. But these battles are necessary if the team is to value significant long-term rewards over short-term statistics.

A team's reputation, efficiency, ability to retain high-level talent, and the success of its mission in general depend on the team's ability to continually rise to the challenge of an evolving technical world. The long-term benefits of team development strategies that include individual team member development far outweigh the short-term hours that must be given to the process of development.

Building a Team Development Strategy

In early 2023, I was reeling from the fallout of the mobile app assessment. I knew that my team was not developing their skills and capabilities enough to keep up with the demands of the industry. Through my own experience, I had discovered one significant gap in the quality of the services we were offering, but what if there were more? What if our web application capability was similarly stagnated and our clients were going to soon find out that we were no longer up to the standard they expected?

My team needed a development strategy that didn't just patch these gaps. We needed to have an ongoing process that drove both the skills of the individual testers and the team capabilities as a whole forward.

Individual vs. Capability Development

There is an important distinction to be made between individual and capability development. A team's capability to execute its services is more than just the summation of the skills of its individual testers. It is that skill coupled with the tools, techniques, processes, and knowledge your team develops and accumulates through its experience, documentation, and intentional development that makes up the totality of your team's ability. Your team cannot rely on its testers knowing how to "do it right" and doing it every time. That approach isn't scalable, and more crucially, it hides the true potential of your team by putting the quality of your product on the whim of whatever skill development your individual team members choose to do or not do. The team as a whole must be developed as well as each individual team member.

We can demonstrate this concept with an example. Let's say there is a penetration testing team that specializes in web application pentests. The team is made up of four members: two junior, one mid, and one senior tester. These four testers conduct several web application pentests a quarter. Each pentest has two testers assigned to it. The team lead decides to assign one junior tester to the mid-level tester and one junior tester to the senior tester. These two groups within the team are then assigned to the web application pentests as they come in. In this scenario, the team lead is going to notice a trend. The group with the senior tester will impress clients, discover more complicated vulnerabilities, and improve the team's reputation. The team with the mid-level tester will consistently perform less impressively. While this isn't a surprise, it's certainly less than desirable. The team's capability to perform penetration tests on web applications is not consistent. Worse yet, with everyone on the team working on a fairly constant basis, there is no improvement occurring. Within a few years, the team will be considered to be much lower quality than other teams that make an investment in improving themselves. When that happens, the team lead will wrongly blame her senior tester. After all, the quality of the assessments was high as long as the senior tester's skills were sharp.

In another scenario, that same team lead divides up the team into two groups in the same way, but this time, she sets aside a quarterly allotment of hours for each tester to attend training. She believes that this approach will prevent the gradual reduction in quality output that other teams experience. Again, she notices a trend. The group with the senior tester consistently outperforms the group with the mid-level tester. The training works well, however, and the skills of the testers are maintained and kept relevant. Unfortunately, the skills are only maintained at a level that established training courses can provide, which is somewhat mediocre. The team lead finds that although training and education are excellent at establishing and maintaining a skillset, they very rarely provide the cutting edge in testing tools and techniques. Additionally, she finds that whenever a member of the team takes another job and is replaced, she has no idea how the quality of the team's product will be affected. She can only hope that the new hire will be able to at least maintain the same level of quality as the tester they are replacing.

One last scenario. Same team lead, same team. This time, the team lead decides to hire one additional mid-level tester. She breaks her team into two groups each with one mid and one junior tester. Again, she allocates a quarterly amount of hours for each tester to attend training. She tasks the senior tester with two responsibilities. First, he is to perform research in the field of web application pentesting. This research consists of staying current with new techniques and discoveries in the field as well as developing his own techniques that are specifically related to the kinds of applications and technologies the team regularly tests. Second, he is to take the results of his research, develop simple tools to implement the new techniques, and educate the team on how to include them in their normal assessment flow.

The result of the approach in this last scenario will be a consistent and increasing level of assessment quality. The research provided by the senior tester will ensure the team is constantly bringing cutting-edge techniques to their assessments. The allocation of hours for training will maintain a baseline of individual skill improvement that keeps pace with the mainstream industry. The lead of the team understands that it is important to ensure the continued development of tester skills and team capabilities.

Hopefully, this example demonstrates the differences between individual skill development and team capability development. Both of these are vital to maintaining a team's quality and relevance.

Setting Levels

Let's pause for a moment and discuss a few terms I've used throughout this book so far. Junior, mid, and senior are generalized levels of skill and experience. These categories are often seen in job posting to give applicants a rough idea of the requirements of a position.

The junior, mid, and senior system can be used internally. It is a simple, common form of setting levels within a team. Three rungs on the skill ladder with perhaps a single technical lead or director at the top. You can call them levels, bands, roles, etc., but the basic idea is that the team is organized through some form of structure based on each individual's skills and experience. As team leaders, we utilize this organization to more effectively apply team resources to the projects we execute. For example, when scheduling a particularly complicated web application assessment, the team leader is more likely to assign a mid or senior resource.

For smaller teams, levels may seem unnecessary since the team leader is already intimately familiar with the technical capabilities of each member of the team. The leader can schedule work and apply resources based on their consideration of the skills of the three or four team members they manage. This works well until the team begins to either change or grow. As the members of a team change, the team leader realizes that the quality of the team's output changes as well. This could be for the better or worse, but the point is that it is largely out of the team leader's hands. They are depending on a team that has the necessary skills available instead of creating one. When the team grows, the team leader loses the ability to remain as deeply aware of the skillsets of each individual.

Levels are how a team standardizes its expectations of its team members. If you correctly set requirements for a level, you will be able to confidently schedule your resources knowing that they have the education and experience necessary for the task assigned. You are not at the mercy of who you currently have on your team. Instead, any new members of the team are expected to adhere to the requirements of their assigned level.

The junior, mid, and senior category framework works for smaller teams such as a startup working in the contractual/professional service side of offensive cybersecurity. It also works for larger teams that work in small teams by breaking the team members up and assigning them to relatively small cells. But it does come with one potential drawback. Generalized categories mean generalized skillsets. This is completely acceptable for most teams, but it may not be the best fit for teams that need a higher level of specialization or want to set more granular expectations.

As an example, a team leader builds out a generalized system of junior-, mid-, and senior-level bands. He sets requirements for 2 years of testing and three industry certifications for a tester to achieve the mid-level. One of his junior testers gets their third certification and is happy to be promoted to mid-level. But the tester earned his three certifications by focusing on web and network-based testing. The team leader finds out that the tester is completely useless when it comes to mobile testing. Mobile assessments are rare for this particular team, and as such, the generalized mid-level category did not have a requirement for mobile assessment skills.

The team leader has three choices in this situation:

1. Update the requirements of the level to include
    all possible engagement types, even those that are
    more rare for the team

2. Switch to a leveling system that allows for more
    granularity

3. Implement a system of supplementary education
    and remove the expectation that every tester should
    be able to perform every type of test

The first option is not a great choice. Your team members cannot be masters of every type of assessment. Implementing expectations that any mid-level tester should be able to conduct every assessment type at a mid-level of quality is unrealistic unless you expect your team to only execute a small set of assessment types.

The second option will work for some teams, but it will require more management overhead to design and maintain the system. As an example, the team could use a system with vertical levels (junior, mid, and senior) and horizontal assessment types (web, mobile, internal network, external network, cloud, etc.). This allows a tester to be a senior web application tester but perhaps a junior internal network tester. It sounds perfect in theory, but in practice, it is difficult to build since management must assign requirements to levels that are 3× (the number of assessment types). It is also difficult to apply this kind of system to the compensation structure like the more generalized system often is.

The last option is more adaptable and organic but also a bit more messy. The idea is that the team lead determines which assessment types every tester needs to be capable of executing. For my second team, this comprised of web application, internal network, and external network. These three assessment types were the most common, and I needed to be able to apply any member of my team to them. These three became my primary assessment types and all others (mobile, wireless, hardware, physical, cloud, etc.) were deemed secondary types. Next, the team lead works with the capability leads (discussed in an upcoming section) of the secondary assessment types. The leads and the team leader would determine how many testers needed to be familiar with each testing type to make sure we would be able to staff upcoming assessments. Of course, as a consultative team, we couldn't be 100% sure what our clients would ask of us throughout the year. So we based our expectations on what had occurred the previous year and our rate of growth.

Once the number of testers that need to be trained in each assessment type has been determined, the team lead and capability leads match team members to the assessment type they have been assigned to. Next, the team lead works with the capability lead to develop the requirements that each team member must meet for their given secondary assessment type to be considered ready to lead an assessment. Finally, the capability lead ensures that any testers assigned to be trained on their capability have the support they need to meet the requirements. That support might take the form of internal team education, industry education, experience, or one-on-one training.

As mentioned, this approach is a bit more messy because the team leader will have to track who is trained on which secondary assessment types in order to properly schedule resources. But it has the benefit of flexibility, and it lowers the overhead required by setting up the team to develop itself.

Regardless of what system you choose to implement in your team, the important point is that levels are a requirement before a skill development strategy can be created. Each level needs to have clearly defined requirements for the testers to hold it. These requirements will be made up the education and experience available in the market which will be discussed further in the Resources and Tools section.

Before we move on, I want to establish one more important point that was not immediately obvious to me as a team leader. An understanding of the skillsets of each team member is the primary tool through which a team leader is able to deliver value to clients. This is a strong statement. I'm drawing a direct line from your ability to apply the right skillset to the client's level of satisfaction in the work product. I'm a firm believer that the proper scheduling of resources based on the identification of skills related to the work at hand is the basis for a successful team, not to mention happy customers.

Level Baselines

If we want reliable levels within our team, we have to write requirements for each level that line up with our expectations of the output of that level. For example, if you have a tester who falls within a general junior level, you can probably expect them to be able to perform basic web application and external network assessments. You are going to need to set educational requirements for the junior level to make sure that the tester can be relied upon to perform those tests to the level of quality we are looking for.

When building requirements for each level, we are asking ourselves, "what does it take for me to be confident that my team members at this level are educated enough to perform the work to the level of quality I want?"

I like to call these requirements baselines. Baselines are the minimum requirements for a tester to attain a certain level within the team.

It's tempting as a team leader to go into your office, pull up a spreadsheet, and work through every level within your team doling out requirements and assigning the relevant training that you believe will get the tester to the correct level of expertise. I suggest a more collaborative approach. Team members are more apt to engage and to be more successful in meeting requirements when they feel that they were involved in the process of creating the baseline. This is the same kind of "player over pawn" mentality that we previously discussed having a significant positive impact on team moral.

Your team members want to feel that they are at least in part players in their own destinies. Additionally, if you've put in the work to create team of motivated and intelligent testers, then you should take advantage of that and seek their perspectives on what courses and other training content will get them to the baseline.

Baselines should be transparent. Any team member should be able to view the requirements of their current level and those above them. Anyone motivated enough to get to the next level will know exactly what that road requires. They should be simple, preferably a bullet list of single sentence requirements.

The difficult part of developing a baseline comes when attempting to define an intangible output, quality assessments, in terms of a bullet list of single sentences. What training will result in the output I want? How do I, as a team leader, know when one of my testers is ready to execute assessments at a high level of quality? The key is demonstrability or validated learning. Simply attending a course with no metric of validated learning is not good enough. There should be no question whether a team member has completed a baseline's requirements because the tester can demonstrate the results of their development. The simplest and often the best form of demonstration is an industry respected certification. There are other forms of demonstrable validated learning, a talk developed and given at a conference, a tool that implements some new technique, etc. We will look at those more in-depth in the section on Resources and Tools.

Baselines are not created once and never updated. They are revisited on a regular basis and updated to keep pace with the changing industry and team requirements. In the same vein, once a baseline has been achieved and a tester given a certain level, they will still have yearly requirements to maintain that level. This helps to combat skill atrophy.

Capability Evolutions

Capability evolutions occur when a team's capability takes a technical leap forward. As an example, a penetration testing team that works in contracts will often be tasked with conducting a phishing engagement as part of the assessment. The classic phishing engagement consists of crafting emails that contain a malicious link and sending them to the unaware employees of the target organization. The pentester attempts to fool the victim by making the link appear innocuous while simultaneously encouraging them to click it immediately. The link takes the victim to a website that appears to be a page that the victim is familiar with but is actually controlled by the pentester. The victim enters their username and password which are sent off to the pentester who is then able to gain access to the target company's applications as the victim.

One common mitigation for phishing and other credential harvesting attacks is multifactor authentication (MFA). Even if an attacker is able to obtain a victim's credentials, the attacker will not have access to the victim's MFA device (usually an app on the victim's phone) and will therefore be unable to use the credentials they have stolen.

If a penetration testing team has a social engineering capability that is limited to the classic credential-harvesting phishing attack, then an evolution of that capability would be MFA bypass techniques to enhance the attack, make it more realistic to what modern criminal hackers are doing, and provide additional value to clients above and beyond what they can expect from the competition.

Levels and their baseline requirements allow a team leader to apply his team members to the projects at hand with a reliably consistent level of output quality. Capability evolutions give the team their edge. They are the spark in the team's reputation, the driving force behind client referrals in the contracting world. Capability evolutions are the reason that people are talking about your team.

To build capability development into a team development strategy, you'll need to identify first which capabilities are prioritized for evolution and second what those evolutions are. The first is easier. The team leader needs to identify which capabilities would have the greatest impact on the quality of the team's output and, more importantly, client satisfaction. One roadblock that I have often run into is a resistance from team members about which capability evolutions are prioritized. Hackers get excited about new exploits and offensive techniques and want to jump in and learn about them. This is a great attitude, but unfortunately, it's hard to always line up what is best for the team with what is currently exciting to research.

As team leaders, we are focused on improving our team's pentest performance and thereby increasing client satisfaction. We are going to want to prioritize the capability evolutions that drive the team toward this goal the fastest. But using the all-important customer satisfaction metric as a club to beat team members into developing capabilities they aren't excited about can backfire and result in poor development results. Again, teams are motivated when they are players, not pawns. Therefore, the prioritization of capability evolutions should skew toward customer satisfaction but should consider what is most interesting to the team as well. When prioritization is handled in this manner, I find that team members are very understanding about the importance of a client satisfaction focus and are more than willing to develop in that direction if they know their pet project is valued as well.

Identifying capability evolutions is not an easy task. It will take time, some amount of research, an understanding of where the offensive cybersecurity community is moving with regard to a specific capability, and an understanding of the subpar aspects of the current capability. This process is not something the team leader can or should take on solo. You have senior team members that are more familiar with the capabilities than you are. While the team leader has a better understanding of how a given evolution will affect client satisfaction, the senior team members will possess an industry awareness and technological understanding of each capability that should be leveraged.

The team leader drives the conversation by presenting evolution suggestions based on the perspectives of the clients. These perspectives might be directly communicated by the client during their previous assessment or they might be identified by the team leader as an opportunity to provide more value to a given client. For example, the team leader might notice that several clients develop applications using the same web application framework. The leader could recommend that research into this particular framework would be a solid evolution for the team to invest time into. The members of the team with the most technical familiarity with the capability should bring evolution suggestions of their own and provide a time and effort estimate for all suggested evolutions.

Even with a lot of thought and effort put into identifying where the capability should grow, there's always a chance that an evolution fails. Perhaps the evolution requires more research time and effort than the team is prepared to allocate. Perhaps the evolution itself is not technologically sound. For example, a team might identify a common web application framework that several of its clients use. The team decides to develop an exploit for this framework as an evolution of their capability given how many clients it will impact and impress. Unfortunately, after spending a significant amount of time researching the framework, the team is unable to find meaningful exploits. This is a cost of doing business. Not every evolution we choose to invest time into is going to be successful.

It is important to handle failures in capability evolutions with agile principles. Fail fast, fail early, and pivot to something else. The team lead is already going to have to take on the difficult task of balancing the time demands of the prioritized evolutions against the time available for research and development. The team cannot afford to get stuck on an evolution that is not producing results.

Capability Leads

The offensive cybersecurity industry develops at an incredible pace. It's not possible and it's foolish to think that any one person can keep up with all of it. This chapter opened with the warning that if you're not getting better, you're getting worse and fast. But how do you "get better" in all relevant testing domains simultaneously?

Let's define first what it means to get better at a specific capability. Getting better at web application pentesting starts with the common industry educational paths. Maybe it's OffSec or SANS or some other institution. These classes pass on the basic principles of testing web applications and can even get a student to a more advanced level with subsequent classes. After the classes have done their best, a tester moves on to on-the-job training (OJT) and experience in actual testing. There they learn to apply the techniques they learned in class and find out the differences between the classroom and the real world.

That's where many pentesters end their educational journey. They continue to pentest web applications and occasionally learn a new testing technique or the weaknesses of a new technology but only when necessary. This is where skill atrophy sets in, and over time the pentester's knowledge becomes less relevant to their always updating targets.

Skill atrophy is avoided by staying current in what is happening in a testing domain even when it is not strictly needed for the current assessment. A pentester who goes out of their way to make sure they're aware of new techniques, new real-world compromises that have occurred, and new tools that are developed will have a constantly evolving skillset that keeps pace with the industry.

This constant evolution through industry awareness layered on top of standard education and on-the-job experience is the definition of getting better. So how do you apply this concept to capabilities? How do you ensure that your capabilities as a team are evolving and keeping pace? A team leader can keep pace with one or two domains of testing, but how do you ensure development across all of them?

A capability lead is a team member, typically a senior pentester, who is assigned to champion a capability. They are the key in the team's self-development and internally driven evolution. The capability leader has the following responsibilities:

1. Ensure every member of the team that is assigned to execute the capability has the education and support to do so

2. Develop the team's knowledge of the testing domain by researching and staying current on what is happening in the testing domain (reported compromises, new techniques, etc.)

3. Develop techniques and tools to apply the latest trends of the testing domain into the team's workflow

4. Integrate new pentesting tools

This might seem like a lot of work, but it can be streamlined. It's helpful to consider your team's schedule from a yearly perspective. Perhaps there are times in the year when your team has very little work and others when they are quite busy. If this is the case, you can schedule the bulk of capability development in the slower times and only require the capability leads to remain current with trends during more busy months.

As an added benefit, a capability lead can add a significant amount of value to the final report or the outbrief by informing the client how their environment or application stacks up to what the criminal hackers are currently doing.

Core and Peripherial Capabilities

It is not necessary nor desirable to train every team member on every capability. For my second team, our clients most often requested web application, external network, and internal network assessments. Therefore, I expected every member of my team to be at least competent in all three. These were considered the core capabilities of the team, and when the capability evolution strategy was developed, they were prioritized. Capability leads that are in charge of core capabilities have their work cut out for them. They have to provide support and make sure that all team members are prepared to execute assessments within the capability.

The other domains were considered peripheral capabilities. They were still important. We knew that we would have several engagements that required us to execute mobile, IoT, and even physical penetration testing so developing the capability was required, but it was not required that every member of the team be prepared to execute them. Peripheral capabilities are still assigned a capability lead and that lead is still responsible for documenting how assessments that leverage that capability should be executed. However, a smaller number of team members will be required to execute each one. For some of the very rare and specialized testing domains, such as hardware hacking and physical penetration testing, there may only be one individual assigned to develop the capability and the associated knowledge base.

The importance between core and peripheral capabilities is less pronounced for teams that do not experience as much variety in their work, such as internal penetration teams. For more predictable teams, your capabilities may be limited to three or four domains, making the process of development more simple and more direct.

Executing the Strategy

At this point, we have our team development strategy. We understand its objectives, and we've broken those objectives down into baselines and evolutions. Before we can put the strategy into action, we'll have to answer two questions. First, what role does each team member play in the strategy? Sure, we understand that each team member is expected to meet our baseline requirements, and we understand that our capabilities need to be developed, but who is going to do what? Second, what exact combination of the available training and educational resources is going to get our team members at every level to accomplish the established baseline? Should we exclusively use established paid training courses? What benefit do technical conferences have within the context of education?

Executing the team development strategy is going to require coordination of all team members. Once again, the team levels are going to come into play. Each level of tester within the team is going to have a role to play. Levels allow us to set general expectations for groups of testers and then fine-tune things as necessary.

Whether you're using a simple three-rung system of team levels or a more complex one, you're going to have some team members that are more on the junior side and others that are more senior. The more junior a member of the team is, the more time they need to spend developing their professional skills to make sure they are delivering quality that match the team lead's expectation for their level.

The more senior a team member is, the more familiarity and experience they will have with the team capabilities and the more they will have to offer to the development of capability evolutions. I don't want to suggest that junior testers don't have great ideas and a lot to offer to the development of capabilities. In fact, when my mobile application testing capability was in shambles, a very motivated junior member of the team put in the work to get it on par with our competitors faster than I would have thought possible. Junior members have a lot to offer, but if they have not yet met the baseline requirements of a junior team member, then the team lead cannot expect them to perform assessments with a reliable degree of quality. They are an unknown quantity. They might do well on a web application test or they might be totally unprepared for it. Until they meet their baseline requirements, their focus should be on training.

Senior team members are at the opposite end of the spectrum. They have met the baseline requirements of the senior level within the team, whether that is a generalized category or within the context of a single capability. There should still be training expectations each year for the senior level, but seniors should be primarily focused on identifying and developing capability evolutions. It isn't that training has no benefit for a senior-level tester, but since the tester's skills are much closer to the cutting edge of the industry, standard training options are less helpful. The development of capability evolutions is training in itself as we will see in the next section.

It's probably obvious that mid-level testers are going to split their time between training requirements and assisting seniors with capability evolution development. As an example, a baseline requirement for a team's mid-level general pentester might include the Offensive Security Certified Professional (OSCP) certification from OffSec. To begin working toward becoming a senior-level tester, the mid-level tester would spend some portion of their allotted training and development hours working on the Offensive Security Experienced Penetration Tester (OSEP). Once the mid-level tester achieves that certification, they might spend the rest of the year assisting the capability lead of internal assessments devise new methods to avoid detection by antivirus programs.

Billable Time

If your team is responsible for executing pentesting contracts to bring in revenue, you might be a bit nervous about the recommendations in this chapter. Capability leads, evolutions, and team member development take time. Where are you going to find that time?

The easiest place, as has been mentioned, is during the slow months of the year when your testers may not have much to do anyway. This is where the bulk of the development and evolution occurs. When your team is busy, it's more difficult especially if you have a billable hour requirement. I have used two techniques to help my team stay current in their testing domains and skillsets while continuing to deliver contract work.

The first technique is to condense the requirements of capability evolutions and individual development during the busier times to the bare necessities. You can't expect a capability lead to write a tool to incorporate a new technique when they are busy executing contracts.

The second technique is more controversial. My philosophy is that staying current with industry trends is an indispensable aspect of delivering the highest level of quality product to my clients. Therefore, I consider the small percentage of time that the team dedicates to maintaining its edge billable time. This is not something to be abused. I wouldn't allow a tester to take a training course during work hours when they are assigned to a contract. But if a team member spends a few hours a week reading up on the latest techniques and trends, that is still time dedicated to giving their client the best test they can.

Resources and Tools

Training and development strategies are developed by identifying and aligning the resources available to the team toward an aggressive vision of where the team could be at the end of a week, month, quarter, and year. The resources available to a leader are going to vary considerably, but generally, they will consist of an allocated budget for team training and an amount of hours the team dedicates to development each week. In addition to these resources, there are a number of categories of tools available to the lead. Again, these may vary, but they generally break down into the following:

- Technical conferences
- College
- Educational courses
- On-the-job training
- Research

Each of these tools has a place in the development strategy, both for the development of team capabilities and team members. It's important to understand the strengths and weaknesses of each tool in order to use it effectively.

Technical Conferences

Cybersecurity professionals love their conferences. We have the big ones like Blackhat and DEFCON and the smaller local ones that usually fall under a local chapter of BSIDES. While these conferences often try to play up the offensive "hacker" side of the industry, they attract professionals and enthusiasts from every domain of cybersecurity and some outside of it. Everyone wants to be a hacker regardless of their day job.

Conferences can be a bit tricky to place in the team development strategy. They are educational in nature. They present talks, workshops, and multi-day training courses that often discuss the cutting edge of vulnerability identification and exploitation techniques. Conference talks are commonly the first place that a new type of vulnerability is presented

117

to the world. In theory, a conference would be a nonstop education-fest for the hacker's hungry mind. However, the reality is that conferences are primarily social events. This is not a bad thing. It is important for team members at every level to meet with their peers and discuss their work. It is important both for the tester to gain different perspectives and see how others have tackled similar problems, as well as for the team leader to gain an understanding of how the OCS stacks up against other similar teams.

Conferences cannot be a primary piece of the team development strategy. While there are exceptions, the training they offer is generally too short, intended for too wide a spectrum of skills, and often exorbitantly expensive. The conference talks are interesting and helpful, but, at least in my experience, it is not common for conference goers to attend more than a handful of talks during the days of the conference. The great benefit of conferences is that they help the team and the team lead build the vision for where team capabilities need to evolve toward. They provide a level of realism and possibly humility to teams that are often siloed from the greater industry where they may develop an inflated opinion of their place in the industry skill hierarchy.

College

Future pentesters start taking the field seriously and building their offensive cybersecurity skills in college. College is probably going to be the place they SSH to a host for the first time and review the results of a port scan. College is great at bringing awareness and some level of familiarity with the various technologies that future pentesters are going to encounter.

That being said, college does not prepare students for immediately starting a career as a pentester. Graduates are ready for pentesting internships and other positions where they are not required to conduct offensive cybersecurity on their own, but unless the student is a very motivated individual who conducts their own study and drives their education in addition to the college curriculum, they will need a few years of IT security experience before they are prepared to provide value as a junior member of the team.

Penetration testers are required to have a moderate amount of familiarity with a wide range of technologies. College graduates are introduced to many of these technologies but not at a level to where they are ready to develop attacks against them and consider possible disruptions caused by an attack. Additionally, it is very difficult for a college curriculum to maintain relevance. Technology updates far faster than college curriculums can.

In the contracting world, college degrees are sometimes a requirement, especially with respect to government contracting. But due to their cost, length, and difficulty maintaining relevance to the current state of the industry, I avoid including them in a team development strategy. Instead, I opt for shorter-term, constantly updating, certification-based training whenever possible.

Educational Courses

Noncollegiate educational courses are a core element of professional skill development. They are short-term, constantly updated to keep pace with the industry, and often associated with a respected certification.

Educational courses fit well into the life of a pentester. Most teams experience an ebb and flow of work throughout the year. Internal teams are very busy when their company is going through audits or testing new defenses. Consultative teams are busy near the end of the fiscal year for their client base since the money for pentesting needs to be spent and company certifications need to be validated. The short-term nature of educational courses, usually no more than a few weeks, allows the team lead to schedule them during the slow months. This gives the tester the time they need to focus on the training and pull all the learning out of the course.

The team lead should validate that whatever courses are integrated into the team development strategy are modern and are constantly having new material added and outdated material is removed. The established providers of offensive cybersecurity courses are usually very good at this. They know that to stay relevant and respected, they must put effort into adding the latest to their courses.

Finally, educational courses offer something that is critical to the validation of skills learned and the identification of level baselines – certifications. Certifications give the team lead and team members a quantifiable identifier that a level of education has been attained. For example, if a team member successfully passes the hands-on assessment for the Offensive Security Certified Professional then the team lead can expect that the tester will have a decent understanding of how to conduct assessments involving Windows- and Linux-based internal networks.

Not all courses provide a certification. That certainly doesn't mean the course doesn't have a place in the team development strategy, it just means that course outcomes will not be verified and will be more difficult to quantify.

On-the-Job Training

As with most industries, the greatest tool for team member education will be on-the-job training. Educational courses are great at teaching testers the techniques they will need to be successful in their assessments. However, the process of applying those techniques and finding the nuances that only the real world can provide is what makes a tester effective.

There are two ways in which OJT provides education: direct mentorship and solving problems. Junior-level testers are developed through OJT primarily by receiving direct mentorship from mid-level and senior testers. Mid-level testers will work on more challenging projects and be expected to solve new problems with the guidance of senior testers.

The process of solving challenging problems requires a tester to gain a deeper understanding of both their testing techniques and the technology to which they apply them. Senior testers are developed through OJT by tackling new problems and developing new techniques to solve them.

This may come off as a very natural process, but anyone that has spent time on a team with poor team collaboration and culture will know that this isn't the case. If a team does not communicate and junior members of a team do not feel comfortable asking questions, then the educational benefit of OJT is lost and the team's output will suffer. It is the team leader's responsibility to create an environment where team members can be developed through collaboration and OJT.

A team leader can use the OJT experience as a metric to determine the type of culture the team has. Are junior testers comfortable asking questions? When questions are asked, who responds? When a question is responded to, does the person who asked the question fully understand the answer? Whenever a question is asked, it is an opportunity for a tester to be further developed. By monitoring the team's ability and willingness to answer a question or to jump in and help with a difficult problem, a team leader can determine if OJT is being used to its maximum potential.

OJT is an implicit part of a team's development strategy. It isn't something that can be quantified easily since it is an ad hoc process. However, it is something that can be inspired and encouraged. Team members can grow the engagement a team has to provide itself with OJT by finding ways in which the team can share in each individual's development, a sort of "all for one" approach.

One example of engaged OJT that I found significant success with is sharing vulnerabilities. Let's say a mid-level tester identifies a SQL injection vulnerability in a web application after working with it for some time. During the next morning's team standup, the mid-level tester announces they have identified a vulnerability and the team congratulates them. The tester does not divulge the specifics of the vulnerability. Instead, they ask a junior tester who has a few free hours to take a look at the application in the same area in which the vulnerability was identified and attempt to find it for themselves.

This scenario provides a real-time opportunity for a more senior member of the team to examine and improve the assessment process of a junior tester. The mid-level tester might identify that the junior is not sure how to test for SQL injections in ORDER BY clauses of the SQL statement. The mid-level tester then works with the junior tester until they understand and identify the vulnerability.

The team lead should encourage this kind of smooth collaborative OJT as an ongoing process of improvement and skill validation across the team.

Creating metrics for how much a team member has developed through OJT is difficult. It's not like educational courses that come with a test and certification at the end. Nevertheless, OJT is one of the most effective ways of developing and maintaining skillsets.

There are two ways to measure the effect of OJT. First, you can survey the team members who have helped to provide OJT to a given team member. You can ask for their opinion as to the growth that the team member has experienced and examples of the improvement. This feedback should be documented and tracked for improvement over time. Second, you can track the output of the team member. For example, how many findings are they generating from their assessments? This is easier for internal teams who have a consistent environment to assess. For consultative teams, the variety of the work will cause differences in the output regardless of the team member's development. If your team experiences a lot of varieties in its projects, you will need to track team member output over a greater period of time to account for the variances. For example, it may take a quarter, 6 months, or even a year to get an accurate picture of a team member's improvement.

Research

Most of the resources we have discussed so far are at least primarily beneficial to individual skill development. That makes sense because developing skills is a process that can be repeated as new generations of penetration testers are ready for it. Research is on the opposite side of the spectrum. It is a tool that is used primarily in service of identifying capability evolutions and then developing the means to integrate them into the team's testing process.

That is not to say that conducting research does not also educate the person performing the research. For senior-level testers who have amassed an in-depth understanding of their specialties through their education and experience, research is one of the few remaining ways that they can continue to develop their skills. Conducting research and testing ideas for techniques, vulnerabilities, and team tooling opportunities require the tester to think of the technology and techniques in new ways. However, the primary purpose of research is to bring new capability features into the team and to keep the team's techniques on the cutting-edge.

Research is done in two phases. The first phase was discussed a bit in the previous section on capability evolutions. It is the phase where the evolution is identified and enough research is performed into the possible evolution to give the senior tester and the team lead a sufficient degree of confidence that the evolution is viable.

The second phase is of course the actual development of the evolution. It is difficult to schedule since it's we can't know the exact amount of time that an idea is going to require to turn it into something functional enough that it can be integrated into team processes. As team leaders, we have to do the best we can to give an idea adequate time while still applying the principle of failing fast, learning from our failures, and pivoting to something that is more likely to succeed.

I have witnessed, as I am sure you have, professional pentesters devoting far too much time to an idea that is refusing to bear fruit. The idea is always "almost there!" Everyone is vulnerable to setting aside agile principles when it comes to a project they are personally invested in. At some point, the reason for continuing changes from the belief that a breakthrough is right around the corner to the idea that so much effort has already been expended on the project that it would be foolish to not see it through to completion. This is the well-known "sunk cost fallacy."

These issues can be addressed by a simple and rigid adherence to guidelines established at the beginning of the year. The team leader sets a transparent metric for when it is time to pivot evolutions. The entire team is encouraged to call each other out when that metric has been reached. This includes junior members of the team informing the team leader that it is time to move on from a project that has missed its metrics. The metrics should represent the progress made on a simple scale. Each evolution should have a set check-in cadence with each check-in being a week apart at most. If the development of the evolution has stagnated and the assigned tester has not made much progress over the course of a few check-ins, it's time to pull the plug.

Finishing the Story

I opened this chapter with a story about a catastrophe that I experienced with my team's mobile capability that was a result of my lack of engagement in my team's development both at an individual and service level. The story continues with me spending a good amount of time in early 2023 thinking through the principles presented in this chapter and discussing them with my senior testers. I'll go ahead and finish the story now and discuss how I responded to the scenario and implemented several lessons I learned, but I want to re-emphasize the disclaimer at the beginning of the chapter. The training programs and certifications that worked for my team at that time may not work for your team. Educational resources change and/or become stale. Certifications may become less respected with time. Most importantly, the needs of your team may not match up with the needs of my team in 2023.

I was fortunate that the early months of 2023 were very slow for my team. This gave me time to dedicate to solving the issue I had identified. As I mentioned before, I was scared, anxious that my team had fallen behind in more than just our mobile capability, and desperate to find a way to get us back to the cutting edge. An additional consideration for me was the fact that I had recently brought three new junior testers onto the team. I was confident in their motivation and ability to learn quickly, but I had not thought to provide extensive training to them outside of on-the-job training with the existing mid-level and senior testers. I have fairly extensive experience in short-term classroom training on offensive cybersecurity topics, but this was a whole new level of challenge that I wasn't sure I could live up to.

I began developing my team development strategy. I created two objectives:

- Develop baseline requirements for every level within the team and develop the testers to achieve those baselines
- Identify and prioritize capability evolutions for every capability

The next thing I needed was a budget. I went to the company's upper management and explained the issues with the team and the need for extensive training for the newly hired junior testers. I have to give my upper management a lot of credit for having the foresight to grant me a significant training budget.

With money in hand, I knew what the limits of my strategy could be. I worked with the team to identify the available training courses, and I tried to line up training with each of the team's capabilities. I selected Offensive

Security (now called OffSec) as our primary source of courses. The reason for that decision was that they had several different levels of material, which supported the levels within my team. Nearly all of their courses are associated with a certification, which would give me validation of my team's developing skills and their price matched up well with my budget.

As a supplement to OffSec's web hacking courses, my team selected the Web Academy from PortSwigger. Again, the training was associated with certification for validated learning, and the price was hard to beat since it was free with a very inexpensive certification cost. The Web Academy also had three different levels, which might have matched up nicely with my team's internal levels of junior, mid, and senior, but we expected our junior testers to learn levels 1 and 2.

Some of our clients gave us several yearly contracts working with Windows internal networks and domains. To better prepare testers of all levels for that work, we selected Red Team Ops and the CRTO certification from Zero Point Security.

The baseline set for junior-level testers was that they must earn the OSCP from OffSec and complete the first 2 levels of the Web Academy. Mid-level testers were expected to earn a higher-level certification from OffSec such as the OSEP or OSWE in addition to completing junior-level requirements. For senior-level testers, we expected that they complete the requirements of mid-level testers and then lead and conduct research and development into capability evolutions.

These baseline requirements may seem a bit light, especially for the senior level. For that first year of bringing a team development strategy to the team, I did not want to place large training burdens on the senior testers while we were simultaneously putting significant effort into evolving our capabilities. While I was not working with that team during subsequent years, my plan would have been to increase baseline requirements for senior-level testers then.

That took care of the development of individual team members. Next, I had to address the bigger, more difficult problem of developing our capability evolutions. I reviewed the assessments we had conducted the previous year and identified areas where I felt we should be doing better. In particular, I felt that our ability to remain undetected by antivirus programs in Windows-dominant networks was not adequate. A lot of our clients came to us due to our reputation of being able to avoid detection. The team had a few individuals who had previously worked at three letter agencies and were familiar with stealth techniques, so this was an important issue.

Next, I spoke with the team's technical director and asked him to work with each capability lead and identify what the next evolution of their capability would look like. I was not ambitious enough to think that we could accomplish all the identified evolutions across all capabilities. But I wanted my team to become familiar with the process of identifying new capability evolutions. My hope was that identifying holes in current capabilities or new features that would improve a capability would become a natural process working in the backs of each tester's mind while they performed assessments.

Several capability evolutions were identified and I set to work prioritizing them. The number one priority was predicably our mobile capability. I felt the program was in shambles and needed to be rebuilt from the ground up to be capable of performing assessments at the level our clients expected. It was the priority since it was currently causing issues with our clients.

It's common that junior testers are focused on their skill development and senior testers are focused on capability development. Of course, junior testers have great ideas and can assist with the development of capability features, but generally speaking, juniors need to develop their skills so that they can provide more value to the team and to clients. Juniors may not have the experience necessary to understand what features a capability really needs.

That being said and as I have previously mentioned, a particularly motivated junior tester on the team was able to both work on their individual skillset and do the research necessary to begin the process of rebuilding the mobile capability. This junior tester became our capability lead of the mobile testing capability, and he and I discussed the tools necessary to create a modern program.

After figuring out what training and evolutions I wanted the team to spend time on, the next big hurdle was giving them that time. After all, we were a team who made money by completing contractual assessments. The term "non-billable" was a scary thing. I was fortunate that I had worked the previous year to help educate my upper management as to the need of not maintaining very high or maximum levels of billing for the team members. Management and I had agreed to try to keep the team at about 80% billable when the work was available.

My team was aware of the flow of our contracts. Early in the year was our time to develop since contracts were slow. The workload began to increase in the second quarter, and by August, the team was billing every available hour until things began to slow down again in late November. This meant that I could use the slow time to focus on training and development while counting on the coming tsunami of work to make up the overall billable percentage.

Final Thought

I provided how I developed and executed my team's development strategy to give you a real-world example of how it can be accomplished. My hope is that while reading it you were able to identify aspects of my approach that wouldn't work in your environment or wouldn't be the most beneficial path for your team. This is certainly not a one-size-fits-all scenario, and you will have to do a few iterations of experiments before you find something that works with how your team does business and the unique requirements of your situation.

CHAPTER 7

Understanding Clients

A greater portion of a team's success comes from its ability to interact and build relationships with its clients than it does from its raw technical ability. This is true for all forms of offensive cybersecurity teams. Technical professionals often brush off the importance of understanding their clients. After all, we have spent years accumulating the skills necessary to assess the security of the client's environment. Aren't we more aware of how the assessment should be conducted than a project manager at the client organization?

The answer is absolutely not. A mediocre pentester who communicates and works with his clients will always far outperform a senior tester both in what they are able to deliver to the client and in the client's impression of the value of the test. As an example, I have worked with and heard about teams whose sole focus when performing an internal network assessment of a Windows domain is to get the holy grail – Domain Admin access. It doesn't matter who the client is. The only question that determines success or failure for these teams is. "did we get Domain Admin access?" The theory is that once Domain Admin access has been achieved, everything else is easy. A malicious hacker who gained access to the network as a Domain Admin would be able to do whatever they wanted so it doesn't matter what this particular client feels is important in the network.

© Michael Butler and Jacob G. Oakley 2024
M. Butler and J. G. Oakley, *The Business of Hacking*,
https://doi.org/10.1007/979-8-8688-0174-7_7

This approach demonstrates a fundamental misunderstanding of the point of offensive cybersecurity. Unless the pentest is being performed solely to fulfill a certification requirement (e.g., PCI DSS), the client will have specific concerns about their security. The pentest report will be used to evaluate and guide their security program. While obtaining Domain Admin access to a Windows domain may be very impactful and helpful to the future of the client's security program, the domain is often not the most important part of the network. For a medical provider, patient data is going to be more important than domain control and that data is going to have separate and additional layers of security. For a company providing software-as-a-service, the domain may not be very interesting at all. Instead, application source code and client credit card data are far more important. Obtaining Domain Admin access may not directly grant access to these areas of client concern, rendering it meaningless.

Companies who hold data that is more important than their Windows domain will prioritize the security of that data over the security of the domain. If a team conducts an assessment without being aware of the client's priorities, they might obtain Domain Admin access but deliver a report that is not useful to the client. While companies that use a Windows domain usually place its security high in their list of priorities, it is rarely the top priority.

Target prioritization is not the only aspect of a test that the client is going to weigh in on. If your team is providing daily updates and maintaining communication with the client, the client will help guide the direction of the assessment toward objectives that will give the client the greatest value and therefore result in a successful test. The client provides the definition of success for each engagement not the pentest team regardless of how technically capable they are.

Types of Clients

We'll start our exploration of client understanding by first defining the various types of clients that are commonly encountered. This is especially important for consultative pentesting teams since they will encounter a wide range of client types with differing motivations and definitions of success.

Understanding Your Audience

While building my second team, the clients that I worked with were almost always highly technical individuals who had worked their way into a decision-making role at their company through years of hands-on experience. As a result, I became very aware of how to talk to decision-makers with a technical background. I learned what they most often wanted and the most effective way to present it to them. I was able to answer questions and soothe concerns before the client even knew they had them. The revenue generated by my team grew by roughly 100% every year that I was in charge. This was a direct result of the reputation my team garnered in technical communities. My team was built to understand and address the concerns and desires of technical clients.

This was of course made much easier by my own technical background. I had at least some idea of what would be interesting to technical clients, and I was able to experiment with different approaches starting from a more mature understanding of the community than I would have been able to in other communities.

I did not consider that there were other communities that I could tap into. Doubling my team's revenue every year was good enough for me. That was until the company I worked for was merged into a much larger corporation. I had new bosses that were very good at their jobs but unfamiliar with the technical client base I had grown. They had different

131

ways of obtaining and retaining clients. While my approach was very much results driven, their approach to client communication and sales was more reliant on cultivating and developing relationships.

As they begin to implement their way of approaching clients, I resisted. I knew my clients. They would be suspicious and uninterested in a salesperson trying to establish a relationship with them. To them, results came first and then trust.

I scheduled a meeting with the new company president to address our two different methodologies of client management. What we both quickly realized was that we were speaking from experience with two very different audiences. While I had learned how to attract the attention of and serve a technical community, the president was familiar with a nontechnical upper-management audience. Neither of us was wrong. Both approaches would work, but they had to be applied to the correct audience.

If the president attempted to apply his approach to the technical audience I was familiar with, they would roll their eyes and begin considering other vendors. If I applied my technical approach to the upper-management audience he was familiar with, they would be confused and feel their time was wasted with technicalities they didn't understand or find any use for.

Whether the team you lead is an internal corporate team or a consultative team working on contracts, you will have at least one audience. Most of us will have more than one. For example, if your team is involved in hospital security, you will have other technical teams, medical professionals, and hospital management as your audiences. It will take effort to understand the point of view of each audience and develop a team that delivers what they are looking for.

Since we are technical professionals, the technical audience will be more familiar and comfortable to us. They speak our language and better understand how we think and how we solve problems. It's very easy to get comfortable with this audience and to not make an effort to understand the point of view of other audiences.

As a negative example of this, I knew someone who took over an internal corporate red team. This individual was brilliant technically, well-liked by his peers, and a great leader. He communicated well with the internal blue team, and together, they achieved a new level of collaboration. The company's internal network began to be far more secure. New attack techniques were quickly tested and defended against for. The organization as a whole was becoming more safe.

Unfortunately, the funding for my friend's team was significantly reduced soon afterward due to a lack of meeting the goals of his upper management. The error he had made was he only considered the technical audience. He did not understand nor address the goals of his upper management. His managers wanted to see explosive metrics. How many boxes were exploited? How many new vulnerabilities were identified? How many times did an unauthenticated pentester find a way to gain remote code execution from the Internet? These metrics weren't being delivered. His manager wanted to be able to boast about the red team's successes and instead found he didn't have any data to boast about.

My friend's approach was technically sound and successful, but in the end, he didn't consider the desires and communication requirements of the two different audiences. If you work in an internal corporate team, you will most likely face a similar situation. Regardless of how many clients you have, you will need to understand how to communicate with clients on their terms.

Internal Teams

If your team is an internal red team or pentest team, your clients are going to be your coworkers and management. Product and network leads will be required to submit their environments and applications through the pentest process so that security vulnerabilities can be identified and remediated before a malicious actor is able to find them.

You will have to maintain a very delicate balance between your team and the team leads that make up your clients. I have worked as a contract pentester on the red teams of a very large commercial company and a very large government agency. Both of those experiences gave me a front-row seat to the wrong way of handling internal penetration testers. The government representative that was responsible for the red team was incredibly adversarial with all our clients. The agencies we evaluated felt that we were coming to "get" them and they weren't wrong. Their natural reaction was to attempt to protect themselves in any way they could. They denied and delayed our access, which damaged our ability to perform a thorough test. They questioned all findings that were reported regardless of how strong the evidence for a vulnerability was. The goal of security was secondary to interagency fighting and sabotage.

The commercial team I worked for was much better but still adversarial. The upper management of the team wanted explosive reports. Less significant vulnerabilities were ignored. We were not allowed to coordinate with other teams to better assess the environments because it would result in less significant findings. The goal of security was secondary to internal politics.

To be clear, some competition between red and blue teams can be healthy and even fun. The issue that I encountered with both the commercial and government organizations I worked for was that the competition was being used by management to score political points and impress their leadership.

Being a leader of an internal team can be tricky. Your team's relationship with its clients may not be entirely up to you. Your management may stoke an adversarial attitude with the leads of the applications you are expected to test. Your clients may feel threatened by your assessment no matter how professional and collaborative you attempt to be.

Inasmuch as it is up to you, you should make every attempt to be professional and collaborative. Your team members should understand that they are to remain neutral even when your clients question their work.

If your team pentests an application and finds major vulnerabilities within it, your report is the technical equivalent of calling your client's baby ugly. While we hope that our clients have the maturity to understand that we are working toward a common goal, that isn't always the case.

If you find yourself in an adversarial situation that you are not able to change, again, attempt to remain professional and neutral. Don't be surprised when your clients attempt to subvert your ability to test their environment or when the blue team plays dirty so they can get a win.

Commercial Clients

Most consultative pentest teams work with a lot of commercial clients. Commercial clients represent the greatest amount of variety among any client type. Their goals, communication requirements, and the type of client representative you interact with can shift significantly depending on the type and size of the company.

The goals of commercial clients will most commonly break down into one of two categories. The first category is that they require a pentest to support certifications such as PCI DSS for processing credit card data, ISO 27001 for validation of an information security management system, or some other certification. As standards have developed and are more commonly required by the market, commercial companies have found themselves needing penetration tests more often to adhere to those standards. Interestingly, very few standards at this point provide direction or requirements for the pentest. There are a few notable exceptions such as FedRAMP which has a list of minimum requirements, but standards and certifications in general leave it up to the third-party pentest team to do a good job. Also within this first category is when the customers of a client expect your client to conduct regular penetration tests as part of their security strategy.

The second category is that the commercial client wants to verify the security of their environment and/or applications. This might seem like a given; don't all clients want to verify the security of their environment? While this might be true, in practice, contracting with a third-party organization to conduct a pentest requires money, time, and management approval. Compared to other types of clients, commercial companies are far more likely to grant their management the level of autonomy and budget control necessary to purchase pentesting services. Clients from controlled sectors, such as government clients, are less likely to be able to request a pentest just to evaluate an environment's security. Controlled sector clients deal with much more red tape so without some standard or requirement driving the need for a pentest, it's difficult to purchase one. This means that commercial clients can more fluidly request pentests to check on their security while other clients will need a formal reason.

Commercial client representatives are likely to be at least somewhat technical. Even when the primary client representative, perhaps a product or project manager, is not technical, they will likely have a very technical individual joining sales calls and meetings with the pentest team to ensure that they are receiving a quality test.

Commercial clients are results driven. The better you can provide hard data demonstrating the quality of the assessment, the more trust you will generate with the client. Since commercial clients are not required to go through an impartial process of selecting vendors, generating trust with them goes a long way toward repeat business.

Controlled Sectors

A controlled sector is an area of the market with a substantial amount of regulation. This might be due to government requirements, such as the Department of Defense contracts, sensitive systems, such as ICS and SCADA systems, or human impact such as a hospital and other medical systems.

Typically, the client representative that seeks your services and is responsible for the assessment from the client's side is a project or functional manager. They have been given the task of finding a vendor to perform a penetration test as required by the regulations governing the controlled sector. As government and industry regulations mature, more and more regulation frameworks are requiring a pentest to verify the security of the regulated environment.

Your client representative is most likely going to have little technical experience, especially with regard to offensive cybersecurity. They will need help understanding how your service will meet the regulations that they have been tasked with.

Tests need to be scheduled with a lot of lead time. Controlled sector clients will need to align several teams to justify and provide access during the test window. There will be more meetings with this type of client than any other type. During the engagement itself, team members may encounter some frustrations with limited access, delays due to needed corrections in paperwork, and shifting client requirements.

Client communication is absolutely critical due to the complexity of the engagement from both sides. However, controlled sectors are also less likely to be on board with ad hoc communication mediums such as chat channels. A regular cadence of short video calls can be a good replacement.

Reporting requirements are going to be more extensive. Controlled sectors are often required to provide the redacted results of a pentest to outside agencies or even the public. This means your team will have to develop an in-depth report for internal dissemination and a summarized report for external parties. Reporting requirements should be discussed early on so that testers do not waste time writing a report in the standard format if a custom format is required. Additionally, since the report will likely be disseminated via meetings, the client will likely request a high-level nontechnical presentation to provide to their upper management.

There is often more than one outbrief meeting. This is because the client representative is again not very technical. They will have a difficult time answering technical questions as they arise when the report is disseminated. These additional outbriefs are a great opportunity to deeply impress the client organization and help secure repeat business.

Client Motivations and Concerns

Clients of all types come with a variety of motivations and concerns. Understanding them is key to helping a client develop an accurate assessment scope and to understanding what you and your team can do to impress them.

Required by Certification

Clients who are pursuing a penetration solely to support and maintain an industry security certification are typically more hands-off than clients with other motivations. These clients are required to have a test, but they don't want the test to be too disruptive. They certainly don't want it to result in an abundance of findings that could delay or prevent them from attaining their certification.

I am not suggesting that you should lay aside professional ethics to help a client obtain a certification most easily. The assessment should be conducted rigorously and as in-depth as possible given the time and scope. However, clients with a certification requirement will appreciate as much time as you can give them. Waiting till the outbrief to inform a client that their PCI network is not properly firewalled off from other network subnets is not going to go over well. These clients do not like surprises. If their environment is fairly insecure, then you may annoy them with the amount of findings that you report. However, if you provide suggestions on how to quickly remediate the findings, offer to perform a retest as soon as the client's engineers can fix them, and inform the client as early as possible, you will ease the client's anxiety and be seen as an ally working to help them attain their certification.

Security Concerns

Clients who are motivated to seek a test because of their concerns about the security of their environment are a pentester's best friend. It's easy to get along with these clients because everyone is working toward the same goal. The client has a healthy respect for the pentest process; otherwise, they wouldn't have requested the engagement.

These clients come with high expectations. They usually find the pentest team they want to work with through the referrals and experiences of technical friends in their industry. They want results and in-depth work. They want to see that you and your team are motivated to perform a high-quality assessment and are easy to work with.

Clients motivated by the security of their environment are far more likely to refer their friends to your company if the assessment goes well. Of course, the opposite is also true. If they are unimpressed, they will warn their friends about your team.

Hacking for Policy Change

Some clients seek out the services of a pentesting team so that they can leverage test results to effect change within their organization. This type of client motivation is not something I expected when I joined the offensive cybersecurity field, and it might surprise you when you encounter it. It can take a variety of forms. The most common example is a middle manager responsible for the technical security of some aspect of the company's environment. This manager is convinced that a team working within his area of the environment is making things less secure, but he doesn't have the political power to do much about it.

He does, however, have the ability to request a third-party pentest. And so he engages with your team to specifically test the area of his environment that he is concerned about. If your team identifies significant vulnerabilities, then the manager is able to go to his upper management with evidence of the security issues and gain support for the policies he wants to implement.

The most extreme example of this that I have encountered when my team was approached by a tech startup. Two members of the startup's C-level management explained to me that their senior programmer was out of control. He refused to listen to management's direction for the development of the primary application, and he held so much critical knowledge about the application in his head that they couldn't replace him. The managers wanted my team to conduct a pentest of the application to prove that the steps their senior developer was taking were insecure and detrimental.

The best that a pentest team can do in these situations is to remain neutral and conduct the pentest as they would without regard to the internal political situation and motivations of their client. Getting in the middle of a political feud never ends well.

Previous Bad Experiences

Clients who have worked with other pentest teams and had a less-than-stellar experience often bring an air of suspicion to a new engagement. The most common reasons that a client is unhappy with an engagement's results are that the prior team failed to communicate well, failed to test everything that was within scope, or failed to convince the client that an adequate level of care, focus, and skill was being applied to their project.

These clients need more management than other clients. They need to be reassured that your team is going to perform to their expectations. These clients offer an opportunity to easily impress them. If you are able to overdeliver in an area that the previous team failed to deliver, then you will likely earn the client's trust. For example, if the previous team did not communicate with the client sufficiently, then your team should make sure that the client is always made aware of testing activities.

Helping the Client

Pentesting is a niche field in the cybersecurity industry. Most professionals in cybersecurity are familiar with pentesting but do not often directly interact with pentesters. Cybersecurity managers and decision-makers know that pentesting is a very important tool in their vulnerability management program. However, they often aren't familiar with the details on how to use that tool.

When a client is seeking an engagement and they contact a sales representative, the representative is equally unqualified to help the client understand how best to use pentesting in their program. It is our responsibility as offensive cybersecurity professionals to work with clients and help them understand how our services best fit their goals. There are a number of ways to accomplish this.

Industry Comparisons

We can rely on clients to be at least fairly knowledgeable about their area of industry or government and the cybersecurity requirements of that area. But interestingly, that knowledge doesn't usually include an understanding of how their specific industry implements offensive cybersecurity. After running a few engagements within a market segment, your team will build an understanding of the unique goals and needs of that segment. For example, the financial technology (fintech) market is extremely concerned about the security of their products. A fintech company's reputation for keeping its clients' data and money secure is paramount to the company's success. Therefore, fintech companies are far more likely to request a white-box style assessment. They want the testers to have all the data possible to help them identify as many vulnerabilities as they can.

If a new client from the fintech market approaches your team for an engagement, you can use this experience to explain to the client what you have done for similar companies and the benefits those companies saw in the approach.

Alternative Approaches

As offensive cybersecurity evolves and your own team develops new ways of providing value through assessments, you will have to educate clients on how things have changed. Pentesting was conducted very differently even just a few years ago. If a client is not aware of how the market has evolved, they'll need help understanding why the new approach your team and the greater offensive cybersecurity community has developed will result in better results for them.

As an example, my experience has been that clients are rarely interested in social engineering engagements. This is most likely due to the specific set of clients I worked with and is not a representative of the industry as a whole. When I presented my team's social engineering services to clients, the client would wave it off and say that they had implemented an automated phishing service and it met their requirements. But when I was building my second team, my technical director developed our phishing infrastructure so that it included MFA bypass features. In future sales meetings with prospective clients, I would bring up my team's social engineering capability. The client would begin to wave me off, and then I'd inform them that we could go beyond what their automated solution was doing. In fact, by demonstrating how MFA could be bypassed, the entire assessment would provide more value since it would be considered more "real-world." Our sales of social engineering engagements increased substantially as my clients could see the value in this new approach.

As your team develops its understanding of what matters to a particular client, you will be able to recommend new aspects of the engagement, new approaches, or even entire additional engagements to meet and go beyond their requirements. This in itself builds trust with a client. You are demonstrating that you and your team are a partner in their journey toward security. You understand their needs and are actively involved in meeting them.

Change the Scope

On many initial meetings with clients, I have cringed when they outline their scope for the engagement. Often the scope is too small to provide them with the level of value they are looking for. Even the best teams can't do a whole lot with a scope of five IP addresses for example. Other times, the client will request that an engagement is conducted in a manner that I know will not lead to the best outcomes.

As an example, I was the subject-matter expert on offensive cybersecurity within cloud environments for my team. Clients with cloud-based environments would come to my team seeking an engagement for an external network pentest just like they had done for their on-premises networks in previous years. While there's nothing wrong with external network pentests of cloud environments, it doesn't lead to the most value for the client in most situations. A white-box assessment where the pentester is given read-only access to the cloud environment can result in a much more substantial report, and it can provide the client with a much better understanding of the weaknesses in their environment.

For these clients, I accepted their scope and then made a recommendation about how we could do more considering it is a cloud environment and a more in-depth review is within the team's skillset. I showed them sample reports and gave them a brief rundown of the types of outputs they would see from what we called a "collaborative cloud" assessment instead of a standard external network pentest.

Clients accepted this change in scope more often than not. When the engagement was concluded, I was confident that the client would be satisfied because I had enough scope to reliably produce results. This had the additional benefit of avoiding a small-scope assessment. It's far more difficult to produce an impressive report from a small-scope unauthenticated external network assessment.

Clients are often very open to suggestions, especially if your team has built any trust with them during previous engagements or from a referral. At the end of the day, the engagement scope is of course at the client's discretion, but they will be informed of the options and the outcomes they can expect.

Client Relationship Pitfalls

We've talked at length about what you and your team can do to improve you relationship with your clients. Now we'll discuss a couple of elements of the client relationship that can make things more difficult for both sides.

No Surprises

I have been in many outbriefs where the pentester who performed the assessment did not communicate with the clients. The outbriefs often start already on the wrong foot. The members of the client's team who are in charge of the environment that was assessed enter the meeting already wary and possibly defensive. The client representative who engaged the pentesting team to conduct the assessment is nervous, wondering if he got his money's worth or if he's going to have to explain a poor assessment to his boss. When a necessary certification is on the line, everyone on the client's side is on edge, hoping that there aren't too many vulnerabilities of high severity. If there are, it could delay or derail the certification project and have a significant impact on the future of the environment.

This is a bad way to start a meeting. If your client is holding their breath at the outbrief, something has gone wrong. Your team has failed to adequately communicate with the client.

If we are to be partners with our clients helping them to achieve their goals and become more secure, we have to adopt a mindset of considering what is best for them. Early notification of vulnerabilities allows the client to communicate with the engineers responsible for the environment and develop a plan for addressing the vulnerabilities. The pentesters on my second team would often meet with clients in the middle of an engagement to explain a new vulnerability that was identified, provide ad hoc recommendations for remediation, and assist the engineering team in developing a working solution.

Again, this more open and communicative approach develops a deeper sense of trust from the client.

Client Sabotage

Whether your team is a contracts-based team or an internal red team, you will encounter client sabotage. The story usually goes something like this:

One day, your senior pentester finds a vulnerability and develops a brilliant exploit for it. The exploit gives your team the holy grail – remote code execution. According to the Rules of Engagement, your team is allowed to leverage this access to start testing the client's internal network. This is a critical vulnerability, and as such, you need to report it to the client immediately. While your team begins to figure out how they're going to avoid the client's security measures and pivot into the internal network, you speak with the client and let them know the situation. The client is impressed and gives you the all-clear to continue the assessment. Your team promptly installs a backdoor program that beacons back to a C2 server.

The next morning during standup, your senior tester tells you that not only is the vulnerability gone but the entire host that held the vulnerability has been firewalled off from the Internet and the backdoor is dead. You contact the client to ask if they know what happened. The client lets you know that they talked to the owner of that host and let them know about the vulnerability. The host was immediately decommissioned. The client suggests that your team move on with the assessment.

As the assessment continues, this pattern repeats. Whenever a significant vulnerability is found and reported, it magically disappears before your team can assess the impact. By the end of the assessment, your team develops a report that is missing much of the impact that the engagement actually produced. It lists vulnerabilities, but their severities are lowered since the team was not able to access them long enough to determine what data could have been accessed.

These situations occur when the client that engaged your team for the assessment has a conflict of interest. They are required to submit to a pentest, but they are evaluated on the security of the environment. An explosive pentest report, which highlights critical vulnerabilities in the environment, will make them look bad.

These are the most sensitive client relationships. They are difficult for the testers who do the work because every big win is followed by immediate disappointment. They are difficult for the team as a whole because it's hard to demonstrate the value your team can provide when they are being sabotaged. If the work is contractual, the client company may seek the services of a different pentest team next time since your team's report was not impressive. If the work is internal, then the client's environment will be viewed as much more secure than it actually is.

This gets even more heated for internal red teams that are tasked with testing the ability of the blue team to detect and respond to attacks. I am not referring to purple teams. Purple teams are collaborative engagements where the blue team works with the red team to identify holes in their detection and response apparatus. The purple team approach does a lot to reduce the unhealthy competitive attitude that can exist between red and blue teams.

Noncollaborative red team assessments of blue team capabilities are important, but when all red team assessments are unannounced and noncollaborative, unhealthy attitudes begin to form. The security teams view themselves as adversaries instead of partners in the security of the environments they work in. The adversarial relationship is often stoked by the managers of both teams who have political and egotistical motivations.

As an example of sabotage between red and blue teams, when I worked as a contractor on a red team for a very large corporation, we would routinely find ways to bypass the security measures within the corporation's networks. This understandably frustrated the blue team. Their frustration was made worse by pressure from upper management who felt that an extreme level of competition between the two teams was a positive thing.

The blue team began to play a bit dirty. Since our command and control servers were held in a cloud environment that they were able to access, they would identify which IP addresses were assigned to those servers and then search their networks for any hosts connecting to them. This allowed them to identify any hosts we had compromised without them noticing through more legitimate means.

Sabotage like this hurts everyone. In the end, the blue team was not becoming better at detecting the red team's methods. The red team's report was impacted by interference that could not occur in a real-world scenario, meaning that a significant amount of the time and money spent on the project was wasted.

As team leaders, we don't always have the political power to do something about adversarial relationships whether they are between a red and blue team or between our client and those responsible for the security of the target environment. Sometimes we will run into conflicts of interest and clients who want to sweep our findings under the rug and minimize the report.

So how do we handle these client relationships? The truth is there is no perfect one solution. Professionalism and communication are key. You must work with your client to identify a solution that fits the situation.

Your client should be informed that their actions are affecting the quality of the assessment. Sometimes that can be enough. I once had a client who enjoyed bragging to other members of management about the successes of my team. Those other members of management would immediately patch their servers or take them offline while the assessment was being conducted. After a conversation about the impact of his talking to other managers, he decided to hold off on bragging until the report was finalized.

Some clients correctly feel that when a vulnerability is identified, they should immediately begin attempting to patch it. However, during an assessment, this can have the unintended consequence of preventing a thorough investigation of the impact of the vulnerability. A solution that many clients find acceptable is for the pentest team to report a vulnerability, the client then begins patching it, but the team is allowed to run a backdoor program on the host to continue the evaluation of the compromise. This satisfies the needs of the pentesters and the security requirements of the target environment.

Another approach I have seen is when the pentest team delays the reporting of a vulnerability until they are able to properly assess its impact or have a firm level of access to the internal network. This is a very dangerous approach for two reasons. First, it is most likely in conflict with the Rule of Engagement and/or other contract documentation. Second, it leaves the vulnerability exposed after it has been identified. The vulnerability might be identified and exploited by a malicious actor, which puts the pentest team in a very awkward position. For these reasons, it's best to avoid this approach. It presents too much risk for the team.

CHAPTER 8

Engagement Security

Engagement security is an often overlooked aspect of managing an
offensive cybersecurity team. We are focused on evaluating the security
of target environments, and sometimes we can be pretty sloppy with
our own.

Team security and safety processes need to be established early in the
team's creation. Adding them later can be difficult as the team will have
already developed its flow and could be somewhat resistant to the often
annoying hoops we have to jump through to keep everything secure.

Preventing Outages

Your team will cause outages. It is a fact in our field. The core of performing
a penetration test is executing nonstandard actions within environments
we are not fully familiar with. Something will eventually break. Even so,
your team should do everything it can to minimize the chances of causing
an outage and learn from outages when they do occur.

Preventing outages begins with documenting and communicating
safety standards for every domain of testing your team engages with.
This is another great place to utilize capability leads. The leads are
experts in their domain and will be the most familiar with potential
causes of outages. Task them with developing safe testing standards and
communicating those standards to the team.

© Michael Butler and Jacob G. Oakley 2024
M. Butler and J. G. Oakley, *The Business of Hacking*,
https://doi.org/10.1007/979-8-8688-0174-7_8

For example, exploits that leverage memory corruption (buffer overflows, heap overflows, etc.) can be quite unstable and dangerous. Capability leads should create safety standards that require a tester to discuss the situation with the client and obtain approval before attempting a memory corruption exploit. This allows the client to make the decision about taking the risk and gives them time to prepare in case they need to compensate for an outage. In either case, the client understands the risks and gives the approval.

When Outages Occur

Even with safety standards in place, my team caused one to two outages each year. It might seem odd, but most of these outages were caused by the senior members of my team. The reason is that senior members are more often assigned to nonstandard or more complex assessments. Nonstandard environments can sometimes be less capable of handling unexpected inputs gracefully.

As one example, a senior tester on my team was performing a web application pentest of the client's primary website. The tester found a Local File Inclusion (LFI) vulnerability. The application took a URL parameter that the user provided as a path to a file. The application would then return the contents of that file. Hoping to turn this vulnerability into remote code execution, the tester decided to download the source code for the main web page so that he could review it for more substantial vulnerabilities.

Unfortunately, the attack didn't go as planned. When the tester leveraged the vulnerability to try to get the source code, the source was instead rendered by the server. The attack was then passed onto the rendered page, which then made the same request again and once again rendered the page. An infinite cycle of requests and rendering occurred until the server's CPU was maxed out and the site went offline.

Outages happen. You must expect them, and you must instill testing requirements that will allow you to confidentially report an outage to your client with a full explanation of what caused it. Hiding an outage or not having enough information about what caused an outage is damaging your reputation and relationship with your client.

The most important factor in preparing for outages is the robust logging of testing activities. All testing activities must be recorded. This may seem daunting to implement and invasive to the testing process; however, the process can be much more smooth than you'd initially assume.

Tester activities can be broken down into the locations that they occur. For example, if a tester is working on an external or internal network assessment, they will perform most of the assessment activities from a command terminal or the interface of a framework such as CobaltStrike. Most terminals log commands automatically, but more robust logging can be implemented and retained so that timestamp and command data are available. All commercially available and most free frameworks include logging of actions that a tester executes.

On the web application assessment side, the primary testing tool is a proxy such as Burp Suite. By default, these proxies log all web requests. If a tester issues a web request that causes an outage, it will be retained in the tool's history.

At a minimum, there are three pieces of information that should be associated with every interaction a tester initiates with the target environment:

- Identification of the tester (e.g., username, tester identifier, etc.)

- Timestamp of when the interaction occurred

- Detailed information on the interaction

Most of the tools that are used during pentests come with some form of logging built in. This logging may need to be extended to include these three pieces of information and to ensure accessibility of the logs by the team leader in the event an outage does occur. If the logging doesn't exist or is insufficient, your team should develop simple solutions to make sure nothing is missed.

For my first team, when an outage occurred, it caused me a great deal of anxiety. I wasn't sure if my team would have all the logs I needed to explain the situation to the client. When logs are not retained, explaining an outage to a client becomes awkward. The tester tries to walk the client through what happened and gives as much detail as their memory allows. In these situations, the client is often not given a full picture of the event, and the team lead is not able to conclusively demonstrate that the outage was not caused by the pentester being negligent.

For my second team, I felt that same sense of anxiety when an outage had occurred, but thanks to the team's commitment to keeping everything logged, I was able to quickly relax. I could clearly explain to the client exactly what happened and provide screenshots from our tools. The clients always appreciated this approach, and instead of an outage causing a breakdown of trust, it built even more rapport.

Benefiting from an Outage

The fact that outages will happen is not an excuse for them. An outage highlights a flaw in your testing processes and safety standards. They are learning opportunities for catching issues that were not previously considered. At the very least, outages can be used to critique a specific testing technique, such as adapting LFI testing techniques to not cause a rendering loop, but often they reveal oversites in the team's methodology.

The least useful reaction to an outage is to blame the client or the environment. For example, if a tester causes an outage by aggressively scanning a client's internal network, the resulting outage is not the fault of the client nor the host that was not able to process the scans. Rather, it is the fault of team leadership for not discussing the possibility of sensitive hosts with the client prior to scanning and the fault of service leadership for not appropriately setting and communicating internal network scanning safety standards.

Handling Negligent Pentesters

When I was running my first team, we received a contract to perform an internal network assessment on a government network. We had built a good amount of rapport with the government representative over the previous few engagements, and I didn't expect this engagement to be any different. A new pentester had recently joined the team. He held many various certifications, and I was very interested to see how he would conduct an assessment since my experience came from a very different background. I hoped he would be able to educate me and the other testers on a more standard way of doing things that he may have picked up from his education.

He conducted the internal network assessment and provided a report. There were a few findings but nothing very substantial. During the assessment, he used the popular command and control framework CobaltStrike and conducted scans and manual tests to identify vulnerabilities in the network.

After the assessment was complete and the client had accepted the final report, I was curious about how he had approached the test. I reviewed the logs from CobaltStrike. I found an entry that disturbed me. After conducting research, I was able to put the pieces together. I determined that the new tester had downloaded a module for

CobaltStrike that ran all the exploits that were loaded into the framework against every available target in the network. It was a miracle that the tester had not caused half the network to go down as he negligently sprayed the network with attacks.

To this day, that event is the single most negligent event I have witnessed in my career. The difficult part of it is that the tester gave no indication that they were a dangerous tester. Their resume suggested they were educated and experienced and they interviewed very well.

If your team fails to establish safe testing standards, then the outages that occur as a result are your responsibility. Negligent team members are those who choose to disregard the established safety standard because they feel the standard does not apply to them or that they know better.

While events like these are thankfully rare, it is important to audit the testing practices of your team members and establish an understanding of how things are to be done for new team members. If you have implemented robust logging, auditing your testers is much easier. Audits don't have to be a negative experience. They can identify flaws in the education of your team and holes in the testing process. If automation is applied, auditing can provide you with valuable metrics on the success and failures of each tester and each technique.

Do No Harm

Our entire field is based on the goal of assessing and helping to improve the security of the client's environment. We cannot degrade their security during our assessment. This might seem obvious, but in practice, degrading client security can easily happen. Like the Hippocratic oath, we must first do no harm to our client's environmental security.

The importance of this principle became clear to me when I was working with my first team. One day, a junior tester approached me very excitedly. He had found a web application with a file upload vulnerability.

He was able to upload a PHP file and then access that file which gave him the ability to run code on the server. It was a big win on a difficult project. When he told me about it, I asked to see the code for his webshell. He showed it to me. It was a simple one-line PHP file that took input from the URL and executed shell commands. I told him to immediately delete the file and remove the access. He was confused and concerned that he might not be able to get the access back if the file was removed. I didn't care. He had failed to put anything into the file that prevented a malicious user from accessing it. There was no encryption, no password requirement, nothing. The webshell had degraded the security of the client environment to the point that a script kiddie who happened to find the file could run shell commands and access their internal network.

Implementing password protections, encryption, and whatever other necessary security mechanisms into a webshell takes time. It's frustrating and annoying to take that time when a serious vulnerability has been found, and a tester is itching to exploit it and see what access they can gain. That's why my team began to prepare secure webshells for a variety of languages ahead of time. They had a proof-of-concept payload that was used to very code could be executed and then a more fully functional webshell with layers of security built in.

This is just one way in which our operations can degrade the security of a client's environment if we are not careful. Another one that I have seen is when a tester opens a port on an Internet-facing host so that they can call into their backdoor program, ignoring the fact that anyone else can call into that program as well.

Whenever we do something that increases the attack surface of our client's environment, we need to ask ourselves if the security associated with that increase is at or higher than the same level of security applied to other areas of the client's network. When in doubt, the team should discuss the risk with the client and get their blessing before adding to the attack surface.

Team Equipment

When my second team was in its first year, we performed most of our testing from virtual machines running on company-issued laptops. Sometimes we used cloud platforms such as AWS when we needed extra power. As we matured, I became uneasy about the client data stored, even temporarily, on our laptops. I dreaded the idea of getting a call from a team member and finding out a laptop had been left at an airport or stolen out of a car. If a laptop was compromised, I would have to assume the worst and inform any client whose data may have been in it.

I came up with a principle. I wanted the security of our team equipment to be such that if I received a call reporting a stolen laptop, I could respond with "I don't care." Of course, losing company equipment isn't great, but I wouldn't be concerned about compromised client data because the laptop wouldn't contain any. This principle became the impetus for creating testing infrastructure in highly secured cloud environments. Our cloud assets were temporary and destroyed after each engagement had been outbriefed. Any data that we did retain was stored in a secured location in the cloud with three factors of security between it and the outside world. The laptops were used for client communications and email, but they did not store engagement or vulnerability-related data. If a laptop was lost, we could remotely log that user out of their communication applications and rest easy.

This approach might not work for everyone, or you might find an improvement to it. The point is that team equipment can hold very sensitive data for a number of clients. Without taking measures to control the exposure of that data, you cannot be sure that your testers are following best practices with data management and security. If a tester relaxes their adherence to the team's security rules, then a client's data may be exposed through team equipment.

Communication Security

The security of your team's communication with its clients is something that should be figured out with the client prior to the start of the engagement. Each client is going to have a different appetite for the security of various communication mediums. Some are going to be very uncomfortable with chat mediums, for example, since they may appear less secure than email communication. Controlled sector clients are especially fond of weekly and sometimes even daily video meetings.

Your team should assemble a basic communication strategy that can be offered and then modified by clients. The strategy my second team used was

- Video meetings for hand-off and kickoff meetings

- Secure email and chat communication for receiving access information and credentials

- Chat communication for daily updates and general discussions

- Ad hoc video meetings for any critical discussions (critical vulnerabilities, complex blockers, possible outages, etc.)

- Video meetings for outbriefs

We supported multiple channels of chat communication (Slack, Microsoft Teams, Signal, etc.) so that we could work with whatever a client preferred, trusted, and could integrate with easily. We attempted to push clients toward chat communication whenever possible so that it was less disruptive during operations. Most clients enjoyed the chat communication, but some preferred a different strategy which we adapted to.

Whatever communication strategy is worked out between your team and a given client, security is going to be an important factor for both sides. This is especially true when communicating vulnerability data. A client may not trust a chat medium to handle sensitive information about critical vulnerabilities in their environment. Also, the client may not want all parties with access to the channel to view that information. As an example, when my team was asked to perform an assessment of a company that was being considered for acquisition by a larger company, members of both the acquiring and potentially acquired company were present in chat channels. The acquired company was sometimes not happy with the idea of raw vulnerability data being communicated to the acquiring company since the acquisition had not been finalized yet. As such, my team would engage directly with the acquired company in separate channels to ensure their security needs were met.

Outside of regular communication, your client will need to feel safe sending your team sensitive access information and credentials for authenticated assessments. Some clients will want to use a secure data transfer method that they own, but smaller clients will usually rely on you to provide one.

Data Creep

In the course of an assessment, there can be hundreds of locations that store or process sensitive data. These locations include a variety of hosts used by the pentesters, chat channels, emails, notes from meetings, formal contract documents, internal team communications, team project tracking software, report development tools, report storage, and much more. Pentesters are very eager to get started on projects when a team is newly formed. If there isn't much data discipline early on, then it becomes far more difficult to implement it later. Without strong data management policies, sensitive data from engagements will remain behind in old communications and files forgotten on laptops. The result is that your team is now a new area of risk for its clients.

The goal of data management for your team should be that after the time frame of the assessment has expired, all sensitive data from every location that it was stored, processed, discussed, or developed is destroyed. This is difficult enough since you can't control the actions of every member of your team with regard to their data discipline, but there are two additional caveats that add layers of complexity.

Clients will often request that you retain their data for some amount of time. The primary reason for this is so that your team can pick up from where they left off and perform a verification test once the vulnerabilities are remediated, usually within a couple of months. Sometimes clients need the data to be retained for compliance reasons. If there is a significant compromise within their organization at some point over the next couple of years, they may need to refer to pentest data to verify that the organization did its due diligence with its security. Finally, clients request that data is retained so that you are not starting from scratch when they request an assessment following the cycle. Several clients that my team would commonly work with would tell us "use the scope from last year" when we asked for targeting information. They assumed we were retaining data from previous engagements to support the current one.

The second layer of complexity is the usefulness of test data to determine the strengths and weaknesses of your team. For example, when you are working on your development strategy for a new year, you may want to refer to the previous year to determine if your team was less successful with web application assessments vs. its mobile application assessments. This data helps to drive the development of your team, where you will spend your training budget and the direction of capability evolutions.

The solution is to develop a data management strategy that allows all test-related data to be stored in a single location with multiple layers of security until that data is either old enough to be destroyed, no longer useful, or the client requires its destruction. The data should be accessible enough that it can be rehydrated when needed to support a new assessment but inaccessible enough that it takes human involvement to access the data.

My team used central Git repositories to share and manage data between testing computers during engagements. This was very helpful when it came to closing out the engagement because we could simply compress, encrypt, and password-protect the repository and then destroy all hosts that had accessed it.

CHAPTER 9

Effective Web and Mobile Application Testing

Web and mobile application assessments are by far the most common type of engagement in our industry. They are the bread and butter of offensive cybersecurity. Even when the client requests an internal or external network assessment, there's a good chance you'll spend time testing applications hosted in those networks. For most teams, application testing is going to be the most important assessment domain.

The good news is that a lot of the tools, techniques, and procedures that work for testing web applications can be used in mobile assessments as well. Your team will save time when developing in overlapping areas, such as API testing, and can use that time to fine-tune testing techniques that are unique to each domain, such as on-device data storage security for mobile applications.

The bad news is that there are also significant differences between the two. The most obvious and impactful difference is the device and its security, which is a major consideration in mobile application assessments but are nonexistent in web application assessments. Your mobile

© Michael Butler and Jacob G. Oakley 2024
M. Butler and J. G. Oakley, *The Business of Hacking*,
https://doi.org/10.1007/979-8-8688-0174-7_9

application capability lead will spend a great deal of their time keeping up with the ever-evolving security standards of mobile devices and updating your team's testing processes accordingly.

Client Goals

The following are a few of the common scenarios that drive a client to request an application assessment:

- Annual or quarterly security validation requirements.

- Prelaunch assessment of a new feature or update.

- Prelaunch assessment of a new application.

- A significant customer of the client requests the assessment.

The goals of your client have much less of an impact on how an application assessment is executed than they do for some of the other testing domains (e.g., network and cloud). Client goals will determine the scope of the engagement, but once the engagement parameters are set, the process of testing is not significantly affected.

This makes application assessments a bit more predictable. Your team can focus on developing its methodology without needing to consider as many outside factors as you would with other assessment types.

Safety Concerns

We tell our clients that since pentesting consists of performing nonstandard and unexpected actions, system outages are always a possibility regardless of the level of experience and education the testers have. However, application assessments have advantages over other assessment types when it comes to your ability to safely test. Application assessments can be performed in nonproduction environments such as staging or quality assurance environments. This gives the tester more flexibility to conduct their testing since they have no fear of crashing the environment. Taking a server down is not going to result in a loss of service or client revenue.

The trade-off is that nonproduction environments may not present an identical experience to what is in production. Staging environments may not have legacy features that are available in production. I've worked with several clients who would provide a testing environment but then also inform me that several much older versions of the application were deployed in production. When given this information, my response is to make sure the client understands that unless we include those other versions of the application in the assessment scope, we can only test the security of the latest version.

Another difficulty in working with nonproduction environments is the lack of data. The application might feel like an empty shell unless it is prefilled with dummy data. Without some kind of data in the application, several vulnerabilities are going to be more difficult to test for. For example, Insecure Direct Object Reference (IDOR) vulnerabilities require other objects present so that the tester can see if they can be referenced in unsafe ways. Pentesting is hard enough given the short time frame testers have to become familiar with and attack an application. If they are also responsible for generating data in the application before they can even attempt to identify vulnerabilities, it's going to significantly affect the quality of the test.

Developers require dummy data in order to execute their unit tests as part of the software development lifecycle so they should be able to provide your testers with a data-filled environment. It is important to bring up this issue early on in talks with the client so a delay in testing can be avoided.

Despite the additional difficulties, the safety benefits of testing in nonproduction environments should make it your first choice for all application assessments.

Scoping the Assessment

Application assessments are usually focused entirely on the identification of as many vulnerabilities as possible. They are true penetration tests without additional red team requirements thrown in. This means that the client is generally more willing to provide additional data, access, or information to support the identification of vulnerabilities. They aren't as concerned about creating a real-world scenario like they are with many network assessments. Your team isn't trying to assess the client's ability to defend itself from an attack, you are assessing the security of the application.

To give your team the best chance to produce an impressive report, you should ask the client for as much access and data as possible. Source code, configuration files, application documentation, etc., are all great sources of data that will help your team be successful.

To conduct a complete assessment, your team will need access to at least one user account at every privilege the application provides. This is because a higher-privileged user will have access to more functionality than a lower-privileged user. Your testers will need the higher-privileged user accounts to identify high-privileged actions and the lower-privileged accounts to test authorization barriers to those actions. Some applications allow high-privileged users to create low-privileged accounts. In these cases, your team may only need the high-privileged account since they can populate the rest of the needed account levels themselves.

Authenticated vs. Unauthenticated

Application assessments should always include both authenticated and unauthenticated attack vectors. Thankfully, it is rare that a client will ask your team to perform a "black box" or purely unauthenticated assessment of an application. The logic behind a black box assessment is that it will better emulate real-world scenarios since a malicious actor will not be given access either.

There are two flaws in this logic. First, it does not consider the most significant advantage a malicious actor has over a penetration tester – time. The malicious actor is not limited to a few weeks or months of an assessment window. They can take their time becoming more intimately familiar with their target application and the organization that hosts it. Second, it does not consider that a malicious actor is not limited in the scope of their attack. They may gain access to the application through social engineering, compromising a different application, etc.

Limiting an offensive cybersecurity team to only unauthenticated testing of an application adds another handicap to the list that professionals already have to contend with.

Whether your team is given authenticated access to the application or not is up to the client. There is benefit to black box assessments, but it is also more difficult to show value to the client. When asked to perform a black box assessment, you should communicate with the client that the added difficulties will likely reduce the depth of the report and the number of findings and then allow them to make the determination of whether the benefits of a black box assessment are worth its difficulties.

Source Code

Offensive cybersecurity professionals are trained to test live applications and environments. Most of us have some kind of coding skills, and some of us are very comfortable with code. But that doesn't mean that an application assessment is the same thing as a code review. If we are going to dynamically test live environments, why would we want source code?

The answer is that access to source code improves testing, even for those who are not expert developers. At a minimum, your team can run automated and free tools to assess the code and see if they can find some of the more simple vulnerabilities. But where source code can really become helpful is when a team member is trying to validate a vulnerability. Vulnerabilities are not often straightforward, and having the ability to look under the hood at the code itself can save a tester hours of struggle and frustration.

I've had a few testers on my teams that were former developers. Access to source code was like cheating to them. They could very quickly move through the application, identify possible vulnerabilities, and then validate them in the code. If they identified a vulnerability, they would search through the code base to see if the vulnerability had been repeated elsewhere.

Having access to source code can give your reports an extra level of detail by including the specific lines of code that created the vulnerability. Your team can include recommendations for how to fix the code to prevent the vulnerability. This is a level of service that clients are not accustomed to.

My second team implemented a simple policy when it came to source code – always request source code from the client. Most clients would say no but some would say yes, and when they did, we were able to produce a more valuable report.

A difficulty you may encounter if you successfully request source code is unintentional scope creep. The client may believe that since they are providing you code, they are getting a source code review in addition to the assessment they paid for. It's important to let them know that your team will not be dedicating time to reviewing the source code. The code is only there to help validate vulnerabilities and provide the client with more information about them.

Stealth

Application assessments are focused on identifying as many vulnerabilities and systemic security flaws in the target application as possible. Stealth testing is not typically useful and therefore is not often requested. The one exception is when the client protects their application with a web application firewall (WAF). Despite the name, WAFs may also be used to protect servers that support mobile applications such as API servers.

WAF validation is very similar in its goals to red team engagements. Your team is responsible for attempting to attack the application and bypass the limitations, detections, and responses of the WAF. The report will document what attacks were blocked and how protections were bypassed. These results help to drive the objectives of the next iteration of securing the application.

WAF validation is not often performed in a vacuum. Rather, it is added to a standard web application engagement. In these cases, your team has two priorities: validate WAF protections and identify vulnerabilities in the application. But performing an application assessment with a WAF enabled will slow down and disrupt the part of the assessment that is dedicated to finding vulnerabilities. This might be acceptable to the client if they want the assessment to be as real-world as possible, but it is not the best way to show value.

To achieve both goals, you can work with the client to identify a time to assess the WAF. Usually this takes no more than 2–3 days. After this time, the client should configure the WAF to allow all traffic from your team so that they can conduct normal application assessment activities.

Testing Domains

Web Applications

Frameworks

Web application testing is one of the most developed areas of offensive cybersecurity. Not only have penetration testers been testing web applications for decades, but there exist both government and nonprofit organizations that have worked to establish standards for web application security and testing procedures.

This is great news for your web application capability. You don't have to start from scratch, instead you can take advantage of the work of hundreds of professionals and build your capability onto of freely available frameworks that have become the industry standard.

There are more general penetration test frameworks such as the penetration testing execution standard (PTES) and the *Cybersecurity Framework* published by the National Institute of Standards and Technology (NIST) and then more specific frameworks such as the *Web Security Testing Guide* published by the Open Worldwide Application Security Project (OWASP) and the Web Application Security Testing (WAST) methodology published by NIST. While the OWASP framework is arguably the most complete and usable for web application testing, it is best to ensure that your capability adheres to multiple standards if you have a wide client base.

Manual vs. Automated

I don't think there's any area of offensive cybersecurity where the limitations of automated testing solutions are more obvious than web application assessments. There are many fully automated solutions that produce great results and can help a penetration tester reduce a lot of the mundane initial work of the assessment. But the lack of automated solutions' ability to consider the context of the environment prevents them from being able to find vulnerabilities that have any subtlety. They are best at identifying known vulnerabilities and performing the first pass of vulnerability testing.

It's important to remember that if the client has even a basic understanding of cybersecurity, they can integrate these tools into their software development pipeline themselves. Your team is not providing much value from these tools alone.

In fact, providing spreadsheets of findings from an automated solution to your client may result in the client questioning the value of your assessment. The goal of a penetration test is to go deeper than what fully automated solutions are currently capable of. Clients are looking for a report of findings that they could not have obtained on their own by buying an automated solution.

Lastly, automated solutions generate a significant amount of false-positive findings. This is again due to the solutions' inability to consider the context of the application environment, and it will take time for your team to go through the findings and determine which are valid. It may be more appropriate to spend that time performing the in-depth penetration testing that the client is looking for than verifying output from an automated scanner.

Automation is best when it can be configured and leveraged by a penetration tester to assist in manual testing activities. The most popular tool of this kind is Burp Suite and it's associated commercial offering, Burp Suite Professional. Burp Suite is a suite of web application testing tools that is intended to make the penetration tester more powerful and to automate tasks when appropriate such as encoding and decoding data. It is not the only tool on the market with these capabilities. Many teams prefer OWASP's ZAP proxy or one of the other freely available web application testing tools.

Mobile Applications

Frameworks

Mobile application testing is one of the fastest changing areas of offensive cybersecurity. This is because we have two industries with major impact on our work that are both constantly evolving – the mobile device and mobile application industries. Both are constantly adapting to new security standards, and your capability will have to stay updated with both to remain relevant. I know from my own experience that a mobile application testing capability can become irrelevant within the span of a year or even 6 months.

Much like web applications, frameworks for mobile application testing and security standards have been developed. Once again, OWASP and NIST are leading the way. OWASP has developed the Mobile Application Security Testing Guide (MASTG) and NIST released Special Publication 800-163 – Vetting the Security of Mobile Applications.

These frameworks provide the bedrock that your team will build its mobile application assessment capability on. They provide the standard that guides the capability through the changes and evolutions of the industry.

Device Difficulties

The greatest challenge in iOS mobile application testing is getting root access to a device. Apple does not provide a path to root access for penetration testers. Instead, the industry relies on vulnerabilities in the operating system software (called a "jailbreak") that they can exploit to gain root access. When a jailbreak will be identified and released to'the public is not predictable and therefore is not reliable in the long term. Without root access, testers are not able to fully test the application since they cannot bypass the operating system's security features.

There are a few alternatives to relying on a jailbreak. The first and most popular is device virtualization. The company Corellium is currently the only provider of iOS virtualization and it can be somewhat expensive. It also may require that your client provide specially configured builds of applications in order for the virtual platform to support it and testing activities. However, it provides a more reliable basis for a mobile application assessment capability and can fill the gaps between when jailbreaks are released.

The challenge of obtaining root access to the mobile device is not as significant for Android applications because Android is a more open system, allowing you to install alternative operating systems and additional tools. However, both Android and iOS application testing can be made difficult by applications that actively detect if they are in a rooted environment. If your client's application has these protections built in, you may require them to provide a specially configured build of the application with root detection disabled in order to support a complete assessment.

Prioritization

There is a commonly shared principle of offensive cybersecurity that an environment or application can never be considered fully secure. There is always a vulnerability lurking somewhere in the code. This is a natural byproduct of both the evolution of testing techniques and the continued addition of new untested code to an environment or application through its development. This principle is shown through every common application. The web server software Apache has new vulnerabilities reported every year. SSH servers seem to have a new significant vulnerability that requires immediate patching about every other year.

A pentester may be given only 2 weeks to assess an application and identify as many vulnerabilities as possible. They will not find them all. So how are they to prioritize the types of vulnerabilities they will test for?

Left to their own devices, most testers will use their intuition to guide their assessment. They will review the application's functionality and find areas that seem more likely to be vulnerable based on the tester's past experience. More junior testers will often try to follow a test flow similar to what worked for them during training courses.

There's nothing inherently wrong with this approach. Testers build up instincts and an understanding of where application security may have been overlooked by the developer. However, it is missing a key element, a consideration of the client's priorities.

Sometimes the client has no priorities and simply needs to have a pentest on the books for compliance. In those cases, the tester is free to test as he pleases. However, clients with more complex motivations will often have input into what they would like to see in the final report.

We'll explore collecting client requirements and desires in a different chapter, but at some point in the pipeline of setting up the engagement, the client should have been asked, "What would you like to see in the final report?" The answer to that question can help the tester prioritize vulnerability types and areas of the application.

As an example, when I have asked clients that question, one of the more common responses I get is that the client isn't very interested in client-side vulnerabilities. They want the big, impactful, and exciting server-side vulnerabilities with a side of remote code execution! Client-side vulnerabilities are often seen as unimportant or boring. The client wants to see interesting results from the amount of money they are spending on the assessment.

These conversations open the door for the team leader to educate the client on why client-side vulnerabilities can be just as impactful, but they also provide crucial information as to the client's definition of value. If the tester works hard for 2 weeks and delivers a final report with a wide range of client-side vulnerabilities, the client will not feel that they have received a valuable assessment.

Taking It to the Next Level
Real-World Demonstration

As technology develops, applications become more complex and it's no different for vulnerabilities. But explaining new vulnerability types and their impact to clients, even very technical clients, can be difficult. For example, clients are often less interested in client-side application vulnerabilities than they are in server-side vulnerabilities. This view isn't entirely wrong. Server-side vulnerabilities are generally more severe because they do not rely on an unwitting victim to trigger the vulnerability. The problem is that many clients will underestimate the impact of a client-side vulnerability simply because it requires victim interaction. This is frustrating for offensive cybersecurity professionals because we know that the lion's share of real-world compromises are initiated by a victim falling for a social engineering attack. But our clients will often wave off XSS vulnerabilities while paying close attention to an SSRF.

As the experts in vulnerabilities, it is your team's job to educate the client and communicate the findings in a way that gives the client an accurate picture of the threat. So how do we accomplish this when it comes to complicated or multipart vulnerabilities?

The most successful approach for my team was to perform a very small-scope social engineering engagement alongside the application assessment. If a tester identified an XSS vulnerability, for example, then we would request approval from the client to perform a small phishing campaign that leveraged the vulnerability. This did a few things. First, it provided all the evidence we needed for the report to demonstrate how XSS vulnerability could be leveraged regardless of whether the campaign was successful or not. Second, if the campaign was successful, the client would be educated on how much easier social engineering can be when leveraging a vulnerability within the client's own trusted application. Finally, if the campaign was successful, the client would have a real-world idea of how dangerous the XSS vulnerability was.

This approach may or may not work depending on your client's appetite for an ad hoc small-scope social engineering engagement, but the point is that the more we are able to leave the theory behind and show the client a real-world threat, the more value we will provide and the more successful your team will be with the given client.

CHAPTER 10

Effective Testing in Cloud Environments

Cloud computing burst onto the scene in the mid-2000s with the creation of Amazon Web Services (AWS). In the decades since, nearly every major corporation and government agency has adopted it at least partially. The scope of today's penetration testing engagements almost always includes networks, applications, and/or services hosted in cloud environments.

The offensive cybersecurity community has been slow to respond to the wide adoption of the cloud. At the time of writing, cloud security is just recently being taught in standard penetration testing classes. Up until now, offensive cybersecurity professionals have not been given the education necessary to contend with cloud environments. Instead, cloud environments have been approached as if they were the same as a classic network deployed in a client's own datacenter.

Cloud assessments provide new challenges, new possibilities, and a whole new testing domain. The uniformity of the environments lends itself to better automation. There isn't much need to develop automation for a single client's on-premises environment since it is nothing like the other environments your team might test and the automation could not be re-used. This isn't the case in cloud environments. Clients will most often use one of the larger providers. Currently, there are three options for large cloud providers – AWS, Microsoft Azure, and Google Cloud Platform (GCP). Writing automation for these environments is far more useful because other clients will use the same platforms for their environment and the automation can be re-used.

If your OCS is not prepared to offer services that directly target and assess cloud environments, it will not be able to meet the needs of clients who consider cloud security to be an important factor in their security and vulnerability management program.

Difference in the Cloud

Centralization

The greatest strength and weakness of the security of cloud environments is the centralization of access control commonly referred to as Identity and Access Management (IAM). Its strength is that it presents a single point and a unified format for the creation of security policies. Security engineers are not required to battle with different security applications from different vendors with different concepts and configurations in different formats as they have done for decades.

The weakness in centralization is that it introduces a single point of failure. The control APIs for all three major cloud providers are available to anyone who can provide valid credentials. This is a major change from what we in the cybersecurity community are used to with classic on-premises networks. An on-premises network has layers. Even a poorly secured network will require an attacker to compromise the external network, enumerate and explore the internal network, gain access to internal hosts and pivot between them more than once, possibly exploit internal applications, identify critical hosts, and finally gain access to them. Compromising a username and password only gets an attacker past the first layer of an on-premises network. Compromising cloud credentials can get the attacker all the way to the critical systems within the limitations of the security policy applied to the credentials. This creates an environment where the defenders must always be successful at preventing weaknesses in access policies while an attacker only has to compromise a poorly configured account once.

Cloud-aware applications and services hosted exacerbate the risk by increasing the possibility of a credential compromise. The applications and services need access to credentials in order to authenticate to and access services provided by the cloud. Therefore, a compromise of an application or service is a compromise of the target's cloud access.

Cloud environments are not inherently more or less secure than on-premises environments. They are different and require a different approach to both securing and attacking them. Cloud environments are much easier to secure, but much less is required to significantly compromise them due to their lack of layers.

Pentest Difficulties

The IT industry is adopting cloud infrastructure faster than security can keep up, and the use of penetration testing in cloud environments is still evolving. As a result, most clients, even very technical clients, will not know how to leverage your services to get the most value.

Experienced clients usually expect a cloud pentest to perform just like an external network pentest. They expect to provide the IP addresses and domains of their publicly facing cloud infrastructure and for the pentesters to assess it. There's nothing wrong with this kind of assessment, but your team will often find that they are not able to produce the same level of value with cloud infrastructure as they are during classic external network testing.

There are two reasons for this difference in output quality. The first is that cloud infrastructure is easier to secure, especially from network-based attacks. Cloud environments offer centralized networking controls and more secure default states. As an example, the default firewall rules of virtual machines launched within AWS's cloud computing service, EC2, allow only SSH access to the open Internet. Additionally, cloud environments provide uniform tools and ease of automation to help enforce security policies. It is less likely that a sensitive service would be exposed by cloud-based hosts vs. a host in an on-premises environment. When this does occur, it is easier to detect and remediate through automation.

The second reason is that much of the typical services that might be found within a classic on-premises network are offloaded in cloud networks to various cloud services. For example, it is unlikely that you will encounter a file storage server in AWS environments since it has an S3 storage service.

Effective Testing

Despite its differences and difficulties, it is possible to provide just as much value to your client through a cloud assessment as you do with traditional assessment types. My experience through personally performing hundreds of cloud assessments led me to develop three approaches that set my team and myself up for success across different types of cloud assessments.

Gather All of the Attack Surface

I was fortunate to be exposed to cloud environments early on in my offensive cybersecurity career. I found them interesting, powerful, and, more importantly, easy to compromise. Very few security engineers were familiar with how to lock down cloud access policies in the early days, which meant that a single compromise would almost always result in a significant compromise of the entire cloud environment.

My early exposure gave me experience in seeing where traditional pentest scoping practices can handicap assessments of cloud environments. Traditional methods consist of gathering a list of in-scope IP addresses and domains, but for cloud environments, the resulting attack surface always seemed to be smaller than I would expect if the same application were deployed in an on-premises environment. I discovered that this handicap isn't because of a lack of attack surface. It is caused by a failure to properly identify the cloud attack surface.

Resources deployed within cloud services can be exposed in a variety of ways, and they do not always have an assigned IP address or domain. As an example, Azure storage accounts and AWS S3 bucket both create full URLs to directly access the data that is being stored in them. AWS SNS topics and SQS queues are typically accessed via the AWS API. These resources can be hidden from the scope of an assessment if the client is only providing IP addresses and domains, but the attack surface they create can often be larger than the resources exposed by traditional IP addresses and domains.

Cloud environments contain a risk that does not exist in on-premise environments. The risk is that sensitive data or critical processes can be compromised without any direct access to the IP addresses, domains, or workstations that belong to the organization. They can and have been compromised through direct access and misconfiguration of cloud resources. Therefore, no penetration test of a cloud environment is complete if all cloud resources are not included in the assessment scope.

This risk, as well as the risk posed by the entire cloud attack surface, is made worse by the concept of "cloud creep." Cloud environments have made launching resources so simple that it can be done by anyone with the right access rights. With just a few clicks in a web console, a user can deploy virtual machines, create storage buckets, and more. Without strong inventory tracking, the size of a cloud environment can grow without control.

There are very few cloud environments that I have assessed that did not have some form of cloud creep. I eventually added a section in my reports just to list all the resources I found in my clients' environments that were created for some forgotten purpose and now sat wasting money and adding to the attack surface.

To help the client develop a scope for cloud assessments that addresses both the issue of cloud creep and ensures that all aspects of the attack surface are included, my team developed cloud resource enumeration scripts. These scripts used the APIs of the given cloud provider to identify all cloud resources within the client's account. We provided these scripts to our clients during the scoping process and ask them to provide us with the results so that we could accurately scope the project. This information was invaluable because it allowed us to show the client the true size of their environment and to begin advising them on how to include all of it instead of just the IPs and domains.

Assumed Breach Scenarios

An assumed breach is a type of proactive assessment where the OCS team is given internal access to a client's network. Usually, the access granted is to a server hosting a publicly available application or to an internal user's workstation. The idea is that the client assumes that its applications and employees are not and will never be 100% secure. So a breach scenario is executed to determine what the impact of a compromise could be and to help steer future efforts in internal network security. Given how quickly a small compromise in a cloud environment can escalate to a very serious situation, assumed breach scenarios can be even more important and effective in assessing a cloud environment than they are in classic internal networks.

Assumed breach scenarios in cloud environments are a high-risk and high-reward assessment type. The reward is that if your team is able to gain access to cloud credentials, the assessment attack surface will expand significantly, and they will have a very good chance of providing a high-value report. The risk is that your team performs the assessment and identifies no findings. Of all the assessment types I have led, assumed breach assessments in cloud environments carry the highest likelihood of a zero-finding report. This is due to a few factors that are related to the differences between cloud and classic networks.

Cloud vs. Classic

When a classic on-premises network is compromised, the attacker will try to identify opportunities to pivot access to something more critical or interesting. This is a network-focused approach and in the world of classic internal networks, it's pretty much the only attack avenue. Everything is connected by the network, and all attacks must traverse it.

When a cloud network is compromised, the attacker will again have access to the internal network of the cloud environment. However, they will find that the network is quite small compared to what they would expect from a classic network that provides the same services. This is because much of the supporting services and backend functions traditionally executed by servers can be offloaded to powerful cloud services.

The difference between cloud and classic networks initially suggests that cloud networks are more secure. After all, there is significantly less attack surface within the internal network. It has shrunk as responsibilities are transferred to cloud services. But the truth is the attack surface hasn't changed, it's just moved. The network is no longer the only means by which the attacker can pivot deeper and gain additional access. The cloud's control plane APIs is an additional and more powerful path.

The control plane attack path is protected by the barriers of authentication and authorization. An attacker must compromise a valid set of credentials in order to access it, and those credentials are limited by the access policies that are applied to them. Making things even harder, the

181

access rights granted to a set of compromise credentials is not something the attacker can just look up unless the credentials are specifically allowed to do so.

The hoops an attacker has to jump through to gain access to the control plane may seem insurmountable, but there is one factor that quickly evens the playing field – if an application leverages cloud services, then it will need access to credentials. Therefore, if an attacker compromises an application server hosted in the cloud, they have a very good chance of immediately gaining access to the credentials used by the application itself.

One of the best examples of the new attack paths available in cloud environments is the metadata service. The metadata service is found in AWS, Azure, and GCP virtual machine environments. It provides a variety of data to the virtual machine as well as credentials to grant the virtual machine access to cloud services within the limitations of access policies. If an attacker is able to compromise a cloud-hosted server at any user level, the attacker can retrieve credentials through the metadata service. I've often used the metadata service to help educate a client on why the scenario needs to consider more than just network-based attack paths.

Compromising a set of credentials is only the first hoop. The attacker must next figure out what access his newly acquired credentials have and the cloud provider isn't going to help. The attacker can try to brute force the access limitations by trying a variety of control actions and looking for any success.

The brute force approach worked for me for years, and it still works today if the cloud security engineers have been lax in locking down access policies. One of the first things I try after I compromise a new set of AWS credentials is to list the buckets in S3. If the credentials have access to list the buckets, they probably have access to list the contents of the buckets and perhaps even pull down the data they store.

As cloud security engineers have become more savvy about locking down access, brute force has become less and less reliable. Skilled cloud security engineers will not allow general actions such as listing buckets or listing the deployed virtual machines. Instead, they lock down the access policies to only allow specific actions against specific resources.

Without being able to view the allowed actions and the resources the actions may be taken against, the attacker is blind and his credentials seem to be useless. But if the attacker has compromised the credentials through a compromise of an application server, then he has all the documentation he needs about the access policies applied to the credentials. The documentation is the source code of the application. If the application is using cloud services, the code must specify both the action and the resource that is the target of the action. The attacker can read the code to learn what the credentials are capable of.

This cyber arms race is important to understand if you're going to give your team the best chance of success in a cloud-based assumed breach scenario. A client may not be aware of or fully appreciate the non-network-based attack paths present in cloud environments. They may create a fresh virtual machine for you to perform the assessment from. This is a serious mistake as it will cut your team off from the code, credentials, and configurations that an attacker would have access to if they compromised an application server. It is not a realistic scenario, and it locks your team into network-based attacks only.

At the same time, you do not want to conduct the scenario from a real production server if it can be avoided. No matter how skillful your testers are, testing requires nonstandard actions, and nonstandard actions introduce instability. You don't want your team to be the reason that a core application server goes down.

The best compromise is when a client creates a clone of a production application server with identical credentials and access configured. Your team is then able to fully test with a realistic scenario from that point.

Collaborative Cloud Assessments

As I became more familiar with cloud environments, I realized that a good portion of the value an offensive approach could bring to the security of the environment was not utilized through assessments that used a more black-box approach. Black-box assessments are quite useful in helping a client determine their real-world risk, but if the client's goal is to develop a holistic understanding of the threats their environment faces, then the tester needs more access. As a result, I developed a new type of assessment that I called the collaborative cloud assessment.

The concept of the collaborative cloud assessment is that the tester is able to use their experience with identifying vulnerabilities in cloud environments and their knowledge of real-world cloud attacks to audit the configuration of all cloud resources and services with the following goals in mind:

- Identify all attack surface

- Identify highly privileged accounts

- Correlate highly privileged accounts with how they are exposed to determine 1) the most likely attack path and 2) the most impactful attack path

- Identify unused resources that are unnecessarily increasing the attack surface of the environment (cloud creep)

- Develop attacks to demonstrate the vulnerabilities caused by insecure configurations

To accomplish this, the pentest team is given full read-only access to the environment. Testers shouldn't need or want to modify anything in the environment, but they do need access to all configuration data. The testers begin by establishing a baseline understanding of the environment. They might use custom scripts or open-source tools to enumerate all cloud resources and collect configuration data.

I have primarily used the open-source version of ScoutSuite to give me an initial understanding of the environment. It's a very helpful tool because not only does it provide you with nearly all the resources and their configurations but also it audits the configurations against Center for Internet (CIS) benchmarks.

Whether you use ScoutSuite, some other tool, or create your own tools, your next step will be to determine the highly privileged user and service accounts. This is important data that will guide your understanding of the severity of risks you identify through the rest of the process. In this context, "highly privileged" is defined as any principal who is able to access sensitive data or execute potentially damaging control actions. The output of this part of the assessment should be a spectrum of user and service accounts and their associated level of privilege.

Now that you have an understanding of the accounts, it's time to work out the likelihood that each could be compromised and then develop the severity of that risk. For example, one of my most common findings from these types of assessments is that a highly privileged service account is accessible by a production application server. In these situations, the security of the entire environment can be compromised if an attacker successfully gains access to the server. For user accounts, consider social engineering attacks. Are the administrators of the environment one click of a phishing link away from compromise?

A compromise of a single resource is not much of a threat to the cloud environment if that resource has no access to the cloud. Of course, any compromise is still important, and a review of resource security is part of the cloud assessment. But the assessment should be driven by what is most impactful and likely before considering less severe attack paths.

Cloud creep is a serious issue, and in the long term, it will have an effect on both the security and cost of the environment. Even if the environment you are evaluating does not have much creep currently, it is important to call out unused resources so that the client can get ahead of this issue. During one assessment, a client informed me that all of their

185

resources were deployed in the AWS Virginia region. I took their word for it for most of the assessment, but near the end of the assessment, I decided to run enumeration scripts across all regions. To my and the client's surprise, I found four EC2 virtual machines deployed in the Japan region. All were accessible by the Internet, but fortunately, they did appear to be compromised. The client realized that just telling their employees to only deploy to the Virginia region was not enough. They implemented account security policies that locked access out of all other regions.

Hopefully, you're beginning to see that the output of this assessment is not a checklist of configuration issues and failed CIS benchmarks. If a client wants that data, there are any number of fully automated solutions that can provide it. This assessment will develop the intelligence needed to direct the client's security program efforts by providing the most likely and most impactful attack scenarios. This intelligence is driven by both the current configuration of the client's environment and known configurations that were compromised in the real world. The final report answers the following questions:

- What is the most direct path to a significant compromise?

- What is the most likely path given the current trends in cloud attacks?

- What impact would a successful social engineering campaign have?

- Is the current system of secrets management sufficient to withstand a moderate compromise?

- What systemic security issues are the cloud security engineers missing?

If you expect to only work with smaller environments, then manually reviewing results and taking notes will be sufficient. However, if your target environments compromise hundreds or thousands of resources, your team will need to develop automation to fill in the gaps of open-source tools and correlate results. The good news is that if your team develops correlation automation for a client using one cloud provider, the automation will work for other clients using the same provider.

Overall, this assessment type is less of a penetration test and more of a white-box assessment or even an audit. The significant difference is that it brings the offensive perspective and an understanding of attack trends to the assessment in order to give the client a clear understanding of what is most important in the future of their security.

CHAPTER 11

Effective Network Testing

Network penetration testing has existed in some form since the 1990s. It is the classic form of offensive cybersecurity, and it is the area that most professional penetration testers are first introduced to through their education. For most penetration testers, network testing is their favorite testing domain for a few reasons. First, it is the most diverse form of pentesting. With web application testing, the tester evaluates an environment, which has been designed and developed by a relatively small number of engineers. With cloud testing, the management of the environment is always the same, only the configuration and size changes. But with network testing, the pentester encounters an ecosystem of applications both new and old working together and built on top of each other to result in something very unique.

Second, network assessments usually have better-defined goals. The testers are told what hosts in the network are considered "key terrain." These hosts are the focus of the assessment giving the testers a very clear definition of success.

Lastly, network assessments can often include an element that does not exist in other forms of testing – stealth. While technically any engagement involving avoiding the blue team is a red team engagement by definition, that doesn't stop clients from blurring the lines between a pentest and a red team engagement.

© Michael Butler and Jacob G. Oakley 2024
M. Butler and J. G. Oakley, *The Business of Hacking*,
https://doi.org/10.1007/979-8-8688-0174-7_11

As cloud technology has become more popular, network penetration testing has lost a small amount of its relevance but it is still one of the most common forms of penetration testing assessments.

Client Goals

Regulations, Certifications, and Standards

Arguably the most common reason for seeking a network penetration test is the requirements of some regulation or certification that the client is attempting to meet. The most common such standard is the Payment Card Industry Data Security Standard (PCI DSS). This standard requires an internal penetration test that validates the segmentation of the part of the network responsible for processing credit card payments. Any company that wants to process credit cards will need to be compliant with this standard, and therefore, they will need to conduct a penetration test.

PCI DSS isn't the only standard that requires a penetration test. SOC 2, FedRAMP, and more also require one. However, with the exception of FedRAMP, the standards don't contain many specific requirements for how the pentest should be conducted. This gives a lot of responsibilities to the client and the organization that's going to perform the pentest to determine what is required to check the box for the certification.

Assessments that fulfill certification requirements can be a lot of fun or they can be quite small and boring. Some clients will use the certification requirements as an excuse to perform a larger pentest of the internal and external networks. In these assessments, your team is asked to perform an in-depth test but to also meet the objectives of the certification. The client often asks for two pentest reports to be developed at the conclusion of the test. One of the reports is strictly related to the topics required by the certification. For example, a PCI report would only discuss the results of network segmentation validation and any finding that were identified in subnets that are related to the PCI certification. The second report would include all the details of non-PCI sections of the network. The client is then able to hand the first report to their PCI auditors without it including details and findings of network segments the auditors have no interest in.

Other clients will scope the assessment so that it only addresses the requirements of the certification. For PCI DSS assessments, this might mean just running a scanning tool that validates that the PCI DSS subnets are segmented and then checking the PCI DSS subnet for known vulnerabilities. These are less interesting but still important assessments. They are also reliable from a revenue perspective for consultative teams. Clients rarely want to change the vendors that participate in their certifications since other vendors may introduce unexpected delays.

Security Validation and Direction

Like other assessment types, clients use the findings of a network pentest or a red team engagement to drive their security and vulnerability management program forward and validate its progress. If you work with a client long enough, you will watch their program mature. Your team will have to work harder to identify vulnerabilities in the environment and weaknesses in the defensive capabilities. This isn't a bad thing or a cause for concern. As corporations grow and change, your team will find that the scope of network assessments also grows and changes. For example, your client may have a relatively secure environment, but if they acquire a smaller company and connect that company's infrastructure to their own, they will have a whole new environment to secure.

When executing a network penetration test or a red team engagement, keep in mind how your team's work fits into the client's program. If the assessment is focused primarily on the identification of network vulnerabilities, are there trends you can identify within the vulnerabilities that would be interesting to your client? For example, during an internal network assessment, my team identified that the administrators were using SSH and SSH keys to access hosts all around the network. While there's nothing inherently dangerous in this approach, my team found out that the administrators were putting their private SSH key on every host to make moving around the network easier for them. This meant that every host was a potential point for a network-wide compromise. A malicious actor would just need to compromise one of the thousands of hosts and they would have access to all of them.

There were a couple different ways to write up this finding. I could report it as a vulnerability and list a few hosts that we had found the keys on. This is completely valid but it's a bit small and less helpful to the client. Instead, I reported the finding as a general failure in authentication management across the network. This helped the client prioritize their program objectives and include a better authentication process near the top. Once that process was implemented, the client asked my team to perform a small test of just hosts that were using the new process to validate that it was secure.

By aligning your findings and your report with the client's program goals, you will make yourself an indispensable ally in the client's security strategy.

External Network Assessments

External network assessments consist of testing the aspects of the client's environment that are Internet accessible. Most clients consider the security of their external network to be the highest priority since if an attacker can't compromise the external layer, the internal layer will be safe even if it's less secure. Cybersecurity professionals might disagree with this opinion, but it is an opinion we encounter fairly often.

Scoping the Engagement

The scope of an external network assessment consists primarily of IP addresses and domains that are owned and/or operated by the client. With the increasing popularity of cloud infrastructure, we can no longer rely on IP addresses to remain static or to point to assets that are owned by our client. Cloud infrastructure cycles IP addresses if they aren't configured to remain static. So if your client is leveraging cloud services, you will need to validate any IP addresses they provide to make sure that those IP addresses still belong to resources your client owns. Domains are more easily trusted since they are controlled by the client.

The size of the scope that the client gives you for the assessment is the primary factor in determining the success of the engagement. Most findings generated from an external pentest come from misconfigurations and failures to update. If the scope of the assessment is limited to a handful of resources, it is less likely that your team will find something significant.

You can get ahead of this issue by communicating with the client early in the process. If the client suggests that they only want a small section of their external network tested, suggest ways in which the scope can be expanded. Explain to your client that a limited scope will yield limited results.

Preparing for the Assessment

External network assessments are the most likely to be conducted in a black box style. Clients will usually provide IP addresses and domains that are to be tested to compensate for the lack of time the testers have compared to real-world criminals. But sometimes a client will opt to provide no information and instead require your team to do all the leg work in identifying the attack surface, validating it with the client, and then starting the test. Your team should be prepared to perform the information-gathering activities necessary to identify the IP addresses, applications, and domains that make up the client's external facing attack surface.

The first external network assessment that I performed was for a Fortune 100 company with datacenters spread out across the globe. The client I was working with did not give me any information other than one domain name. They asked that I find the rest of the attack surface information myself just like a real hacker would have to do. I was underprepared to say the least. I realized I did not have any automated infrastructure for combing through public repositories of Internet information to identify what belonged to the client. Even if I did, I didn't have the kind of powerful scanning engine I would need to gather information from the attack surface I could identify.

After that experience, I made sure that the teams I ran put in the effort to build out infrastructure that had the power to quickly identify and enumerate the client's attack surface.

The data that makes up the client's attack surface is commonly referred to as open-source intelligence (OSINT). This is a term from the military that is a combination of the words open-source and intelligence. OSINT is any data that can be gathered from the Internet that helps identify or attack a target. In penetration testing, OSINT is primarily made up of the IP addresses and domains that create our clients' attack surface. But it can include much more than that. OSINT can include repositories on sites like GitHub if the client participates in open-source projects, web forums where the client's applications are discussed or where employees of the client unintentionally disclose sensitive information, YouTube videos where the client demonstrates their product, and much more. All of these sources can be very helpful. For example, my team once compromised an application by getting credentials for a demo account from a YouTube video.

The most important (and fortunately easiest to automate) are the IP addresses and domains. In the past, this information would come from Domain Name System (DNS) servers and WHOIS records, but in the modern Internet, DNS servers are rarely configured to dump the records of a specific domain to anyone who asks. Fortunately, there are many repositories of Internet information created, maintained, and updated by curious people performing research on how the Internet operates. Two examples of these kinds of repositories are the Standford Internet Research Data Repository and the Sonar Project by Rapid7.

I have personally used data from both of these projects to identify attack surface. My team built scripts to pull and process the data and to search it for identifiers associated with our client.

Unless the client is providing all your attack surface information, your team must validate any IP addresses or domains it finds before testing them. The Internet is rapidly changing, and the information in these or other projects cannot be totally accurate.

Enumeration

Before your team is ready to take on any significantly large-scope external network assessments, they need to develop a scanning infrastructure that is powerful enough to handle the task. Running Nmap from a laptop is only going to get you so far. Once the scope includes a few thousand or even tens of thousands of targets, you're going to need something more robust.

There are all kinds of scanning solutions both free and paid. These are a great place to start, but there is no replacement for controlling the types of scans that are run and the format of the data they generate. Developing your own scanning cluster is not difficult and can be achieved by any team member with a basic understanding of scripting. The cluster should be capable of distributing a target list evenly among its servers, and it should at least perform port and web content enumeration. Your team can use servers that you own, cloud-based virtual servers, or even serverless options.

Regardless of what automated scanning infrastructure option you choose, it's important to understand that scanning can be dangerous. You are enumerating every port and making a significant amount of requests to any identified web server. This creates a significant processing load on the target servers that could disrupt their normal operation.

This is much less of a concern for external network engagements than it is for internal network engagements. If these servers are on the Internet, they are routinely being scanned by both innocuous and malicious projects. While I have never heard of a pentester disabling an Internet-facing server through scans alone, your team should always consider the load they are putting on the target servers.

Kicking Down the Front Door

After your team has identified and enumerated the attack surface of the client's external network, it's time to prioritize targets for additional scans or manual testing. Targets can be sorted into one of three categories:

- Primary application servers
- Secondary support servers
- Miscellaneous targets

Primary application servers are the network's front door. They are where the vast majority of customer traffic is directed and handled. Support servers run necessary services to support either the customer's experience as they access the client's applications or they support the backend operation of the application servers. Support servers should generally not be exposed to the Internet unless absolutely necessary.

Miscellaneous targets represent the rest of the attack surface. Some of the servers may seem random and even unnecessary. You might assume that some of them are exposed to the Internet accidentally and no one at the client's company has found out yet.

Given these three categories, where should the testers begin looking for vulnerabilities? While it may seem obvious that the miscellaneous category is going to have the highest chance of hosting vulnerable services, I have seen many experienced professionals target the primary application servers in an attempt to kick down the front door. There's one problem for them. Front doors are made of steel. Kicking them doesn't do a whole lot. It's much easier to break a window, which, in this case, means targeting the miscellaneous servers.

The majority of the budget and time that the clients spend on security goes toward locking down their primary application servers and the workflows that are related to them. There are certainly vulnerabilities lurking somewhere with the primary application's code, but they are going to take time and effort to draw out. Effective pentesting means prioritizing the lowest-hanging fruit while considering the greatest benefit to the client. The miscellaneous servers are that lower-hanging fruit. There usually aren't enough of them to take a lot of time checking into, but they can often offer the fastest route to a serious compromise.

Stealth in External Engagements

From time to time, I will have a client that requests an external network assessment with an element of stealth. My response is to explain to the client that a stealthy assessment is not nearly as useful for the external network as it is for the internal. With the plethora of cloud-computing platforms with easily rotated ranges of IP addresses, there is no way to prevent a malicious actor with unlimited time from enumerating the network. It isn't typically feasible for a client to block the IP ranges of all cloud platforms.

External network assessments that are required to use stealth are significantly less effective because they must blend in with normal traffic and slowly enumerate targets. So much time is spent on the enumeration portion of the assessment that the vulnerability identification and exploitation phases are rushed.

If a client wants to validate their ability to detect and block malicious traffic coming from the Internet, your team can perform the validation as a small part of the assessment. Pentesters can set up multiple attack boxes across different cloud platforms and determine what level of malicious traffic is possible before it gets detected by the client's security systems.

With that validation complete, the client should grant your team's IP address access to conduct the external assessment unhampered. This accomplishes both goals of validating defenses and identifying vulnerabilities in the external layer.

Internal

If your client falls into the typical philosophy of focusing security on the external facing layer, then you will find that their internal network is far less secure. I've worked in very large networks full of thousands of hosts with virtually no segmentation and no gateways between the various levels of the network. Without segmentation in place, the entire scope of the internal network is open to the tester or the malicious actor that is able to gain access. With that much available attack surface, something's bound to be vulnerable.

Scoping the Engagement

Just like with external networks, more scope means more findings. More scope means that your team will develop a better awareness of the network and be able to advise the client on vulnerability trends instead of just presenting a list of findings.

The scope is going to be made up of internal IP address ranges. There could be a few domains mixed in if they use internal DNS servers. Of course, there's very little research your team can perform using open-source resources since the internal network specifics will not be in any repository. Again, like external network engagements, the client may provide the relevant IP addresses or they may expect you to enumerate them yourself just like an attacker would.

Internal network engagements can be initiated in a number of ways. Here are the most common that my teams have encountered:

- Assumed breach

- External compromise

- Access provided

The assumed breach scenario builds on top of the black-box assessment by providing access to your testers in the same way the client would expect a malicious to gain access. Most commonly this means that your team will be given access to a user's box as the scenario will be that a user has fallen victim to a phishing attack and their box has been compromised.

In my opinion, the assumed breach is a very proactive and effective way to position an internal network engagement. The client is aware that they cannot be totally secure, and it is only a matter of time before a compromise occurs. So to get ahead of that eventuality, they contract an assessment to determine the worst-case scenario of such a breach. Then they use the data from the assessment to drive their security program forward so that when a breach occurs, they'll be ready.

For your team, the assumed breach scenario gives your report validity, which can be very helpful with internal network engagements. Some members of the client's staff may be uninterested in findings from an engagement in which the testers were given access. Clinging tightly to their idea that the security of the external network is paramount, they'll say of course you had findings! You didn't have to contend with the security of the external network! The assumed scenario helps to cool this response by providing a scenario in which access was gained without the need to compromise the external network.

The external compromise approach will give you the most unquestionable report possible, but it is also far more difficult. This type of internal network engagement starts with an external network test, and the client assumes your team will be able to breach it and establish their own access to the internal network. Depending on your team's skill with network penetration testing and the size and security of the client's attack surface, this may or may not be possible in the time given. But if your team pulls it off, your report will demonstrate how a malicious could gain access to the internal network and what damage could be done there. It's a very high-stakes, high-reward approach, and the outcome is not predictable.

For clients that prefer this approach, I voice my concerns. I let the client know that since the time we have with their network is limited, it is not the same as a real-world attacker. Since I want to provide value to the client, I suggest that my team performs the external network assessment, and if they are not able to establish a foothold in the internal network within a specified time, we should move to an assumed breach scenario assessment to ensure that the client still receives an internal network assessment report. For example, if the length of the test is 3 weeks, then my team would work the first week on the external network, and if they have not yet gained access, then the client would provide access. The team would continue to test the external and internal networks to see if they can find a way in with more time, but the quality of the report is not dependent on the testers finding a way in.

The last way that internal network assessments are conducted is when the client simply provides access. This is usually done in the form of a VPN connection or through a jump box. These assessments are the easiest to set up since you simply connect to the client's network, but they are also the least defensible when it comes to questions about realism. For clients that have a mature idea of cybersecurity, this can be a great approach, especially since using tools over a VPN is much easier and faster than if you are forced to go through some backdoor program like is typically the situation for assumed breach assessments. However, if you are concerned that your client may not value your findings as much because your team was given access, one of the approaches might be better.

Stealth

Many internal network assessments that are not being conducted in support of a client's certification will include a requirement that your team attempt to bypass the detection and response capabilities protecting the environment. These assessments may be fully red team engagements where your focus is on accessing more and more sensitive areas of the network without getting caught or they may be a hybrid where you have both an objective to avoid getting caught and to identify vulnerabilities.

The ability to avoid detection while enumerating and attacking a network is a separate skillset from just looking for internal network vulnerabilities. It requires the tester to be educated on and consider the impact all of their actions will have in the network. It requires them to be familiar with alternative ways of gathering information without raising alarms and to execute attacks while blending in.

Philosophy of Stealth

When I first began to develop my skills in detection avoidance, I was taught that the less traffic or "noise" I generated, the harder I was to detect. The theory makes sense on the surface. If you don't want to be caught, then keep quiet. The SYN Stealth scan that Nmap uses by default follows this philosophy. The scan is used when a tester is trying to identify open TCP ports. Nmap initiates the TCP three-way handshake by sending the first SYN packet. If it receives a SYN-ACK packet from the target, then it knows that the target port is open. In standard TCP protocol, Nmap would be expected to send the final ACK of the handshake, but in order to minimize the amount of traffic it is sending across the wire, Nmap does not by default. It saves one packet per TCP port that it scans.

There is a glaring flaw in this philosophy and it can be seen in the SYN Stealth scan. How many devices on an internal network behave in the way the SYN Stealth scan does? How often is the final ACK packet never sent by legitimate hosts? The answer is that it very rarely if ever occurs. So anyone who is familiar with the SYN Stealth scan and reviews the traffic in the network will find Nmap scan sticking out like a beacon.

The goal is not to reduce noise. The goal is to blend in. The stealthy tester will execute the absolute minimum amount of nonstandard traffic in the network. The next question should then be how do we define "nonstandard" traffic?

Whether traffic is considered nonstandard or not is determined by three elements:

1. Who is sending the traffic?

2. Who is the destination of the traffic?

3. What is the contents of the traffic?

Network detection and response tools are becoming more and more capable of baselining normal network behavior. They do this by identifying which hosts talk to which hosts and what their communication looks like on the wire.

If you're not familiar with what detection technology is used in a client's network or with how it is configured, you should assume the worst until proven otherwise. Assume that the client has behavioral analytics as well as signature-based detection and try to stay under the unknown thresholds of when your nonstandard behavior will trigger an alert.

While I am primarily referencing stealth on a network level, this philosophy of stealth also applies at the host level. The client's security engineers will deploy detection mechanisms to their hosts, especially Windows-based hosts. The stealthy tester attempts to execute the minimum number of nonstandard actions within the host in order to avoid detection. This means attempting to behave as a user whenever possible.

Enumeration with Stealth

Let's put this philosophy into practice. A tester from your team has just gained access to an internal network by finding a vulnerability in the external network. They have no information on what detection capabilities they are up against. They know the client wants them to attempt to pivot deeper into the network and locate a Windows domain. The client requested that they do so without being detected. How do they conduct their enumeration, vulnerability identification, and (hopefully) exploitation all while remaining undetected?

A question I often asked when interviewing potential new team members was, "Let's say you've gained access to a host on an internal network. You know that the blue team is watching for a compromise. How can you enumerate the network using the highest level of stealth?"

I eventually did away with the question because it felt like too much of a "gotcha," but the answer I was looking for was that network enumeration could be started without running any scans or generating any network traffic. The host itself holds a lot of network information through several of its configurations. The host file, route configurations, ARP tables, etc., are all great sources of information that begin to build a picture of the network. Tools that display network connections are the most helpful because they give you specific IP addresses located deeper into the internal network. Even more helpful, the IP addresses they give you are known to connect and communicate with the host that you compromised. These IP addresses should be more fully enumerated first because the traffic between them and your compromised host will not be suspicious.

The initial stage of stealthy internal network enumeration is the identification of subnets that actually have hosts. This is especially important if your client's network uses a large private IP address scheme such as 10.0.0.0/8. You are not going to be able to scan that whole range, and it would most likely get you caught if you tried. So instead, you use all the sources of network information previously mentioned to identify the subnets that have hosts deployed. It is not likely that the engineers who designed the environment put only a single host into a subnet. Subnets are used by engineers to organize hosts under the application they support or the function they execute. So if you identify one host in a subnet, there is a strong likelihood that the other hosts in that subnet perform functions in the same category.

Once you have exhausted the network information you can pull from the compromised host, its time to start creating some network traffic. Again, since you don't know where the detection thresholds are set, you will need a strategy of slowly increasing the nonstandard traffic you are generating to gather the data you need. The following is a simplified version of the strategy I have used:

1. Identify internal IP addresses and subnets using host resources and network connections

2. Perform scans of the IP addresses on three or four common ports only

3. Investigate results and determine if more enumeration is necessary to identify significant vulnerabilities

4. Conduct additional enumeration by slowly scanning the rest of the IP addresses in each identified subnet using the same three or four common ports

5. If required, expand port range at about four ports at a time

6.   Repeat until enough attack surface has been identified that the tester feels they have a good chance to identify significant vulnerabilities

The idea behind this strategy is to avoid behavior-based detection by blending in with traffic between hosts that regularly communicate and then expanding into subnets. By sticking to common ports only, we can perform some very helpful enumeration while also identifying additional targets for more targeted enumeration if necessary. The four common ports I use are 22, 445, 80, and 443. These help to identify the most likely target operating system and to determine whether it is running web services on standard ports. I prioritize web services because in my experience the most commonly vulnerable points of an internal network are custom web applications.

This strategy may work for your team, or you may need to develop something that more reliably blends your activities in your clients' networks.

Prioritization

Target and vulnerability prioritization is the key to ensuring an effective test by preventing testers from developing tunnel vision and spending too much time on vulnerabilities that are not bearing fruit. For network assessment, targets are prioritized based on two factors:

1.   Client interest

2.   Likelihood of vulnerability

Client interest is determined by whether the target will get you closer to achieving the client's goals. The target host might be a critical part of the client's services or it might be able to get your team one step closer to critical targets.

Determining the likelihood that a target contains exploitable and significant vulnerabilities seems impossible at first. Most teams will leave it up to the penetration tester's intuition to select the order that targets are assessed. After all, the tester has built up a sense of which targets are more likely to be vulnerable through years of vulnerability identification and exploitation. This intuition is valuable and it shouldn't be dismissed. However, it is also possible to document it into a process. Developing a target prioritization process leads to more consistent results and the opportunity for more powerful automation to take on at least a portion of prioritization tasks.

As an example, my team developed the following list of host attributes that we used as a baseline in prioritizing the order in which targets were assessed during an external network engagement. Note that many of these items are derived from the "don't try to kick in the front door" principle from earlier:

1. The host has services running on nonstandard ports (8080, 4443, etc.).

2. The host is not running or directly associated with the operation of a primary application or service.

3. The host is running older versions of services compared to other hosts in the network.

4. The host is running custom applications.

5. The host does not have a domain name or the domain assigned to it is not part of the client's primary domains.

The more attributes from this list a target had, the higher of a priority it became. For external network assessments, the client's interest was almost always "can you breach the external layer?" Therefore, prioritizing the targets that were most likely vulnerable was also the most direct path to satisfying the client's goals.

Safety

Internal networks are the most sensitive area of a client's infrastructure. This is especially true for clients in controlled sectors. Whether it's electric companies, hospitals, or airlines, clients in controlled sectors will have areas of their network that are especially sensitive. These areas must be identified before the assessment begins. During the assessment, the client needs to be informed whenever testers will be interacting with critical hosts. If any disruption occurs, the client will need to react quickly. While conducting an assessment of critical hosts, the tester should be in communication with the client preferably through a chat channel or a video call so that information can be passed quickly and the tester can ask questions before engaging with the target.

Critical hosts should be assessed separately from the rest of the network. When it comes time to scan them, they should be only hosts included in those scans. Critical hosts can often be more sensitive than the hosts we typically encounter. This is for two reasons. First, if a system is responsible for regulating power for a region, the team responsible for it will often resist attempts to update it. Updates could cause a disruption which is unacceptable. Second, the critical system is running software that may not have been designed with Nmap or other pentesting tools in mind. Pentest tools, even when it seems innocuous, may cause serious issues with the software running on critical systems.

The testers conducting the assessment should enumerate and evaluate sensitive hosts separately from the rest of the network. Scan speeds should be turned down significantly so to reduce the possibility of any disruption.

Taking the Test to the Next Level

Early OSINT

Gathering data about your target environment can begin at any time. It is the one aspect of penetration testing that is not reliant on the Rules of Engagement being signed. This is because gathering open-source information does not require direct interaction with the target environment. You are pulling data from other sites (Internet information repositories, GitHub, YouTube, etc.) about the target site. You do not need client permission to do so as long as there is a strong boundary between gathering information from third-party repositories and directly engaging with the client's network.

Pulling data early in the process can help identify what your team is up against and guide your conversation with the client when it comes to designing the expectations and scope of the engagement. If your team has developed automated open-source information gathering, then you can pull information about the client environment without even taking up the time of your team.

Always Gather OSINT

Even when your client gives you all the IP addresses and domains within scope, your team should still pull as much open-source information as possible. The weakest part of your client's network is the part they are unaware of. This is especially true of cloud environments where the concept of "cloud creep" can cause untracked resources to be deployed and possibly exposed to the Internet.

If you identify attack surface that was not included in the scope, you can show it to your client and ask whether they feel it would be helpful to include it.

Testing Host-Based Detection

If your clients expect your team to perform internal network assessments, you will have to contend with endpoint protection and develop methods of bypassing the security agents on the endpoints you compromise. This can be very difficult and sometimes close to impossible. My team worked on one engagement where even opening a command prompt on a Windows host sent an alert and quarantined the process. There is an entire industry working to make endpoints, especially Windows endpoints, as secure as possible.

There are two ways to make your team far more effective in avoiding endpoint detection. The first is to remain at the cutting edge of the offensive cybersecurity community and its efforts to defeat endpoint detection. This is an area where capability leads can be very helpful. Having a senior tester on the team dedicate time to understanding and implementing the latest industry techniques will significantly increase your team's chances at remaining undetected.

The second method is to develop or have access to an environment where your team can test tools and techniques against endpoint agents prior to the start of the assessment. Creating such an environment is not difficult, but acquiring licenses for endpoint protection software can be. There are freely available agents that can serve as a starting point for your testing. If you work in a corporate environment or one of your clients is interested in sharing their environment with you, you can more directly test against a real-world deployment.

CHAPTER 12

Reporting

An assessment is only as good as its report. The report is your final
opportunity to communicate the value that your team produced for the
client. Most of the reports I have seen from other teams use an internally
developed format to communicate the number and severity of findings
as quickly and directly as possible. Tech professionals don't like writing
reports and it shows.

The first time a penetration tester creates a pentest report, they will
typically download one of the freely available pentest report templates
from OffSec or SANS. Then they fill out the fields, change the styles and
logos to match the company, write up their findings, and deliver it to
the client.

These early report formats achieve the goal of documenting and
communicating findings to the client, but even for internal corporate
teams who have less incentive to impress their clients, the report can seem
rather amateur. Even worse, most of the value that the team produced
during the engagement is lost when it is boiled down to just the findings.

Designing the Report Template

Use a designer. Even for internal corporate teams, a report designed by a
designer is going to have an edge of professionalism that your team cannot
replicate. If you work for a decent-size company, there's a good chance
that the company either employs or contracts with a design or branding

© Michael Butler and Jacob G. Oakley 2024
M. Butler and J. G. Oakley, *The Business of Hacking*,
https://doi.org/10.1007/979-8-8688-0174-7_12

company. I've paid as little as $500 to get a professional report template that impressed my clients for years. Most of my competition did not use a designer, and so our reports looked far better. We sent a sample report to all potential clients after our first meeting so that they could compare the final product they are paying for against offers from our competitors. I have no doubt that the report was responsible for a good portion of our revenue growth.

If you cannot or choose not to use a designer, then the next best option is to find reports developed by some of the larger penetration testing companies. They have no doubt put serious time and money into their report formats. The reports may be a bit more than you need, but they will give you an idea of what you should be aiming for when developing the style of your team's report.

Report Sections

If you look at the table of contents for the free pentest report templates, they have some variations of the following sections:

- Introduction/Foreward
- Executive Summary
- Methodology
- Findings
- General Recommendations
- Various Appendices (scope, risk rating methodology, etc.)

All of these sections are important but they miss a lot. A client receiving this report will not have any information on what attacks were attempted but were succesfully defended against. This is critical information for the client to determine whether the improvements they have made to the security of the environment were successful or not. The team is also not given the opportunity to make general observations or recommendations. If they have identified trends of vulnerabilities in the environment or processes that make the environment less secure, they do not have the space in the report to document and communicate that information.

My team developed a report that included all these basic sections as well as ways to more fully document the value the assessment produced. In the next section, we'll discuss all the common sections of a pentest report and the additional sections my team developed.

Introduction/Foreword

The introduction/foreword is a one-page writeup of the basic details of the assessment such as who the client is, who the assessment team is, the dates of the assessment, and other related information. This section uses the same language for every report with only specific details changed such as the client's name, dates, etc.

Executive Summary

The executive summary is one or two pages long. It presents a summary of the major points of the assessment including a numerical or graphical representation of the number of findings at each level of severity. It also includes a general ranking of the security of the environment based on the knowledge and expertise of the testing team.

This part of the report should be designed so that it still functions if separated from the rest of the report. Your client may want to pass a summary to their management without including all of the report details.

This section should include at least one graph but no more than two. The graphs can visually show the findings and their severity and (for bonus points) how the client's organization performs compared to similar organizations that your team has experience with.

Most of the words in this section should not change between reports but the graphs and data obviously will.

Methodology

This section is entirely boilerplate. It is only updated when a significant change is made to your team's methodology. You should have a writeup of the methodology for each primary testing domain and plug in the ones that are relevant to the assessment. If the writeup is longer than two pages, I recommend moving this section to near the end of the report so as not to push the findings too far down.

Assessment Narrative

This is the first section that is not found in pentest report templates that we'll discuss. The assessment narrative tells the story of the test. It is broken into subsections representing each phase of the test. For example, an assessment that included an external network, web application, and cloud testing phases would have three sections.

I cannot overstate the importance of this report section. It is the section that my team would spend the majority of every outbrief discussing with the client. It is the representation of nearly all the value of the assessment.

Every tester involved in the test is responsible for adding a summary narrative of their work into the greater assessment narrative. Whomever is primarily responsible for the success of the project is responsible for taking the various narrative pieces and putting them together into one cohesive story. The story discusses what the testers attempted, what failed due to the security of the target environment, what succeeded, what security measures were bypassed, and the specifics of how vulnerabilities were identified.

During the outbrief, each tester should present their section of the assessment narrative to the client paying extra attention to ensure the client understands how the findings were identified. The client should feel free to ask any questions at this time or to point out information that the testing team was not aware of.

At the conclusion of the outbrief or after the client has read the assessment narrative themselves, they should feel fully informed on the important points of what occurred during the test.

The attack narrative is your second greatest tool in demonstrating value to the client and hopefully impressing them with your work. The first is, of course, communication with the client at all points of the assessment.

Findings

I suggest not changing too much from the standard pentest report templates. Every report that I have seen has a very similar way of communicating findings. Clients are used to this format and might find it annoying if it is changed too much in your team's reports.

Findings are organized by severity unless the assessment has multiple phases. In that case, the findings are organized first by phase and second by severity. Each "finding" is a block of information that discusses the following:

- Vulnerability title

- Severity

- General information about the vulnerability type

- Specific information about the vulnerability and its possible impact if exploited

- The IT assets in which the vulnerability exists

- Recommendations for remediation

- References to re-enforce the team's determination that the finding is legitimate

- Steps to reproduce the finding

The important principle of every finding is that it must be defensible. This was not something I was taught early in my career. I felt that since I was the expert, it was up to me to rank vulnerabilities at the severity level that I felt warranted based off my experience and education. A lot of testers use this method but it is fundamentally indefensible. If the severity of a finding is called into question by the client, the only defense the tester can offer is their professional opinion. Their opinion is not worthless, but it is also prone to change and develop as they become more experienced. This becomes a serious issue in a team environment where two testers might rank the severity of a vulnerability very differently. How is the team going to produce consistent results based on the opinions of its testers?

When my team considered this challenge, we solved it, at least mostly, by implementing the same system used when new vulnerabilities are publicly disclosed. The system is the Common Vulnerability Scoring System (CVSS) calculator provided by the Forum of Incident Response and Security Teams (FIRST). A tester puts values into the calculator, and it derives a severity based on several factors such as the ease of exploitation and additional access a success exploit would grant to an attacker.

The CVSS calculator is an industry standard but it isn't perfect. Some of its inputs such as Scope and Attack Vector can be vague and confusing. There are times that it over or under rates the severity of a vulnerability. It will still occasionally require adjustment based on the professional opinion of the testers. This adjustment and the reason for making it should be disclosed to the client in the findings section.

While not 100% bulletproof, using the calculator reduces most opinion-based severity rankings and provides the client with the logic behind a finding's rating. If a client disagrees with the severity, the ensuring conversation is not personal. They are not calling the opinion of one of your team members into question. Rather, they are suggesting that the calculator did not consider some important factors. The CVSS calculator is not the only system of ranking vulnerabilities and your team may find a different system works better to provide more accurate and defensible severity ratings to your client.

General Recommendations

The recommendations section presents the client with ideas on how they could best respond to vulnerability trends and systemic flaws in their environment. While this section should always be completed ethically with the client's best interest in mind, if your organization offers services that could support your recommendations, this is the place to discuss them. I highly recommend that if you plan on recommending any follow-on services from your company to your client, you bring an expert in those services to the outbrief. They will do a better job of answering any client questions than your team may be able to.

Types of Reports

In addition to the full report we have discussed so far, there are other formats for reporting that clients may request.

Executive Summary

As previously mentioned, clients will often want a separate executive summary document from the detailed report. This summary should not be overly technical since, as the name suggests, it will be read by management and perhaps even upper levels of management. This should be the easiest alternative report format requirement to satisfy since you are simply cutting out the rest of the report and providing the executive summary.

Presentation

In my experience, a Word document or PDF was good enough for most clients, but occasionally, a client will request that your team develop a presentation to better present the report to members of management or of other departments. This is especially common when working with government clients. The government client representative has several different parties to whom they must report. It's not uncommon for one penetration test to create three or more meetings to relay and discuss the findings.

If you have automated the creation of your report, then developing a presentation may not be difficult to add to the automation. But if you're like most teams who mostly put together reports manually, developing a presentation can be a pain. This is another area where the assessment narrative can be very helpful. Since it already breaks down the assessment into a progressive story, it can be used to lead slide development.

Summary of Findings

When a client is required to provide the results of an assessment to their customers, auditing agencies, or other third parties, they may not want to disclose all the details of each finding. That level of information is not needed nor helpful to third parties. In this situation, your team can provide a report that includes the Executive Summary and a Summary of Findings. The Summary is a table of the findings that lists their severities, provides a high-level description, and notes whether the finding has been remediated yet.

Automation

Reporting is a tedious manual process of filling in a document template with the specifics of the engagement. My second team was very adept at automating tedious workflows. They developed code to compile a report from text files. The testers still had to fill out the text files, but all the boilerplate text, graph generation, text and image formatting, and more were automated. They successfully reduced the process down to the one part that could not be automated.

Your team may not have the time or the skills to develop that kind of automation, but the good news is you may not have to. Penetration testing has come a long way, and there are more commercial companies offering products to support it. There are now open source and commercially available platforms for report generation. These range from highly automated but more expensive options like PlexTrac and Dradis Pro to freely available options that require more time in setup and configuration like pwndoc.

My approach has been that I should do what I can to ensure testers spend the majority of their time testing, developing team capabilities, or developing their skills. This means reducing time spent on things like report writing unless absolutely necessary.

Demonstrating Findings

Visual communication methods are always going to be more impactful than text in a document or words spoken during an outbrief, especially when you are trying to communicate complicated topics within a subject matter your audience may not be entirely familiar with.

Your team works with vulnerabilities every day. When they aren't attempting to identify new vulnerabilities during an assessment, they are working on their personal skills and the team capabilities to identify and exploit vulnerabilities in the future. Your client is probably not spending nearly this much time in offensive cybersecurity even if they are more technical. Most of their time is spent either managing projects or performing security engineering, development, or some other tech-related work. Even when they understand the vulnerabilities from a technical point of view, they may not fully grasp the impact or be able to answer the question, "how bad is this really?"

The first step that most penetration testing teams take to communicate more visually with their clients is to include screenshots in their report. Specifically, the screenshots document each step in the exploitation process of the identified vulnerabilities. This both provides evidence for the vulnerability and conveys what an exploit would look like.

Screenshots are a great first step and can even be used in the assessment narrative to highlight certain points. For example, if a tester attempted to provide an XSS payload to a web application and received a message stating the payload was considered invalid and would not be processed, the tester could include this in the assessment narrative when discussing successes in the client's defenses.

Most teams stop at screenshots, but if a visual medium is best at communicating vulnerability impact, your team should work to identify other ways in which it could be leveraged. One that I have seen from time to time is video documentation of a vulnerability being exploited. I have rarely seen video demonstrations as part of a team's reporting process, but I often see them at hacking conferences when a speaker wants to display a new tool or exploit. Video isn't necessarily easy to fit into standard reporting methods, but there are alternatives such as GIFs.

The Future of Reporting

Reporting assessment results is going through an evolution. The evolution seems to be rather slow, but I do not believe that Word and PDF documents will continue to be the standard. Document formats are not useful in a code-driven world. Today, most clients will pass a pentest report to a security analyst who will then manually create and assign tickets based on the findings. This is a slow process that is at odds with the goals of automation.

Clients have not yet required assessment findings to be presented in a more usable format, and so one has not been developed and adopted by the industry. Companies who develop products that automate pentest report generation are already positioning themselves to communicate findings in more usable formats. For example, PlexTrac has developed integrations with JIRA so that tickets can be automatically generated.

The difficulty with future-proofing your team's reporting capabilities is that there is no agreed-upon format. If your team works with multiple clients who use a variety of ticketing applications or configure their ticketing system differently, then you will have difficulty developing a way of presenting findings in a format that can be easily ingested into their systems.

As the industry develops standards, there will no doubt be a time when vulnerability reporting formats are standardized and document-based pentest reports will become mostly obsolete. For now, your team should stay informed on the trends of pentest reporting and develop automation for long-term clients to more fully integrate into their security program.

CHAPTER 13

The Wedge

Your team has conducted a world-class assessment. They communicated with the client throughout the whole process, so the client is thoroughly aware of the value that your team delivered to them. The outbrief goes smoothly, and the client accepts the vulnerabilities your team reports, discusses remediation suggestions, and tentatively suggests a time when your team can verify their patches.

Now what?

If you're like most penetration testing team, your job is done. You say goodbye to the client and hope to see them next year or at best next quarter when they need another test. Your team turns its attention to the next assessment on its roster unaware that you have just missed out on an incredible marketing opportunity.

The kind of trust that is established with a client after an assessment is completed is something salespeople dream of. Not only has your team built rapport with the client, but at the end of the outbrief, the client has technical challenges that they may need help overcoming.

In the world of marketing, offensive cybersecurity services are what's known as a "wedge" – an initial point of relatively low-cost services that prepare and drive the client toward additional long-term and higher-cost services through leveraging the trust that is established.

© Michael Butler and Jacob G. Oakley 2024
M. Butler and J. G. Oakley, *The Business of Hacking*,
https://doi.org/10.1007/979-8-8688-0174-7_13

The difficulty in executing the wedge is that the technical professionals present at the outbrief are not salespeople, and most loathe the idea of being used to sell a service. So we arrive at two questions that need to be answered before we can implement and leverage our wedge:

1.   How do you upsell?

2.   What should be you upselling?

How to Sell

There are thousands of books, videos, and conferences on the subject of sales and marketing. In my experience, most of the traditional "hard-sell" methods that they teach do not work in our field and will, in fact, drive the client to a competitor. I don't say this without experience. The company that I built my second team at put a lot of effort into marketing and sales teams near the end of my time working with them. The company pivoted from involving technical people in the sales process in favor of experienced salespeople who lead inital sale and upsell efforts. The result was a drop in revenue.

Prior to these efforts, my team had driven incredible revenue growth year over year by implementing the client processes that we have already covered in this book. We were selling without trying to. We built trust and a reputation, which allowed us to attract additional clients without a marketing budget.

These sales techniques may work better for a nontechnical audience. If your client representatives are management types looking for a vendor to fill a need, then a tech-heavy sales pitch will probably have the same effect on them that hard-sell methods have on technical people. However, I have rarely seen nontechnical people personally attending sales calls and conducting vendor selection. Even when they are in charge, they bring a technical individual from their team to make sure the vendor isn't just blowing smoke.

While reputation and trust are the most consistent ways to generate growth within a market, they also lock you into a market and most likely a geographic region. Reputation can only spread as far as word of mouth. It has difficulty jumping city, state, or country borders.

As my friend and colleague Kaden Pieksma broke it down, there are three ways to market in the offensive cybersecurity world:

1. Build trust and reputation

2. Provide the right service and the right time

3. Traditional marketing (e.g., Internet advertisements)

To achieve the first option, your team must have a quality product and communicate that quality to the client at all times throughout the assessment and afterward.

The idea of the second option is that when a person finds that they have a need for a service they have little experience with, they will often go with the first vendor that comes to mind. If a very proactive marketing team contacts possible future clients through email, phone calls, and any other medium, then those clients will have the name of your company in mind when they need pentesting services.

This is a volume-driven form of sales. Success won't come often since it relies so heavily on the right timing. Therefore, you must increase the number of clients you are contacting to increase the number of sales you get. To be successful using this method, a marketing team will need to interact with hundreds of potentially new clients on a weekly basis.

This is not a spam campaign. It's important that your company is representing itself well in its contact with clients. The chance of a sale increases with the number of clients you are contacting, not with the amount of time you contact a single client.

I have little experience with the third option, so I cannot speak as to its likelihood of success. In my opinion, if your company plans to make online ads a significant part of its marketing strategy, then it will need to identify a niche or a feature of your services that clients are looking for. You can't compete with the big established players in the market in general pentesting advertisement.

The Audience

After the company where I built my second team was acquired, the new company president approached me to discuss ideas on our sales strategy. I explained to him that our high level of success at retaining and increasing our client base over the past several years was a direct result of all the effort we put into building trust with our clients. Clients that trust you recommend you to their friends. To build that trust, we had to make sure that our services provided more demonstrable value than our competitors. Our clients were almost always technical enough to understand whether they were getting a good service or not and we had to respect that.

Salespeople had been largely unsuccessful. In fact, only a handful of engagements were generated from sales efforts. The rest were from referrals or community involvement. Additionally, salespeople were not able to close deals once a client was interested in talking with us. They simply weren't technical enough and were not able to explain why our offensive cybersecurity services were better than the other options in the market. So either myself or the team's technical director would attend every sales call and sell our services to our technical clients.

The new president was very surprised by all of this. It contradicted most of his professional experience. Salespeople were supposed to sell, and technical people were supposed to execute what was sold. I told him I was worried about that kind of approach because it wouldn't go over well with our technical clients and we would lose existing and future clients.

As we continued to discuss the situation, we both came to a realization. We were talking about two different audiences. The audience I was familiar with was technical and knew when they were getting anything less than the highest quality service. The audience the president was familiar with was managerial and would choose their vendors based on ease of integration, clout in the marketplace, price point, and their relationship with the vendor.

Approaching these two very different audiences requires two very different approaches. If I had used the sales techniques I developed to attract a member of upper management, it would likely go over their head since they aren't as technical as the clients I was used to. Likewise, if the new president tried to approach technical clients by convincing them that we were a big deal in the marketplace, we would lose the sale.

Before you enter any scenario where you intend to execute an upsell, first identify who your audience is and what approach they are likely to respond to. I am not an expert in sales or marketing, but I have had a lot of success when it comes to selling and upselling to a technical crowd. This chapter is going to be focused on what works with technical audiences.

Recommendations

The assessment outbrief puts you and your team in a position to easily make recommendations to the client from a trusted position. If you abuse that position, the client will recognize that you are prioritizing making a sale over what is actually best for them. Technical clients are very sales-adverse. They can tell when the conversation goes from what is best for their environment to a practiced sales pitch.

Moreover, your cybersecurity professionals are not going to feel comfortable recommending company services if they are not the best fit for the client's situation.

Your team should be familiar enough with the upsells that they believe that they provide value. If possible, your team should be involved in the services or products on some level so that they can understand and discuss them with the client from an educated, good-faith position.

Recommendations are strongest when they follow the results of the engagement. For example, if your company offers cloud security engineering services and your time identifies weaknesses in the client's cloud environment, you have a natural and strong upsell that your team can believe in, and the client can accept without feeling like you are just pushing additional services.

What to Upsell

The services and/or products that you upsell to your clients are going to depend on the direction your company would like to grow and what markets are readily available to it. But the pentest wedge is not a magical place where any upsell will work. The client trusts your team and is prepared to hear recommendations, but only within the context of the recently completed assessment. It doesn't make sense to upsell cloud security services after completing an exclusively on-premises assessment.

I have found three categories of services and products that work within our context. There is a natural step from pentest reporting to these services and products, and the client is in a position to be more open to them.

Defensive Security Services and Products

Perhaps the most obvious upsell is defensive cybersecurity services. Offensive cybersecurity naturally feeds defensive cybersecurity. At the end of a pentest, the client knows that they have work to do. If your company has defensive cybersecurity professionals available, you can simply offer those services or any related products to assist the client in responding to the flaws in their environment.

If this is an upsell that you anticipate, you should invite a member of your defensive services to the outbrief. Not only can they explain how their services could be used to help improve the security of the environment, but they can assist in recommendations for remediating the identified vulnerabilities.

Training

If your team was able to find vulnerabilities within the target environment, then there is an opportunity for training those involved with securing the environment. This is especially true when the vulnerability appears to be systemic. For example, your team identifies a cross-site scripting vulnerability due to faulty user input sanitization in a web application. Since the same developers that created the vulnerable code work on other aspects of the web application, there might be several instances of similar vulnerabilities. The developers of that application should be trained on how sanitization should be handled so that the current and future code base will be properly secured.

If your team is able to demonstrate vulnerabilities and trends of bad security practices, the client may be interested in training services to help get their team back on track. Training might take the form of self-paced web modules, remote instruction, or on-site classroom instruction.

Additional Testing Services

Attempting to upsell the client into additional penetration testing services is the most difficult of these three upsells. The client has just been through an outbrief where they were informed, in detail, about the vulnerabilities in their environment. They feel beat up. They see a lot of work addressing these vulnerabilities and the environments that contain them ahead. They may be already putting together ideas on which team needs to tackle each of your team's findings. Their hands are full, and they aren't usually going to be interested in hearing about how you can make them even more full through additional testing.

At the same time, your team has just demonstrated its proficiency in offensive cybersecurity. The client and their team are, hopefully, very impressed and open to ideas about continuing to work with your team. If relevant, your team can suggest additional tests of other environments or applications that were not in scope for this assessment. You can voice concerns about indicators of security flaws that you would like to pursue. For example, if the assessment is focused on a web application, your team might uncover that the server is running as an administrative-level user or that there might be very little network segmentation on the internal network. You can voice these concerns and recommend a follow-up assessment.

If your OCS offers long-term, continuous, or quarterly testing, the outbrief is a good time to bring it up and recommend it so that vulnerabilities are identified more quickly. But in doing this upsell, you have to consider that the client may have just spent their annual offensive cybersecurity budget on the assessment you already performed. You will need to find a way to make the price point of any additional testing services work with their possible lack of budget. For example, you might significantly discount the upfront price for continuous testing services and expect to recoup that discount over the next few years as you retain the client. This approach should be considered carefully since clients who have received discounted prices may continue to expect them.

Final Note

Upselling a client should be approached with caution. You have built trust with your client and that should be respected. Any additional services or products you offer the client should genuinely be in the client's best interest and be based on identified security gaps, rather than primarily driven by the desire to increase sales. The delivery of value should be emphasized and prioritized with upselling as a secondary, ethical practice that arises naturally from demonstrating expertise and building genuine trust.

CHAPTER 14

Cyber Arms Dealing

Having covered more traditional cybersecurity service and product paradigms in other chapters, we must also address the concept of cyber arms dealing, the business of selling hacking tools and services to governments, militaries, and criminal organizations for profit. We will define cyber arms therefore as cybersecurity solutions developed and sold in such a way that they are to be utilized in the carrying out of intelligence gathering and warfighting. This is not to say such solutions would not also be capable of being used by criminals in the same way. However, it is not in the authors' intentions to advocate for such a behavior.

The delineating line between cyber arms dealing and simply selling offensive security tools comes down to intent and customer characteristics. For instance, there is no good reason to price in exclusivity when selling an implant to offensive security companies. On the other hand, if a country were purchasing a cyber implant or backdoor for the purposes of intelligence collection or cyber warfare, that customer would want to know they were the only ones that would have that too. This is for many reasons, but perhaps chief among them are attribution and utility. Such customers wouldn't want their backdoor rendered useless if another customer of the cyber arms dealer got the same tool caught and uploaded to the collective antivirus community. Similarly, such customers would not want to have their actions or the actions of others potentially attributed to each other, that's how you possibly start wars. Before tying cyber arms dealing into the primary thread of business and hacking, it is necessary to cover the

M. Butler and J. G. Oakley, *The Business of Hacking*,
https://doi.org/10.1007/979-8-8688-0174-7_14

concept of cyber warfare. Understanding the legalities and implications of dealing cyber equities to organizations or entities interested in those activities is paramount to understanding both the profitability and risks involved.

Major Misconceptions

Before we get into what these sorts of products might do and thus why they would be produced and sold, we ensure we understand what they can't do. Further, we must understand the business risks associated with what we call cyber arms. Resulting from the knowledge gaps in technology and legality, there are major misconceptions which challenge the successful implementation of the cyber domain as an adequate and appropriate warfighting environment. These misconceptions directly impact the business cases for developing and selling solutions that are utilized to that end. The following are not representative of the totality of challenges faced in conducting cyber warfare and related activities, but in our opinion, they are some of the most pervasive.

Exploitation is Warfare

Cyber exploitation and intelligence-gathering activities by foreign adversaries are continually referred to as cyber-attacks. This use of vernacular permeates from the media into the minds of those who ingest it. For this and other reasons, cyber activities which are not attack effects or battlefield preparation are constantly referred to as attacks or cyber warfare. We have established that this is incorrect. Title-fifty activities are not acts of war whether they are committed by the United States or other nations, and we need to remember that.

When a foreign spy is discovered in the United States, they are not shot, but they are tried, convicted, and incarcerated or depending on their political or diplomatic status simply expelled. The US government itself has taken this same stance with cyber actors in its charging through the Department of Justice and Federal Bureau of Investigations of attributed uniformed hackers from China and other countries. This should further enforce the fact that for a cyber activity to fall within the legal and authoritative realm of warfare, it must actually be a fully attributed state-sponsored attack effect.

Even when conducted by uniformed members of a foreign country as part of state-sponsored cyber intelligence gathering, it is just that intelligence gathering under US title-ten (or similar) authorities and not requiring or party to title-ten warfighting actions and authorities. As such, it would be outside the legality of most national, and certainly international, for a state to respond to such exploitation or intelligence-gathering activities with their own cyber-attack effects. This would certainly be viewed as an unprovoked warfighting action and potentially a declaration of open conflict.

Business Impact

Exploitation activities do not correlate directly to acts of war, and therefore, tools that facilitate such activity are not exclusively tied to warfare nor to be viewed as weapons. The similarity between exploitation tools which give access to ethical hacking and cyber warfare environments means that they can arguably be produced and created for either reason. Therefore, a company wishing to provide exploitation development and sales can do so without walking a tightrope of legality and optics for working to create these products. As has been previously discussed in this chapter, exploitation sales would look most like cyber-warfare-related business activity only when offered with customer use right exclusivity.

Ease of Attribution

There is not a widespread appreciation for the sheer difficulty in attributing cyber activity. This is the case for exploitation, intelligence gathering, and attack effects launched within the cyber domain. Especially where cyber-attack effects, which are acts of war, attribution must be with absolute fidelity if a response is to be launched. We need to remember that a response to an act of cyber warfare can be as severe as a missile launch or invasion.

There are essentially two ways in which a cyber-attack effect can elicit a warfighting response within a realistic time window. The state which launched the cyber warfighting action can openly admit the act as part of a declaration of hostilities against its enemy. The only other situation that responsibly allows for warfighting responses to a cyber-attack effect is when the attributed perpetrator is a state with which the victim and responding state are already in open conflict. These two scenarios revolve around open acknowledgment of motivation for the cyber-attack. Short of the perpetrator admitting it was a title-ten-type action, in cyber, there is essentially no way to know the intent of a cyber activity without it resulting in an attack effect or being admitted as an effort to bring one to bear. When part of a declaration of hostilities or ongoing conflict, motivation is admitted or assumed.

Business Impact

The business implications from the difficulty of true attribution in cyberwarfare mean that a company wishing to create and sell products that are a party to warfighting actions does not need to worry about their resident country being dragged into a conflict. While this fact is helpful in driving down the risk of participating in such a business model, a company may want to invest in strong sales terms and agreements that are able to be disclosed in the case of a foreign entity pointing the finger at the cyber manufacturer as being responsible for actions carried out using their sold tools.

Return Fire

In cyber warfare, there is no realistic concept of return fire. If we ignore the previous misconception and assume attribution is possible, there is still no feasible situation where it would happen so fast that cyber or other actions could subsequently be launched against the unit or asset which launched the attack effect. Remember, a tool which delivers an attack effect can be installed days, months, or even years prior to being executed. Further, even if the enemy hackers are discovered placing the attack tool, without execution having happened, there is no way to completely know, or more importantly prove, the motivation of that action. When the necessity for timeliness is combined with the near impossibility of attribution in the first place, return fire seems a laughable concept. Cyber-attack effects should be directed as a strategic decision as part of a greater and wider conflict, not as part of a tactical response to an ongoing firefight.

I like to compare the ridiculous concept of returning fire in the cyber domain to the following example. Imagine a US patrol in Afghanistan accidentally came across a Soviet-era land mine, placed decades earlier to deter Afghan advances. The land mine is stepped on by one of the patrol members and it explodes. The mine was placed by Soviet soldiers who are potentially dead of old age and are certainly no longer even in the country of Afghanistan. What target might the surviving members of the patrol return fire against? This may seem like an exaggeration, but it would be just as easy for the members of that patrol to go back in time and return fire against the Soviet soldiers who placed the mines as it would for a victim of a cyber-attack effect to attribute, target, and respond in a tactical manner to the assets which launched the cyber-attack with their own cyber-attack capabilities.

Business Impact

The takeaway from tactical cyber not being as realistic as it is generally believed to be revolves around product satisfaction from consumers. As a developer and provider of cyber arms, it is in the best interests of a business to sell products that are not promises of magical beans, fairy dust, or cyber silver bullets that can take the enemy out of the cyber battlefield mid-hack. This is especially true given the types of customers one might have in selling cyber arms and the danger in misleading such entities. There is an easy line to draw to criminally degrading national security in knowingly selling over-hyped and inadequate warfighting tools to one's own government.

Target Dictation

There is this idea that once targets are found in the cyber domain, commanders can simply direct them to be attacked and it will be so. What makes the return fire scenario even more improbable is the fact that target dictation in the cyber domain happens as the result of vulnerabilities being present and weaponized exploits existing. Commanders and decision-makers cannot dictate which targets are susceptible or which capabilities exist. So even in a scenario where we ignore that attribution is extremely difficult and successfully targeting for return fire next to impossible, we may still be unable to respond to that target with cyber-attack effects. Let's assume attribution was essentially immediate and with enough fidelity to responsibly dictate a response against the enemy who conducted it. We must also assume that the enemy that conducted it has not simply been attributed but that the location from which it is obfuscating its communication pathways or accessing the Internet to conduct cyber operations has also been located and with enough fidelity to adequately target it. For return fire to happen while the aggressors are still carrying out cyber-attack effects would also mean that the infrastructure identified as being actively used by the enemy is vulnerable to an exploit in the arsenal of the responding state and that an attack effect that is viable on the enemy device is available.

Business Impact

The business consideration based on the difficulty of target dictation is like that of the impossibility of return fire. In both cases, the best business practice would be to not perpetuate the misconceptions by offering products that can overcome those challenges. No cyber bullet will tactically neutralize, and enemy cyber activity and no cyber bullet will magically allow for immediate and accurate target dictation. Regarding target dictation, it is best for a cyber arms dealer to educate the purchaser of their wares on the need for access to the target, via cyber or physical means, to enable the purchased capability.

Profitability and Risks

We have framed the cyber arms dealer business model by laying out major misconceptions surrounding cyber warfighting activities and how they can positively and negatively impact the business of hacking. Next, we will cover the difference between services and products at a solutions category level, before delving into the various products and the unique profitability and risks that come with them.

Services

This will be a quick discussion relating to the sales of cyber warfighting services. By services, we mean things like denial of service for hire, information operations for hire, providing access to networks or devices as a service, and so on. While developing an exploit for a system is not illegal, it is illegal to use that exploit against a device without the owner's authority.

We will then treat any cyber warfighting services for hire as having an extreme cost benefit challenge as it relates to discerning the legality of such actions. It is no secret that in the warfighting business, organizations like Blackwater and later Triple Canopy provide warzone services, with varying degrees of ethical and legal challenges. Profitability of such an activity, within the cyber or physical domains, is extremely reliant on the palatability and by-country acceptance of providing those services commercially. Therefore, the authors have chosen to mention said services but delve further into the details of using them for a successful hacking business.

Intelligence

One exception to these cyber arms service business risks may be the practice of open-source intelligence (OSINT). As an offered service, gathering openly available intelligence, which does not require illegal or US Title-50-like authorities, could be done without managing legality and ethics concerns. This does not mean it isn't without profitability challenges though. Corporate industry readily pays for OSINT from known vendors to gain business intelligence; however, as it relates to selling this service as part of cyber arms dealing, it would seem akin to selling investing advice to Berkshire Hathaway or Blackrock. Sure, you may offer OSINT as a service, but the entities purchasing cyber arms products also gather intelligence through other authorities and with other tools. Further, if they wanted OSINT, they already have the personnel and solutions to do it essentially for free.

Products

Unlike services, most cyber arms products give a level of non-culpability, in that you are selling a knife and not a murder weapon. This is not a blanket mitigation for business concerns in developing cyber arms but an important discriminator for products over services as categorical favorites in profitability for a cyber arms dealer.

Product Concerns

Because of why and to whom they are being sold, cyber arms products have unique challenges to contend with from a usability, effectiveness, and strategic implication perspective. If we are to sell cyber arms products, we must acknowledge and understand the way these products will be employed, maintained, and protected by our customers.

Resource Availability

In the same line as the misconception that targets in the cyber domain can simply be chosen based on a decision by a commander, there is the incorrect assumption that tools are readily available. We don't just mean the exploit and attack tools but also the ability to even communicate with a target once it is chosen or operate interactively on that target with an access tool if it can be exploited.

The difficulty in attaining the technological resources involved in cyber warfare coupled with the potential ease with which control or ownership may be lost would have to weigh so heavily on every warfighting decision it might paralyze the cyber operator and the commander alike. Let's assume a cyber-attack effect was launched, and the victim not only attributed the perpetrator but identified the infrastructure they were actively using to launch more cyber-attack effects against other assets of the victim state. The commander picks that infrastructure as a target and cyber-attack effects as the appropriate response action. Let's even assume the victim state has both a working exploit against those systems and an attack effect that will nullify the enemy's cyber warfighting capability. The decision that is now faced by the commander is, is it worth it? Remember, using an exploit and or an attack effect potentially risks the loss of control or ownership of that resource.

Imagine a patrol in enemy territory is engaged by enemy small arms fire. Now imagine that the patrol leader must weigh the fact that if he or she responds in kind with small arms fire from their M-16 assault rifles, there is a chance that the M-16 weapon as a resource might be lost, not to the patrol, but to the entire state military. This is an unrealistic situation in the domain of land warfare, but in the cyber domain, it is very real, and assuming all other challenges leading to an ability to return fire or engage an enemy with cyber-attack effects were satisfactorily accomplished, there is still the question of whether the risk to the cyber resource itself is worth it in the given scenario. Would you be willing to risk an exploit and attack effect resource in a cyber return fire response against enemy cyber infrastructure if that same exploit and attack effect would be needed to shut down enemy air warning radar ahead of troop deployments and air strikes? This is further in support of the fact that cyber domain warfighting activity should be strategically planned and weighed at the theater or global level and not a part of tactical responses in ongoing battles as the potential implications of cyber resource utilization are so far-reaching.

Shelf Life

There are resource assumptions beyond the misconceptions about the general availability of cyber resources both in general and in a target-specific sense. There is a notional concept that these resources can be stockpiled and kept off the shelf so that when the time comes for use, the potential for their loss is less damaging to the overall cyber warfighting capability. The fact is that this is simply not the case. Even if a state had the ability to create stockpiles of different exploits, access tools, and attack effects, there is no guarantee that when the time comes that they are utilized, they are effective. There is an entire global industry sector dedicated to securing cyber systems from being subject to exploitation, unauthorized access, and attack.

An attack effect or exploit may still work and the vulnerability enabling their execution on the target may still be present, but the security industry may have developed signatures based on similar capabilities already seen or simply improve heuristics to the point that they detect the tools as malicious and stop them. Cybersecurity companies don't care if a tool is an amateur hacker backdoor or a state-created zero-day exploit. They are doing their best every day to stop all types and sources of potentially malicious cyber activity. This means that even if the ability to stockpile cyber resources were realistic, stockpiling them in the first place may be a wasteful endeavor. Aside from the security industry, there are also any number of other states, organized crime entities, and hacker groups trying to also develop cyber resources, which may be almost identical to what is stockpiled. These facts also further complicate that decision paralysis on whether to risk losing a cyber resource through its utilization as it may be lost at any time even if never utilized.

Control and Ownership

We have established various resource types involved in cyber warfare and their importance to the success of the warfighter and the effectiveness of commanders and decision-makers. We will now cover the concepts of resource control and resource ownership as well as their uniquely amplified impact in the cyber domain. The threats to resilience and mitigations to them covered in Chapter 12 cover for the most part threats posed to cyber warfare resources by the operating environment and defensive capabilities of the enemy and industry security apparatus. Loss of resource control and ownership are exceedingly more dangerous to the mission at hand and to the overall success of waging a cyber war and represent a loss of capability containment and potential damage to innocent noncombatant individuals and systems. Loss of control and ownership also potentially lead to state-developed capabilities being brought to bear against itself or its allies by enemy targets.

Resource Control

Resource control is the ability to start, stop, direct, interact with, and manage a given resource and its activity. Losing control of a resource, in any domain of warfare, occurs when that resource is still being used or active but no longer being wielded by the perpetrating force. Though upon destruction a warfighting resource is no longer at the control of the perpetrating state, it is not actively being utilized by another entity or acting on its own without control and will not be covered under resource control. Destruction of a resource is considered final, if destruction is complete, and not under the purview of resource control and the factors that mitigate the loss of resource control. The other qualifying attribute of resource control loss is that though no longer under the direction of the original wielder and owner, the resource itself is not being recreated simply retargeted.

Think of the soviet warfighting equipment left behind in Afghanistan when the USSR finally decided to pull its ground forces out of that country. Thousands of AK-47 assault rifles and other weapons were now under the control of local Afghan tribes. This is a loss of control of those individual resources because they were not all destroyed and were now being used by other forces, enemies in fact of the Russians. What is worth noting in this scenario is that though the Afghans not had at their disposal thousands of AK-47s, tanks, heavy machine guns, and other weapons, they were still not in a position to now create their own. When the AK-47s became unserviceable or tanks broke down and other weapons failed, they would be discarded, and the Afghanis would then once again be without those resources as they had no way to recreate the resources themselves.

The United States suffered a similar loss of resource control when ISIS forces took many weapons left behind for Iraqi forces by the United States and used them against on-combatants and US allies and troops. Like the Afghanistan example, the ISIS fighters had no capability to replicate the US weapons left behind and used them until they no longer worked at that point of discarding them. If the ISIS forces ran out of ammunition for a particular US weapon, it would be discarded, and if a US Humvee broke down, it was likely discarded. In this way, loss of resource control can be seen as temporary, lasting as long as the resource itself is likely to last.

Resource control is not limited to a loss of the resource where it falls into the hands of an enemy or another operator. There is also the concept of containment and a loss of control where the resource is not in the hands of a particular external operator but is no longer under the direction of the perpetrating state. This loss of control can still be enemy-initiated. If you consider a drone or unmanned aerial vehicle (UAV), there are many examples and even open-source information on the Internet on how to jam communication links to UAVs and drones. If the enemy is unable to take over control of the drone but can hamper its ability to take direction or fly resulting in its crash, control of that resource has still been lost.

Resource control can also be as benign as losing the ability to communicate with a GPS satellite. The satellite may still perform its GPS mission but without control from a ground station may be unable to adjust orbit to avoid a collision or falling into the earth's atmosphere. Similarly, without enemy involvement but more dangerously, loss of control could also be represented by the automated tracking and firing mechanism in the Phalanx CIWS-radar-guided 20-mm cannon engaging birds and other nonaggressive targets with fire. This is what happened when a Japanese-based Phalanx CIWS locked on to and shot down a US plane during an exercise. Thankfully the crew was safe, but this is clearly a dangerous example of control loss.

Resource Ownership

Resource ownership is the ability of a state to maintain the unique ability to recreate a warfighting capability. Once the enemy or another state is able to recreate the same capability, the resource is no longer owned by the perpetrating state. Resource ownership is more a concept of exclusivity

versus the operability concern of resource control. In traditional warfare
resource ownership is a concern but the timelines involved in an enemy
being able to recreate a weapon or other warfighting resource are timely.
Once a weapon system is understood enough to recreate it, the enemy still
has to find the resources to manufacture the capability and then bring it to
utilization. In the cyber domain, this timeline can be much faster, making
the danger of resource ownership loss potentially an immediate concern.

Let's consider the first nuclear bombs developed by the United States,
which were developed in a long, secretive, and herculean effort. Given the
deadliness of this resource and the labor required to create it, the United
States certainly would want as little risk as possible regarding the potential
loss of ownership. If another country or countries during World War Two
were able to recreate the resource, resulting in a loss of ownership by the
United States, the bomb would no longer be a US-only resource. Even with
such a high concern for maintaining exclusive ownership of the nuclear
bomb capability, the United States still tested and even used this weapon.
This was done without fear of endangering the exclusivity of the weapon
because, in use and testing, there is next to no information that an enemy
could glean to further its own nuclear bomb efforts. There was no chance
that in using the bomb against Japan that the Japanese Empire would be
able to recreate the capability.

Resource ownership in the cyber domain is a more immediate threat
to the use of a particular resource, particularly tools. Whether an attack,
access, or exploit capability, once a cyber resource has been used on an
enemy system, there is a chance that it might be caught and forensically
analyzed. Upon analysis, the enemy will likely be able to leverage the same
capability within a significantly short time window. This means that unlike
the nuclear bomb example, a cyber-attack, once used has the potential to
almost immediately be turned against similar targets by the initial victim.

Resource ownership can also be lost when it is not recreated
but becomes so understood by the adversary that they develop
countermeasures effectively nullifying it. If a resource is no longer viable

because the enemy has made it completely ineffective, it can no longer
be considered a resource in that conflict and is therefore no longer a
resource owned by the perpetrating state. During the raid on Osama Bin
Laden's compound in Abbottabad, Pakistan, one of the stealth helicopters
delivering the SEAL teams crashed, most of it was destroyed, but the tail
portion fell on the outside of the compound wall and was mostly intact.
Pakistan allowed the Chinese to take and analyze the tail portion of the
aircraft. If the Chinese were able to reverse engineer the stealth technology
on the helicopter tail section and make their radar able to detect it, the
United States would no longer own that stealth resource in a conflict
with China.

Exploits

Exploits are used to gain remote access, escalate privilege, and in general
manipulate a target system in ways its owner does not intend. The danger
is relatively low for a remote-targeted exploit resource that is taken and
utilized by an external entity. Even in possession of a tool that launches the
exploit, without the ability to recreate it themselves, they are unlikely to be
able to target it adequately against other systems to constitute controlling
it themselves. On the other hand, tools that perform local privilege
escalation can be executed on any target with a similar vulnerability. It
is therefore a realistic possibility that a privilege escalation tool could be
discovered on a victim system by the enemy and then taken and used by
that enemy on other systems.

The loss of control over an exploit resource can also occur if a remotely
exploiting and self-spreading virus begins exploiting systems outside of the
intended target range. With the self-spreading virus going after unintended
systems and if the perpetrating state cannot cease the weapons activity,
it has lost control of that resource. This can occur when things like device
addresses are used as targeting logic for such cyber tools. The virus may be
meant to spread to any target in the enemy within a specific set of network

addresses; however, if one of the infected systems is taken to a place where it can communicate with a different network that uses similar address schemes, the tool may spread there too.

Losing ownership of an exploit resource is something that should be carefully considered prior to leveraging it. Cost benefits must be weighed in the decision to use an exploit that is unique to the perpetrating state. Once an exploit is utilized, the enemy may notice it, and having captured network traffic or forensically gone through the victim system are now able to similarly leverage the vulnerability through their own similar weaponized exploit. At this point, the perpetrating state has lost ownership. An exploit resource that is exclusive to the perpetrating state is one that is viewed as a zero-day exploit, in that no other entity has the same capability and the security industry does not know of the capability. This is an extremely valuable resource to be protected and safeguarded. If ownership is lost, it puts the perpetrating state in a potential race to defend itself from the same capability.

In fact, if an enemy was able to recreate a previously exclusive zero-day exploit, the perpetrating state might even decide to make it publicly known to the security industry in hopes of heading off the enemy's ability to utilize it. This is not a danger to all exploit resources, many systems we have come across in offensive security assessment are well known, decades-old exploits with available patches and fixes. Just because an exploit is known and no longer exclusively owned by a state does not mean that potential targets have fixed their systems against it. If in a specific conflict however, the enemy observes the exploit, and instead of recreating it for themselves simply nullifies the ability for the perpetrator to leverage it against their systems, the perpetrating state has summarily also lost ownership of that resource.

Mitigating the risks associated with exploits is a tempered approach to their use. Even in situations where a perpetrating state uses a publicly known exploit against an enemy system, once the enemy learns of the exploit, they may update their systems making them invulnerable. In this case, exclusivity and ownership were not a concern, but the exploit still ceases to be something the perpetrating state can utilize. The concepts of ownership and control loss of ownership come with significant concerns of not only limiting the capability of the perpetrating state but potentially endangering others. Say a perpetrating state acts irresponsibly and lets a powerful exploit fall under the control or shared ownership of an enemy state who then uses it against all of its enemies. Does the perpetrating state share some responsibility for letting this exploit into the wild so to speak? What if criminals now use that exploit to target innocents? These questions may seem excessive due to being cyber domain activities, but they can still be warfighting actions that ultimately impact noncombatants and that is worth contemplating.

Business Model

Cyber arms relating to exploits can largely be viewed as vulnerability research and exploit development. Often, turning a vulnerability into a working exploit is referred to as weaponizing the vulnerability. There are two methods for prioritizing these activities. A cyber arms business might want to sell weaponized exploits for use. In this instance, vulnerabilities are identified as well as turned into working exploits to be sold to military and government customers. This could be done in either an opportunistic or directed manner. Opportunistic sales of exploits would revolve around happening to come across weaponizable vulnerabilities during broad research directed by the cyber arms dealer itself. If a vulnerability happens to be found, the company can weaponize it and offers it up to buyers. The other business case would be customer-directed research and development. To that end, a customer might approach a cyber arms dealer with a contract saying it will fund efforts to find vulnerabilities and create exploits against specific technologies it cares about. These two cyber arms business cases mirror the differing vulnerability research models of traditional security companies where bug bounties pay opportunistic researchers who happen to find issues in software and fuzzing for a service against specific software is customer-directed vulnerability research.

Access Tools

Of all the examples we will discuss regarding loss of control, access tools as a resource are overall the least impactful when this happens. One way control of an access tool might be lost is if the enemy discovers its presence on a system or systems and begins manipulating the access tool's environment on that system so that it behaves in ways the enemy wants. The enemy may not be able to reverse engineer the functionality of an access tool used to pull back information out of a network, but they might be able to determine what files on the system the access tool is monitoring for and collecting. If this is the case, the enemy can control what information is making it back to the perpetrating state that installed the access tools.

Control can also be lost without enemy intervention. Earlier we discussed how a satellite used for GPS may lose its ability to communicate with its ground station and operators. This didn't stop it from sending GPS signals but means that control of that resource was lost. Similarly, an access tool, which beacons out to the Internet every so often to receive tasking may be on a system that is moved to a network that can't talk to the Internet. If a laptop, for instance, was exploited and an access tool installed that monitored Twitter posts for tasking was taken inside a secure facility with no network connection, the tool itself would still be trying to reach out for tasking but would be unable to reach Twitter. Though this situation itself means that the perpetrating state loses the ability to communicate with that system and the access tool, it could lead to the discovery of the access tool on the system as it is continually trying to reach out to the Internet from a non-Internet-connected network which may be caught by defensive software or devices as being anomalous or malicious.

If the access tool was discovered due to this loss of control, it could lead to a loss of ownership. Discovering an access tool on a secure network, an enemy may perform forensics on the device and ultimately learn how to recreate the access tool for their own use. The command-and-control aspects of an access tool may not seem very valuable or pose a significant risk if they fall into enemy hands, but there are other portions of an access tool that might. If an access tool, for instance, had previously unknown stealth capabilities, able to get past security scans, or new persistence mechanisms able to survive a reboot or a hard drive wipe, these would be dangerous resources if the enemy can determine how to use them. Like the exploit example, the enemy could also simply incorporate this new knowledge into their defensive capabilities, meaning any existing similar access tools are either discovered or nullified.

We have already discussed the concepts of environmental keying to prevent access tools from being used on systems they were not meant for or even executed for forensics analysis in a lab. Anti-tamper capabilities can delete the tool upon inspection by enemy security personnel as well. Access tools should also address the loss of control resulting from an inability to receive new tasks. A solution to this might be setting up a certain number of unsuccessful callout attempts now resulting in the tool uninstalling itself or a similar functionality to insure that eventually, upon loss of control, it will do its best to avoid a loss of ownership of that resource.

Business Model

Vulnerability identification and exploit development are a high-risk, high-reward business scenario due to the dynamic nature of cyber exploitation in general. Conversely, developing access tools would be a difficult business line to dominate or exploit for much profit. Access tools themselves are cheap and easy to develop, with the uniqueness and marketability of such products being determined by their ability to avoid detection and persist on a system. The risk to business for access tools revolves around the ease of development and unknown competitor capabilities. A competitor's access tool could have similar enough functions, persistence, or obfuscation methods that, if their customer got using it, it could result in a compromise of your access tool business line as well. This is a challenge for exploit tools also, but they are fewer and less often developed, whereas the bar of entry to providing access tools is much lower, and thus, there is more competition to accidentally relegate your own products.

Attack Effects

There is the possibility that control of attack effects is lost in a similar fashion to exploits. If the tool is discovered on a system, there is a chance that even without fully understanding or reverse-engineering the tool, an enemy is able to execute it against systems similar to the one it was designed for. It would be safe to say that the danger for both loss of control or ownership is higher with an attack effect that an exploit or access resource. This is because exploit and access resources are typically intended to not be noticed. Attack effects, on the other hand, are warfighting actions designed to have a noticeable effect on enemy systems.

Though an attack effect itself is not going to spread by itself (that would be an exploit), there is still a potential for a loss of control. As in some of the examples covered in this book, attack effects may be executed from a launch point machine against a remote one. What if that launch point machine was a virtual machine or backed up in its entirety and then deployed to other networks within the enemy state? This would result in the attack effect being launched from copies of the original launch point but in networks that were not the intended target of the attack effect. This not only poses a greater danger to a loss of ownership, but the loss of control means the perpetrating state may be responsible for acts of cyber war being inadvertently launched against noncombatants.

Losing ownership of an attack effect is also a serious concern. Having an enemy able to recreate an attack effect means it could be used against friendly systems and other third parties. Just as with exploits, publicly known and available resources can be used to carry out attack effects, including operating system commands that come installed with software like Microsoft Windows. It is not very concerning if an enemy learns that the perpetrating state used the del command to delete files in a cyber-attack. On the other hand, if the attack effect was exclusive and therefore a resource of only the perpetrating state, the enemy coming to share ownership of it is a serious loss of capability and a potential danger to wider global cyber systems.

Precautions should be taken to avoid the replay like issues of the virtualized launch point example or the recreation of tailored attack effects by an enemy to use against friendly forces and those uninvolved in the conflict. To this end, if a specialized attack effect is needed, then it should be tailored as much as possible to the specific target at hand. This way if the enemy is able to capture the capabilities and recreate them, they will similarly have an extremely limited target set of potential victims. This does go against resiliency efforts at making an attack effect that is likely to be useful longer and against a wider array of targets, but if the attack effect is dangerous enough, then it is a worthwhile sacrifice to ensure it is not effectively repurposed by the enemy.

Business Model

Once a cyber warfare actor has exploited and maintains access to a machine, deploying an attack effect is the final course of action. Akin to the access tool, there is a low bar of entry for attack effects in most cases. There are any number of ways to encrypt drives, disconnect devices, or otherwise affect a system once privileged access is gained. Many of these methods can occur by simply using existing commands on a system. Therefore, attack effects are another low-risk, low-reward product line for a cyber arms dealer. Exacerbating the profitability challenge for attack tools though is that they come with some level of culpability and legality concerns that make them a more troublesome business model to execute, to the extent that it is likely not worth it.

An exploit and an access tool can be realistically developed for and used in ethical hacking as much as they can in warfare. Creating a tool that destroys file systems and disrupts systems though, that only has a place in war and crime. Further, from an ethics and legality standpoint, more tailored attack effects, such as one that say, impacts microcontrollers responsible for gas line control, would be developed solely for nefarious purposes. The optics of creating such tools, even as part of a legal cyber arms business, are going to not be worth it.

Obfuscation Infrastructure

If discovered by an enemy, the perpetrating state may lose control of its obfuscation resources with little to no effort by the victim state. Denial of service attacks are unsophisticated but effective. If the obfuscation infrastructure is identified as being related to operational resources found in the enemy cyberspace, the enemy can simply send so much traffic at the obfuscation infrastructure that the perpetrating state can no longer communicate through it. Control can also be lost of such infrastructure if the larger networks, which obfuscation and redirection systems are a part of, have communication issues. If an Internet service provider for the third-party network which hosts the obfuscation infrastructure is having issues, it can affect operations by the perpetrating state no longer being able to communicate with, through, or control its redirection points.

Losing ownership of obfuscation infrastructure is especially dangerous to missions, conflicts, and a cyber war in general. Losing ownership of obfuscation infrastructure would happen if the enemy or another entity were able to exploit and gain privileged access to that system without the knowledge of the perpetrating state. If this happened not only would the system no longer obfuscate the activity of the perpetrating state, but the enemy could use its new access to stealthily hamper ongoing operations, have direct knowledge of capabilities and activities, or worse, continue attempts to swim upstream toward the perpetrating states own frontend and backend infrastructure.

Every precaution should be taken to maintain the security of obfuscation infrastructure to avoid possible compromise by enemy hackers. This can be accomplished through both security software and standards as well as efforts to avoid attribution to operational resources. If the obfuscation systems are not tied to operational resources in the enemy cyberspace, then the enemy will not have reason to target them with denial or hacking attempts in the first place.

Business Model

The design of obfuscation infrastructure for cyber warfare operations differs from traditional infrastructure in some ways from traditional networking infrastructure, largely in the way it is implemented. However, this is a product that should be created and delivered, not operated without being owned in some way by cyber warfighting entities with proper authorities. In this way, obfuscation infrastructure as a cyber arms product does not benefit from the follow-on operation service contracts that accompany many information technology infrastructure offerings. Aside from delivery of such architectures to customers to authorized operators of cyber warfighting activities, maintenance contracts might be the only way to turn that delivery into longer-term profit.

Summary

In this chapter, we have discussed the concept of cyber warfare and the major misconceptions that surround that paradigm. How such misconceptions impact a cyber arms business was discussed as was the profitability and risk associated with offering services and products to potential customers in this arena. Further, the challenges to resources used by cyber warfighting customers were detailed, as was their impact on business. The types of products that could be developed and sold were outlined, and related business models were presented. The main takeaway from this entire chapter for both vendors and customers of the cyber arms industry should be a cost benefit. As a consumer, is it worth it to procure these products from a vendor or develop them in-house? As a producer, is it worth the effort and ethical implications to pursue various cyber arms business lines?

CHAPTER 15

New Frontiers

In this chapter, we are going to touch on two emerging sectors of the cybersecurity industry that hacking businesses can exploit. The systems that these offerings would target in the respective areas are space systems and artificial intelligence (AI) systems. A space system is any system or system of systems that involves operating space-resident systems, henceforth referred to as space vehicles (SVs) as well as any interconnected terrestrial attack surface. An AI system is one that utilizes automated decisional computation to perform and/or learn to perform tasks. Both types of systems represent challenges and opportunities when operating a business around hacking and offensive cybersecurity.

An Introduction to Space Systems

The most basic example of a space system is where there is a device on the ground transmitting and/or receiving to a device in space that is transmitting and/or receiving, think Sputnik. This is a far cry from some of the extremely complex systems of today, considering the International Space Station (ISS), it regularly makes maneuvers using on-board propulsion to move out of the way of space debris that is on a collision path with it. In the case of the ISS, it can be flown from onboard the station itself as well as by individuals at a ground station on Earth. A simple example of one space vehicle and one ground station is shown in Figure 15-1.

© Michael Butler and Jacob G. Oakley 2024
M. Butler and J. G. Oakley, *The Business of Hacking*,
https://doi.org/10.1007/979-8-8688-0174-7_15

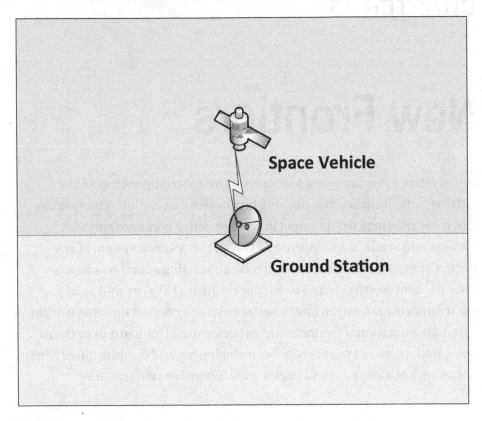

Figure 15-1. *Basic space system*

The Ground Station Design

When considering the space systems of today, however, the ground station may resemble something like what is shown in Figure 15-2. There is a software-defined radio (SDR) responsible for receiving the signals from the space vehicle and turning them into communications via demodulation. At this point, if there is encryption of the communication stream, it will then be decrypted and ultimately passed to a flight control computer running the software that communicates with and controls the space vehicle and keeps track of its flight operation-related data. Potentially on the same computer but as a different function of the ground station would be the payload control which handles the operation of the payload portion of the space vehicle and keeps track of payload data being sent back down to earth. Certainly, a single suite of software could be developed to handle both functions and often that is the case. We are only separating them to highlight their differences.

One other facet of the ground station that I will not cover in great detail at this point is the antennae itself. This is the dish or other type of antennae which allows the SDR to receive the signal wave from the air and or transmit it back to the space vehicle. The process from the ground station perspective is just the opposite, where a communication stream is crafted using a protocol like IP and then encrypted, if necessary, then modulated and sent as a radio wave via the SDR and antennae into the air to the space vehicle.

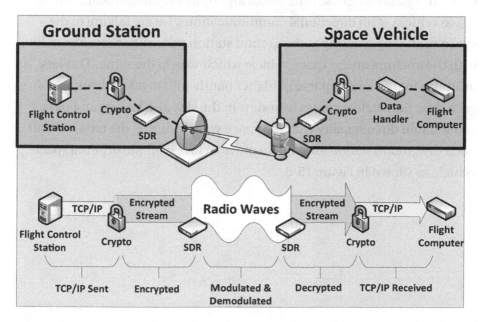

Figure 15-2. *Detailed space system view*

Space vehicles have evolved in parallel to ground station as far as complexity and capabilities go. Like the ground station, there is an SDR to turn the radio wave signal into a communication stream. Next, there is a computing device we will refer to as the handler which receives the communications from the ground station and directs them as necessary to the flight computer or payload computer. The flight computer is responsible for controlling the functions of the space vehicle with regard to flight. What those functions are will be covered in the upcoming section on space vehicle functions. The payload control computer is responsible for manipulating the payload of the space vehicle. A payload is the portion of the space vehicle carrying out the mission it was designed for.

Ground Station Functionality

Ground stations often use directional antennae to communicate with the space vehicle. With directional communications, we are talking to the space vehicle by pointing at the ground station transmitter receiver in line with the antenna on the space vehicle which will do the same. This lets us utilize frequencies capable of higher bandwidth to take advantage of each time the satellite comes into view in the sky, also known as a pass. To maintain directionality with the space vehicle during the pass, we will need the ground station antenna to move in lock with the orbiting space vehicle as shown in Figure 15-3.

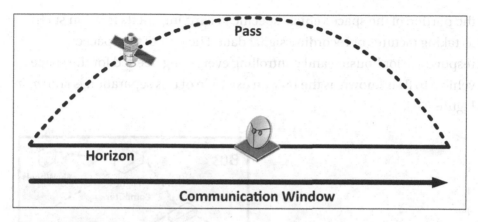

Figure 15-3. *Diagram of a pass*

Communication with a space vehicle moving relative to the earth's surface requires more than the ability of the ground station to move its antenna and take advantage of the full pass for a longer communication window. It also requires that the ground station have a really good idea of where the space vehicle will start its pass so that it can already be facing the correct location on the horizon and not waste time spinning the antenna around. This situation becomes much more complex if you have a single ground station that will communicate with multiple satellites since instead of simply waiting for one satellite to come over the horizon it will have to address and deconflict multiple orbits.

Space Vehicle Functionality

The space vehicle in general has several required functions in addition to similarly to the ground station having to maintain the ability to communicate and receive tasking. It has to be able to carry out its mission as well as maintain communications with users on the ground and stay in the correct orbit and achieve necessary positioning. This means maintaining communications needs, maintaining space vehicle flight requirements, and enabling payload operation. The payload refers to the portion of the space vehicle specific to carrying out its mission such as taking pictures or recording signal data. The part of the spacecraft responsible for housing and controlling everything needed for the space vehicle to fly is known as the bus, an example of this separation is shown in Figure 15-4.

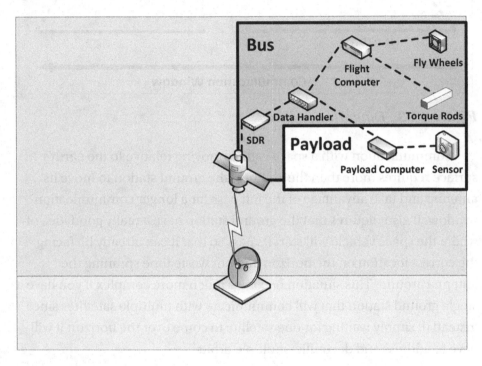

Figure 15-4. *Payload and bus*

Space System Business Challenges

The unique aspects of space systems attributed to their operating environment and related operational challenges make them one of the last great frontiers for cybersecurity applications, including ethical hacking. This section will briefly cover both types of space system constraints and how they impact the compute that would be hacked within the space resident portions of those systems. Paired with the introduction to space systems presented earlier in this chapter will allow the reader to fully grasp the implications of foundational problems at the intersection of the cyber and space domains. We will discuss how each of these problems interacts with the business case of hacking such systems and cybersecurity in general.

Environmental Challenges

Computers and other digital technologies operating in outer space face a slew of threats and risks. Radiation is generally understood to be bad for electronic devices, and space presents both single event doses, in the form of solar flares as well as the overall accumulation of radiation exposure over the life of a space vehicle. Temperature extremes when in and out of the sun and the vacuum of space as well present challenges to component designs to ensure that they can function in space and for the duration of a space system's mission.

Operational Challenges

Operationally, space vehicle components must also survive the extreme vibrations of launch, which differ from launch vehicle to launch vehicle. Testing components to see if they can survive such vibrations and still function as well as testing them against the previously mentioned environmental challenges are requirements that must be passed before a space system is even allowed to be launched. Once in space, the SV must deploy from its launch vehicle, detumble, attain its appropriate orbit, and then perform its mission while also maintaining enough power through generation using solar panels and limiting the draw on power from computing and communication devices.

Space System Attack Surface Problems

The following are the foundational issues faced by attackers, defenders, and ethical hackers of space systems as well as how those problems impact the business of hacking in this emerging niche of the cybersecurity industry. This list of issues for space systems is not exhaustive; instead, it has been kept to those problems which have a direct impact on the business of hacking.

The Cost Problem

Space systems have a cost problem, though to be fair, all cybersecurity solutions have a cost problem in that they are largely seen as a tax to be paid as minimally as possible as opposed to being part of potential profit. Space systems and their owners are simply hyper-cost-sensitive, not just in dollars but also in terms of other limited resources onboard space-resident systems such as bandwidth, power utilization, processing power, and storage. There is the utmost respect for flight heritage, and if something hasn't been done or installed on an in-flight space system before, most system owners will opt to accept the risk of malicious activity over the risk of being the first to try something.

Offensive security practices on space systems will have to contend with all these issues as well as the fear from said owners in ethical hacking activity causing an operational problem with their space vehicle. This will be a very hard business to crack into and will require not only exceptional hacker talent but a familiarity with aerospace engineering and operations to enable the type of discussions necessary to communicate cost benefit and acceptable risk.

The Test Problem

Currently for space specifically, there is a bit of a test problem. Where other environmental and operational risks are both mitigated during design and development as well as exercised, for cyber, this is not the case. For the structural integrity of a space vehicle's components, things are done like specifically torquing each bolt to a prescribed amount of torque determined by engineers. After this is done though, the space vehicle is still exercised through a vibration test to ensure that it holds up under the shaking it will experience during launch and deployment.

In some cases, government regulations dictate a validation of security controls on space systems tailored to their being a space vehicle or normal network like a ground station. This is similar to making sure all the bolts have been tightened with the correct amount of torque. The closest thing in the cyber domain to something like a vibration test would be to combine software testing and red teaming to actually exercise the code and computational activities on the space vehicle and ensure they are not easily compromised by an attacker despite having met validation checks of a cybersecurity risk framework. Without both compliance and an exercising of the space vehicle and ground station security apparatus, space systems will have an elevated and partially unknown cyber risk posture. This leaves open an opportunity for well-informed and experienced offensive security practitioners and businesses to step in and find innovative ways to exercise the cybersecurity apparatus of space systems in a way that aligns cybersecurity tests and evaluation of space vehicles and their infrastructure more closely to the other testing done in the space industry.

The Adaptation Problem

All noncyber risks to a space vehicle can be considered mitigated when appropriate steps are taken to burn down that risk and those steps are verified, validated, and exercised. In the case of risks to the integrity of the space vehicles' physical components, the risk of breaking during launch can be mitigated by appropriate construction and torque definitions, verification that they were followed during the build, and validation through being exercised in a vibration test.

At that point, the risk can be considered acceptable and that's the end of it. With cybersecurity issues, not only do solutions need to continue to improve but they need to evolve with the threats. A cybersecurity risk mitigation solution for a space vehicle today might be nullified by a different vulnerability and exploit being discovered and weaponized tomorrow. As space systems adapt to cyber threats, those threats are also adapting to overcome the defenses of the space systems. More than any other cybersecurity offering, red teaming and penetration testing offer the most effective way to adapt system defenses to counter evolving threats by probing and remediating existing solutions and identifying the need for new capabilities.

The Defense in Depth Problem

Another problem with current space system architectures and operations is the overly abundant trust between the systems that make up these systems of systems. It has resulted in most current systems having no defense in depth beyond the ground station. From the ground station up, everything is completely trusted, and the space vehicles and other ground stations trust what they get from each other completely. This is in part the case because it is more computationally efficient to trust what you are receiving from component to component on a space vehicle as well as from the ground station to the space vehicle and vice versa. This is also the same for mesh communications.

Implementing a little suspicion and verification of what is being passed from component to component and system to system in the space system will go a long way in preventing ease of attack and ease-of-attack proliferation across space systems. As computational resources on board space vehicles become more powerful, there will be enough resources to perform more permissions and rule-based security, and if a space system can afford the resource cost of implementing security solutions, they should. Offensive security practices can go a long way in illustrating this issue and just how dangerous it is through assessment of space system architectures to show the need for further layers of defense in depth.

The Modernization Problem

The last problem for cyber and space that I want to cover is the modernization problem. This is really manifested in two forms. First, there is a need for modernization, and second, there is a need to modernize correctly. The need for modernization is because the operating systems and software currently in use by space systems are stripped down resource-conscious power budget-constrained devices trying to squeeze everything, they can out of a space vehicle to accomplish the functional mission necessary. What this leads to, though, is that via a compromised ground station, an attacker is essentially attacking the computing devices of yesteryear with limited if any security implementations, but leveraging the tools, exploits, and computing power of today.

As onboard computers grow in capability onboard space vehicles, they will stop running one-off software, tiny, and real-time operating systems and begin using Linux or Unix distributions. This makes it easier for those developing code for space vehicles as their code is more traditional, more portable, and easier to implement. They also get the benefit of having access to much larger communities of support. In general, it is just easier to implement functionality via software from a more modern operating system. While this makes it easier for developers to write code that runs effectively on the space vehicle, it also makes it easier for attackers to write malware that runs effectively on the space vehicle.

As space systems modernize and start using operating systems closer to what is seen in many places terrestrially, the attack surface of space systems will go from foreign to many attackers to familiar. I say this not to dismay such modernization but to caution that as choices are made to move from something like VxWorks or OpenRTOS to things like CentOS or BSD that the full capability of those operating systems is utilized. Not just from an ease of coding and higher functionality standpoint but also to leverage the more mature security solutions available to such operating systems like stateful software firewalls, mature permission management, and the like.

The danger is that to make the development of a space vehicle easier, the choice is made to use the Linux operating system, but the security software and settings available to that Linux operating system are not used, installed, or running in an effort to still keep the operating system as lightweight on resources as possible. In doing so, the space vehicle would be an extremely targetable and familiar target to malicious cyber actors. As developmental decisions to modernize are made, they need full implementations of modern solutions, to include the security functions that can be utilized with them. Modernization will continue to push the digital components of space systems to look less bespoke and more like systems ethical hackers are familiar with. While this means attackers will have an easier time, it also means a wider group of hacking businesses will be able to realistically start participating in protecting space systems.

An Introduction to AI Systems

There is an ever-growing list of ways to define artificial intelligence (AI) systems, to enable them as machine learning (ML), large language models (LLM), and so on. For the purpose of this book, we will not look to define where the line between AI or ML and something simpler ends, such as automation. For this section, we will refer to all these systems that take in data in one form or another and algorithmically process and/or learn on it as AI.

AI System Business Challenges

The red teaming and hacking of AI systems then will revolve around several aspects of those systems which constitute risk worth protecting by hiring hackers. AI systems need to protect and understand the risk to data that will be ingested and has been ingested as well as algorithmic models that have been developed or trained and will be trained.

Data Poisoning

Data poisoning is when attackers seek to have an AI system ingest improper, invalid, or malicious data. This might be done to create a poison, an incorrect or malicious output from the algorithmic model. It can also be a method whereby attackers intend to get a learning model to learn improperly. The opportunity for hacking to provide protection and thus present a business case is to prove the integrity of input validation for learning and nonlearning models to increase trust in their ability.

Model Abuse

This challenge is where a model is trained to effectively perform a task, but attackers identify a way to abuse optimizations in the model to impede its implementation. A good example of this is when researchers found out that simple tickers placed on the side of the road were making certain car autopilot software veer away or stop altogether. This was because the sticker represented a shape that the models generalized to mean something like a pedestrian. Like data poisoning, offensive security offerings can prove a means to evaluate trained models against potentially problematic inputs before they become a problem in a postimplementation scenario.

Prompt Safety Escape

As of the writing of this book, large language models have been trending. As these highly interpretive systems continue to learn and take in human input requests and turn them into useful results, there has been constant research into breaking free of the safety constraints placed on the input from prompts. One example is building a bomb. If you asked one of these LLMs how to build a bomb, guard rails in the prompt mechanism will stop the LLM from providing you results. The issue is it is very easy to overcome these guard rails and very difficult, if not impossible, to generate comprehensive prompt protections. The reason for this is the very reason LLMs are effective, they are not strictly syntactical and are meant to interpret any type of human input. Therefore, as many different ways as a question can be asked, the LLM can answer, and when a new protection is put in place, one just has to ask, in a slightly different phrase or series of phrases, how to build a bomb.

Safety escapes in such systems are not a novel concept, LLMs have just made it much more difficult to protect against. Think about self-driving cars and their autopilots again. Many of them require a driver to place their hands on the wheel every so often or monitor eye movement and direction to make sure that a driver is paying attention while the autopilot is engaged. In this example, we can consider someone placing gloves with weights on them on the steering wheel to convince sensors a human is still paying attention to be a safety escape like the prompt escapes of LLMs. The issue is not new but has certainly evolved, and with regard to LLMs' ability to take in infinitely varied prompts, there is no better resource than adversarial-minded and creative ethical hackers to help these technologies develop safer prompt and response mechanisms.

Leaking

Call a plumber, no wait, call a hacker, our AI system is leaking. There are two concerns with what an attacker may be able to pull out of an AI system. Where data poisoning and model abuse focus on inputs, this is a problem of outputs. If an AI system is not careful about the way it responds or what it gives as a response, there are methods for attackers to pull out data that was ingested as part of using or training the system. This can be particularly precarious in situations with protected information such as healthcare data. If thousands of people were used to create a mode to identify cancer, but the outputs weren't correctly protected, an attacker might be able to pull out individual health information. Further, an attacker might be able to identify the model itself, which is often going to be considered patented and/or intellectual property, which is vital to an organization. If attackers and prompt get repetitive output from an AI system, they can figure out how its algorithm and training works. This would enable the three previous AI system issues as well as likely mean a huge competitive loss for an organization using that AI system. As with the other AI system challenges, hackers are the best nonmalicious resource available in the cybersecurity industry to help AI system designers and users figure out how to protect themselves from these threats and risks.

Conclusion

Both the space and AI areas are hyper-complex, dynamically evolving niches of the cybersecurity industry and malicious hackers are fast adopting methods to attack them. This means any business involving ethical hackers will have quite the foot race ahead of them to stay abreast of these threats and provide cost benefits to their customers. These and future frontiers of cybersecurity must be viewed as both a business opportunity and a challenge to those looking to profit in the business of (ethically) hacking them.

CHAPTER 16

Infinite Cost Benefit

Doing well in business involves many things going well, but two core principles that drive profitability and/or return on investment are optimizing cost benefit and understanding the type of game you are in and playing accordingly. The offensive security solutions created by hackers specifically, and the cybersecurity industry as a whole, are no different. Interestingly, in cybersecurity, cost benefit is more a trifecta than a coupling of producer and consumer. In the business of hacking, cost benefit must be considered from the viewpoint of the cybersecurity solution producer, the cybersecurity solution consumer, and the actors attempting to compromise entities protected by such solutions. Further, that trifecta of participants in the game of cybersecurity needs to know whether they are playing an infinite or finite game and if the solutions at their disposal enable effective play.

Understanding Cost Benefit Perspectives

Within cybersecurity, there are different ways of evaluating cost benefit depending on the perspective involved. It is essential to understand how cost benefit is evaluated by all those involved in cybersecurity to come up with truly appropriate evaluations of cost benefit. It is also important to understand that cost benefit is applied differently by different stakeholders within the game of cybersecurity. The business of hacking takes on

© Michael Butler and Jacob G. Oakley 2024
M. Butler and J. G. Oakley, *The Business of Hacking*,
https://doi.org/10.1007/979-8-8688-0174-7_16

different measures of return on investment for producers of cybersecurity solutions, those who consume them, and the malicious actors those solutions mitigate.

Cost Benefit to the Producer

Cost benefit for cybersecurity producers will be impacted by the marketability and adaptation of their solutions as well as the performance of those solutions to enable return customers. Regarding the business of hacking, marketability is going to be impacted by brand and presence but also bolstered by the continued increase in compliance requirements for different government organizations and industries to have ethical hacking assessments performed against their systems. Performance and return customers will most likely be based on metrics such as the ability to find and compromise vulnerabilities as well as the ability to convey the impact of necessary remediations to the customer. In more unfortunate situations, offensive security assessment becomes less about the findings and more about satisfying the compliance check box. In this sort of producer–consumer relationship, both of those nonmalicious stakeholders are in a race to the bottom to provide/procure the fastest, cheapest service that allows for the satisfaction of compliance requirements. This is a bad look for ethical hacking and has a negative impact on security posture.

Cost Benefit to the Consumer

The more familiar perspective for most of us when considering cost benefit is to do so as the target of potential attack. In this perspective, the focus is on the perceived value of various aspects of the organization and how much should be spent to burn down the risk to those assets. In our case, we are talking about burning down cybersecurity-related risks to such assets. Consider a credit bureau as our target. There are several major entities, I will not pick a specific one, so let's just call them

TransExperiafax. Now, though TransExperiafax offers credit reporting, monitoring, and protection to the people whose credit files they keep, most of their money is made from data analytics based on the files they keep. Let's say Transexperiafax makes an annual revenue of 2.5 billion from selling its data analytics to other companies. Also, they were recently the victim of a cybersecurity breach, and when it was announced, they lost 10% of their stock market cap, which equated to a 1-billion-dollar loss for the year for their shareholders.

If we think about how TransExperiafax might evaluate cost benefit itself as a potential target of future attacks, those two values are probably key. The 2.5 billion annually and 1 billion due to a breach are likely to be the strategic cost benchmarks to determine how much they are willing to spend on cybersecurity efforts toward protecting those year-over-year values and mitigating or avoiding catastrophic events. Using these numbers maybe TransExperiafax decides they'll spend 1% of the 2.5 billion annual risk plus the 1 billion potential loss values, each year, spread over 12 months equally. Their cybersecurity spending would look like Figure 16-1 below.

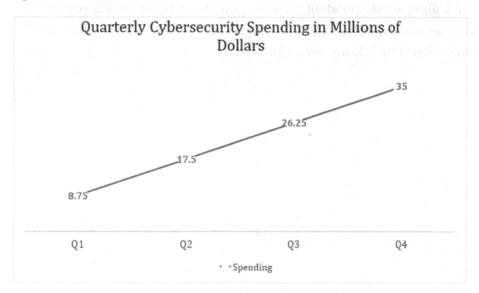

Figure 16-1. *Target cost benefit*

Cost Benefit to the Attacker

Unfortunately for TransExperiafax, the enemy gets a vote on cost benefit too. At least, they will have their own way of evaluating it. In what way does the attacker evaluate cost benefit? The easiest way for us to consider this is to make an assumption (probably a fair one) that the most likely malicious actor to target TransExperiafax is going to be an organized crime activity, potentially somehow tied to a foreign government but not necessarily. If this is the case, then they are looking at TransExperiafax as a potential profit. TransExperiafax maintains some 500 million personal credit files and another 50 million company credit files. If we say the average company is 10 people, that means there are essentially 1 billion personal credit files worth of data they maintain. If the average credit file on the dark web sells for $5, that means the potential profit of compromising TransExperiafax is $5 billion. So, the attacker is going to evaluate the cost benefit of their malicious cyber pursuits against a potential $5 billion payout.

Using these numbers, maybe a criminal organization has decided they are willing to risk spending 1% of the potential 5-billion-dollar payout over a year, divided quarterly. Figure 16-2 below shows what their cyber operations expenditure would look like.

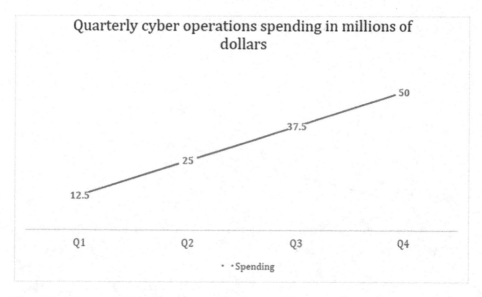

Figure 16-2. *Attacker cost benefit*

The point is that a target organization who is only able to see half of the cost benefit perspective picture is going to do cost benefit analysis on cybersecurity implementations without all the necessary information. If TransExperiafax did this, they would evaluate how much they should spend on cybersecurity using a 1- to 3.5-billion-dollar benchmark. Would they spend more or make different decisions if they knew that to the attacker, they looked like a $5 billion payday?

Appropriate cost benefit analysis for cybersecurity products, capabilities, and services needs to at least consider both sides of this analysis and incorporate them into their decision process. Figure 16-3 below illustrates the disparity in spending based on perspectives and shows that the attackers would always be spending more than the defenders. A key point too though is that this is just one attacker, maybe there are three, maybe there are many more, maybe they all go after TransExperafax this year, maybe each year, and maybe consecutively.

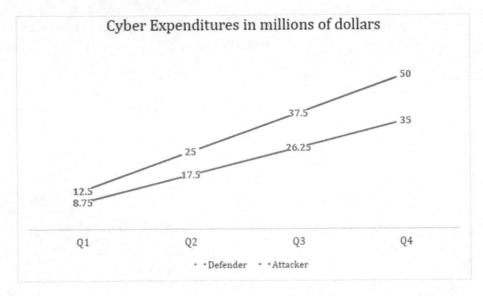

Figure 16-3. *Comparing spending*

Understanding Cost Benefit Implications

While understanding the different perspectives of cost benefit is beneficial, it is also necessary to track the implications of implementing a given product, capability, or service. This means that even if on the surface a cybersecurity thing may look cost beneficial, we must also consider how the implementation of that thing alters the rest of our architecture. Primarily this means understanding how risk and work move around an organization as a result of such implementations and if those implications potentially negate the benefits of face-value cost benefit analysis.

Risk and Work Are Never Destroyed

Much like matter, it is hard to destroy risk and effort. Ok, with cybersecurity, it is not so absolute. However, when cybersecurity things are marketed, sold, and consumed, they are often done in a way that is dismissive of risk and work implications and instead focuses heavily, if not entirely, on the up-front change and cost benefit.

Poor Evaluation of Cost Benefit Implications

As an example of poor implications evaluation, let's consider the example of implementing automation through declarative languages. Put very simply, this is coming up with an easily understandable set of commands that when executed by individuals perform complex tasks behind the scenes. For instance, the declarative command "newhost" might execute several scripts in the background to execute commonly performed tasks when a new virtual machine is set up. It leverages a virtual machine API to create the virtual computer, adds it to the domain, creates a user profile on the machine, and installs antivirus and a suite of tools necessary for people to perform their job functions.

The face value of such an implementation is that instead of having a systems engineering team having to manually go through those tasks for each new machine, they can simply type "newhost" using the declarative language interpreter, and all the scripts and execution are orchestrated in the background through automation. This allows for the gaining of efficiencies in setting up times for new machines, saves hourly wages paid to admins as they set up hosts, and reduces the risk of mistakes by humans during the setup process that could make machines vulnerable. Easy sell right? Unfortunately, these benefits don't take into account where certain risk and work have moved to, and at what point the moves become worth it.

Good Cost Benefit Implication Evaluation

Using the same example, let's walk through what implications should be included in the cost benefit evaluation of a solution like this. There are several impacts to an organization when automation of this nature is put in place. Instead of spending a few hours here and there setting up a new machine for each new hire, an immense amount of work is put in upfront to set up the automation mechanisms themselves. There is a clear need to understand what this work looks like and at what point the upfront cost starts to pay off and for how long it pays off. If it costs $100,000 in billable hours to set up the automation but each machine set up only costs $100 in billable hours, we would have to have a thousand new machines set up before we start to see cost benefit in this regard. That might be easy in a very large organization; however, in a smaller one, it might not make sense to pursue this type of automation.

There is also the fact that such automation, scripting, and orchestration require specialized skillsets in a system engineering team that were not required before and additional personnel may need to get hired or time spent training them. These issues would add more impact to the cost benefit analysis on implementing this solution. There is also the important movement of risk. Sure, human error is less likely to happen as humans are performing less actions. On the other hand, a single mistake at the orchestration level could not put every subsequent machine creation at risk. This is another implication that must be considered in any cost benefit analysis, where did the risk move to?

A Litmus Test for Cost Benefit

To this point, we have covered detailed methods and examples surrounding the concept of cybersecurity cost benefit, which in truth is simply true cost benefit for an organization. I would like to describe something I use as a quick litmus for cybersecurity things before I even go down the road of a comprehensive cost benefit analysis.

I refer to it as the 1-9-90 principle. The values may vary over time, but the point being made is that essentially, there are three types of threats that make up 1%, 9%, and 90% of cyber actors. Roughly 1% (probably less) of cyber actors are nation-state-level cybersecurity threats, another 9% are APTs and organized crime, and the other 90% are unorganized crime and script kiddies:

- The 1% are undeterrable, unpreventable sources using almost completely, if not completely, unknown capabilities, and the best way to deal with such risks is to find ways to accept that they could happen and find ways of living with them such as resilience and redundancy solutions.

- The 9% are potentially detectable but unlikely to be preventable as they use both known and unknown capabilities.

- The other 90% of cyber threats are those that must be prevented as they involve only known techniques and tools that can be scanned for and/or caught by existing security tools.

So how does the litmus work? Well, if someone says they are developing a tool that can prevent nation-state-level APTs or detect them, you should take that claim with a grain of salt. As a purchaser or implementer of such technology, you risk having sunk costs and resources into something that can't possibly deliver on what it claims. This 1-9-90 principle can be a great guiding resource for R&D as well as you should focus on developing solutions that are aimed at mitigating specific threat actor sophistication in the most efficient and feasible ways. On the other end of the spectrum would be someone saying we should just accept the risk of the 90% when you could easily thwart such known capabilities why would you spend money on being resilient against them? Figure 16-4 below illustrates this principle through a simple matrix.

	Tools / Techniques	Type of Actor	Risk Mitigation
1%	Unknown to public	Nation state	Accept
9%	Unknown and known	Organized crime	Detect
90%	Known to public	Unorganized crime	Prevent

Figure 16-4. *1-9-90 principle*

If we look back at the moving target defense (MTD) example from Chapter 1 and apply this litmus, we probably wouldn't have to bother with further analysis. As the concept claims to PREVENT a 1% capability like a zero-day, it would fail out litmus as striving toward an inappropriate method for risk mitigation. Of course, 1-9-90 could be .001%, 9.999%, and 90% or have some other variance, the point is more that the majority of threats can be prevented, those that can't be prevented we should try to make sure we detect but we should also acknowledge that there are unpreventable threats that we need to find a way to accept by being resilience to their manifestation. As with any rule or principle, there are surely exceptions, this is simply a quick sniff test ability to provide litmus to the cost benefit analysis of a given cybersecurity paradigm.

The Infinite Game

Simon Sinek is a British-American author and public speaker who wrote a book and has given countless talks, including TED Talks, on the concept of the infinite game which is a similar take in ideas to James P. Carse's work Finite and Infinite Games. Full credit to Simon for bringing the concept into public light and conveying it in such a way that it can be applied to almost any situation. Essentially, the concept is that there are finite games and infinite games.

A finite game is one where there are known players on known teams playing by established rules with a specific win condition. In such finite games, the players are playing to win the game, think of a sports game, or chess. Infinite games are those with known and unknown players on known and unknown teams who can join, leave, or return at any time and where the rules are always changeable. Infinite games do not necessarily have a start or a beginning, and the players are not playing to win; they are playing to stay in the game, think business, or an insurgency.

The Lesson

As applied to business, warfare, and other areas, the most important aspect of finite and infinite games is that the players know what type of game they are in so they can play with the appropriate motivation. If we look at one of Simon's examples, in the Vietnam War, the United States was playing a finite strategy, trying to "win," whereas the local opposition was trying to simply stay in the game long enough for the United States to drop out. Similarly, this played out recently and to a successful conclusion with the opposition playing the right game and the United States playing the wrong game in Afghanistan as well. The United States was trying to "win" in Afghanistan where the Taliban was simply trying to stay in the game until the United States dropped out. When a player does not know the type of game, they are actually playing they cannot optimize play or hope to improve their position.

Infinite Cybersecurity

The cybersecurity industry and its customers face an infinite number of adversaries that are infinitely varied in their sophistications and motivations, and we have been doing so with a decidedly finite mindset. The crux of the finite and infinite game concept in application to cybersecurity is that cybersecurity is an infinite game. New threat actors can target a defender at any time, some may give up targeting a vendor at any time. The attackers do not play by any rules, and the goal of the defenders should be to keep playing (operating their business or organization in the face of threats). Instead, as we have already covered to some degree, the cybersecurity industry talks a lot like American generals and politicians did regarding the conflicts in Vietnam and Afghanistan.

Applying the Theory

The best way to apply this is to identify the cases where we can gain an advantage on as many attackers as possible while intelligently ceding that there are some (nation states) where there is no ceiling or timeline for us to shortcut. In those cases, we must simply attempt to close on their curve as much as possible. Within the cybersecurity industry, the proactive and infinite gameplay-minded hacking industry is uniquely positioned to embrace infinite game theory. As cybersecurity is an infinite game and the cyber domain the playing field, we will be most successful when our business practices align with the type of game being played.

Adversary as a Service (AaaS)

Typically, some of the most powerful defensive operations an organization can undertake are robust monitoring capabilities and threat-hunting campaigns. Unfortunately, monitoring and, to a greater degree, threat hunting rely on admittedly outdated and nonstandardized intelligence to help them zero in on malicious activity in the network. Even frameworks like MITRE's ATT&CK are based on often aged, incomplete, and largely open-source information. This means that hunting based on these facts is likely to find you someone reusing a capability, forgotten access or tools, or help you walk your way down a false flag operation. This is of course because the bad guys also have access to this framework, so they know how different actions, techniques, and tools are attributed.

What if instead of heavily relying on threat intelligence, we created our own intelligence, as an adversary such as a nation state might? After all we have access already, we know our own strategic outcomes and goals and how we are going about them. We know our own IT refresh cycles, upgrade, and update schedules, etc. Why not create intelligence about our own organization like a nation state might and leverage that kind of information to inform things like hunting and monitoring as well.

Performing this type of activity is a sort of pseudo-red teaming that when coupled with proactive assessments afforded by penetration testing and red teaming can help an organization mitigate risk based on self-knowledge and largely agnostic of threat specificity. By not focusing on individual threats and instead focusing on self-knowledge, informed intelligence defenders might be able to force multiply their ability to combat larger groups of potential threats.

In a way, this is the next step to practices like resilience. With resilience, we take an understanding of ourselves and our needs to inform risk-reducing practices aimed at keeping an organization in the game. Having an organic adversary as a service capability allows us to red team our own resilience decision matrix and inform threat-hunting campaigns in a way that supports the continued pursuit of strategic goals and withstands as many threats as possible without trying to fight off specific threats.

Attacking the Curve

A former colleague of mine asked an interesting noncyber question that really got me thinking about how to attack the curve (a heavy graphical representation of the curve I am talking about soon to follow). He asked: "How long might it take an adversary to find and weaponize a vulnerability in something like routing infrastructure?"

I was not sure, but that was not the point, I said perhaps 3 to 5 years maybe. His next question was: "What if every 3 years, then, we just switch our routing infrastructure to a new brand entirely, such as from Cisco to Juniper, moving the target on the adversary?"

Now there is a lot to poke at, but broadly, this is a very interesting concept. We can't have a steeper or continuous curve like some nation states might in targeting us (if we think our organization is actually the target of such efforts). However, maybe we can attack the adversary's efficiencies in the aspects of time and resources as they play an infinite game with us.

Before we go through the graphs to follow, I must assert that there is a distinct difference in how you approach attacking the curve when talking about criminal organizations and other lower-tier APTs compared to nation states. As we mentioned, the former has cost benefit in mind, the latter have national security in mind and their curve can be steep and unending if they feel it necessary. For nation states, cost benefit in this sense is not really a consideration.

Cost Benefit Refined

In Chapter 3, we discuss cost benefit and how the adversary and the organization may have differing opinions on what cost benefit cybersecurity or cyber-attack spending looks like, which effects an organization's ability to adequately resource its protective strategies. Instead, below we will show how adversaries like criminal organizations might approach their cost benefit line as it pertains to spending time and money before leaving the game if they have not gotten access or information necessary at that point. Figure 16-5 shows an adversary spending personnel hours over time to achieve a compromise with a limiting cost benefit line. The adversary is going to spend a lot of hours upfront trying to gain access and information while later spending a few hours to siphon out data. They will either abandon the attack if it looks unlikely to have cost benefit or be successful.

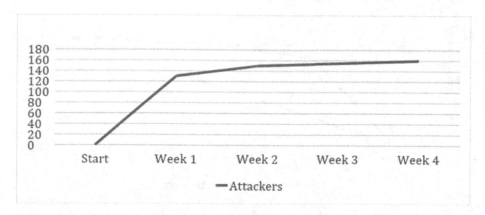

Figure 16-5. *Attacker personnel hours*

On the other hand, the defender will spend personnel hours in a predictable way, with their cybersecurity person working 40-hour work weeks over the course of the month as shown in Figure 16-6.

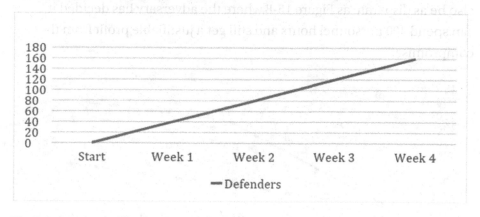

Figure 16-6. *Defender personnel hours*

Figure 16-7 shows the two alongside each other.

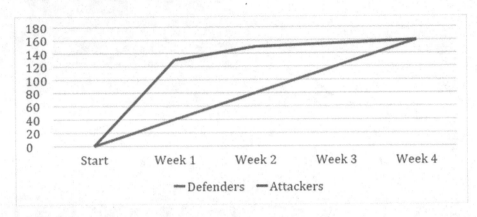

Figure 16-7. *Defender and attacker personnel hours (limited to 160)*

It is important to accept that the more realistic scenario is probably that the adversary is willing to spend more than 160 hours in a month or have more than one person in the initial phases, which means it could also be as disparate as Figure 16-8 where the adversary has decided it can spend 400 personnel hours and still get a justifiable profit from the compromise.

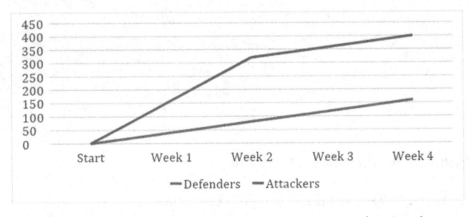

Figure 16-8. *Defender and attacker personnel hours (realistic)*

Figure 16-9 is a different way of portraying Figure 16-7, and Figure 16-10 is a different way of showing Figure 16-8 to highlight the area of the surface between the two curves.

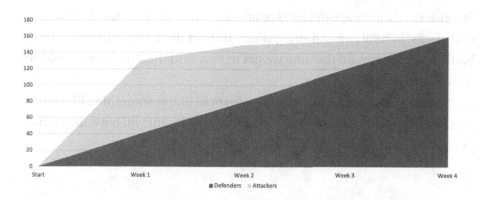

Figure 16-9. *Highlighted defender and attacker personnel hours (limited to 160)*

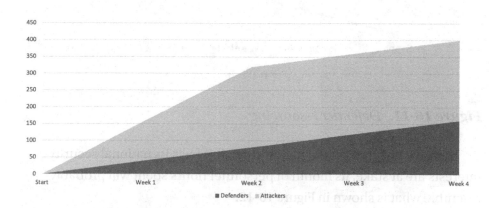

Figure 16-10. *Highlighted defender and attacker personnel hours (realistic)*

What Figures 16-9 and 16-10 do a good job of showing is the shaded region between the line graphs. This shaded area is essentially a mathematical representation of the disadvantage faced as a surface area. Anything a defender can do to decrease this surface area is a worthwhile approach to cybersecurity. In these examples, our adversary has a bounded finite battle in the greater infinite cybersecurity conflict. If we as defenders can increase the surface area or lower or move the defender's line of cost benefit, we can successfully impact their ability to win a finite battle and also extend the time we get to play and that they have to play in the infinite game.

So what does it look like when we instead graph something like an APT? Well our one-person cybersecurity department will have the same personnel hour graph, shown in Figure 16-11.

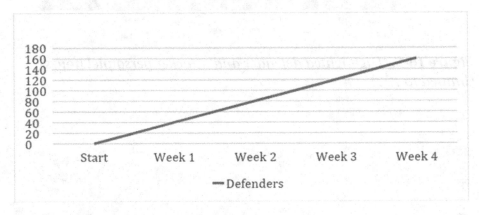

Figure 16-11. *Defender resourcing*

But now the attacker is a nation state that feels its national security interests are at stake, its month of personnel hours spent will probably resemble what is shown in Figure 16-12.

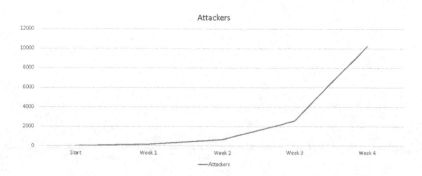

Figure 16-12. *Attacker Resourcing*

The striking difference in effort and the advantage of the attacker regarding time is shown in Figure 16-13.

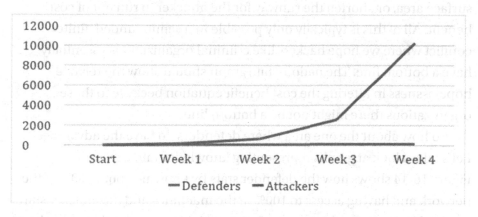

Figure 16-13. *Contrasting Attacker and Defender Resourcing*

Now when we shade in the surface area of disadvantage, we get a stark representation of the imbalance involved.

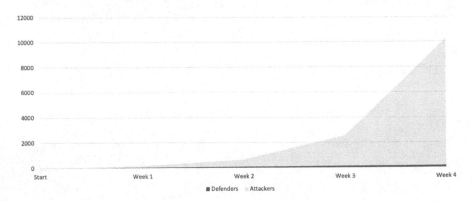

Graphs for resources or expenditure would look much the same as the ones we have done with time so I will not repeat them. These graphs represent a surface area of disadvantage that can be attacked by doing things to increase the defenders' surface area, decrease the attackers' surface area, or shorten the runway for the attacker to run out of cost benefit. All of this is typically only possible in a semibounded, finite conflict where we hope hackers like criminal organizations essentially have a bottom line. The nation-state graph should show the relative hopelessness in altering the cost benefit equation because to those organizations there might not be a bottom line.

So how about the one area where defenders do have the advantage? Let's take a look at graphs representing knowledge and access.

Figure 16-14 shows how the defender stats by knowing about 100% of the network and having access to 100% of the machines and the attacker starts at zero, but how over the course of a 1 month compromise those numbers change. Ultimately the attacker has access to half the network and ransoms it to the defenders.

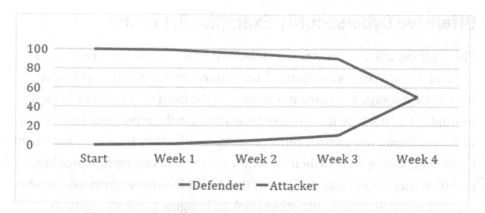

Figure 16-14. *Knowledge and access*

Figure 16-15 shows the shaded surface area advantage that the defender has in regard to knowledge and access. Attempts at continuously maintaining this advantage are our best chance in playing the infinite cybersecurity game for as long as possible.

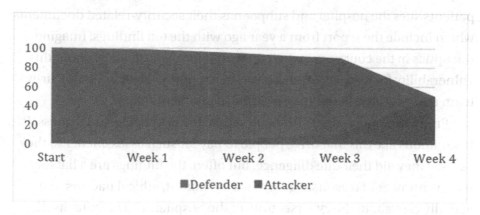

Figure 16-15. *Defender advantage*

Offensive Cybersecurity Example: Reporting

There are countless times when an offensive cybersecurity event is carried out and the end-results are ignored, thrown out, or destroyed. This is done for several reasons. The customer, if they are the head of IT or security for example, may not have the funds to fix anything in the report and knows they won't get them even with the report as evidence. So, they have the assessment conducted so they can tell their boss they did it or check a compliance box, and then they throw away the liability that is an offensive security assessment.

The example I use in my other book is, imagine a hospital gets an offensive cybersecurity assessment done and there are ten findings. Say they do have funds to fix everything, but it will take a 3-year period to cover all ten remediations, so they prioritize them and get to work securing their network. Now, a little over a year in they have remediated four of the ten findings and are working on the fifth when an attacker leverages finding six to get into their network and steal HIPAA data for their patients. One of the patients sues the hospital and subpoenas their security-related documents which include the report from a year ago with the ten findings. Imagine the optics in the courtroom when they say, "look you all knew about this vulnerability for over a year, and it was in a report you got from a security team and now it was used to compromise my clients' data."

Pretty bad optics, right? Probably a case the hospital loses I'd guess. It is situations like this that drive people to pay for such assessments so they can say they did their due diligence, but often, the findings are a liability for any number of reasons. Again, if we are honest, ethical hackers may actually care about the cybersecurity of the hospital. The hospital itself cares about protecting its financial interests and the offensive security vendor cares about keeping its professionals employed and expanding its customer base. The great cybersecurity professionals are the ones that find ways to help make the hospital more secure within the constraints of neither the vendor they work for or the hospital actually having cybersecurity as their strategic outcome.

Conclusions

Good cybersecurity cost benefit is accomplished when you implement a cybersecurity product, capability, or service where the introduced cost is positively offset by the risk it mitigates. Accepting that cybersecurity is an infinite game, it is imperative to acknowledge that solutions such as ethical hacking enable infinite gameplay while others may be finitely oriented and are therefore less cost beneficial. The intended takeaway is that you as the reader can assess cost benefit in your own terms and that you can do so situationally in a way which explores not just what a product, service, or capability aims to provide, but whether it truly provides cost benefit at the strategic, organizational level.

Index

A, B

Acquiring talent, 25
Adversary as a Service (AaaS),
    284, 285
Amazon Web Services (AWS), 156,
    175, 178, 179, 182, 186
Application assessments
  authenticated/
     unauthenticated, 165
  definition, 164
  high/lower privileged
     accounts, 164
  impressive report, 164
  source code, 166, 167
  stealth testing, 167
  WAF validation, 167
Artificial intelligence (AI)
    systems, 268
  abuse optimizations, 269
  data poisoning, 269
  leaking, 271
  safety constraints, 270

C

Client management
  approaches, 142, 143
  assessments, 73

chat channel, 76
Domain Admin access, 129, 130
engagement time, 76–79
handoff meeting, 75
high-quality assessment, 74
industry comparisons, 141, 142
internal red/pentest
    teams, 133–135
kickoff meeting, 75, 76
motivations/concerns, 138
  experiences, 140
  industry security
    certification, 138
  policies, 140, 141
  security concerns, 139
motivations/definitions, 131
outbrief flow, 79–82
project execution
  engagements, 83
  operational checklists, 90, 91
  penetration testing, 90–93
  post-engagement, 89
  pre-engagement
    processes, 85, 86
  reporting/pentesting, 88, 89
reporting
  requirements, 83–85
scope creep, 86, 87